The Fire in the Mountain

The Fire in the Mountain

Sicily, Etna and Her People

HELENA ATTLEE

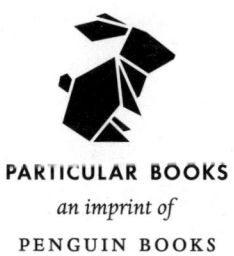

PARTICULAR BOOKS
an imprint of
PENGUIN BOOKS

PARTICULAR BOOKS

UK | USA | Canada | Ireland | Australia
India | New Zealand | South Africa

Particular Books is part of the Penguin Random House group of companies
whose addresses can be found at global.penguinrandomhouse.com

Penguin Random House UK
One Embassy Gardens, 8 Viaduct Gardens, London SW11 7BW

penguin.co.uk

First published 2026

001

Copyright © Helena Attlee, 2026
Map copyright © Neil Gower, 2026

Penguin Random House values and supports copyright.
Copyright fuels creativity, encourages diverse voices, promotes freedom
of expression and supports a vibrant culture. Thank you for purchasing
an authorized edition of this book and for respecting intellectual property
laws by not reproducing, scanning or distributing any part of it by any
means without permission. You are supporting authors and enabling
Penguin Random House to continue to publish books for everyone.
No part of this book may be used or reproduced in any manner for the
purpose of training artificial intelligence technologies or systems. In accordance
with Article 4(3) of the DSM Directive 2019/790, Penguin Random House
expressly reserves this work from the text and data mining exception.

The moral right of the author has been asserted

Set in 12/14.75pt Dante MT Std
Typeset by Six Red Marbles UK, Thetford, Norfolk
Printed and bound in Great Britain by Clays Ltd, Elcograf S.p.A.

The authorized representative in the EEA is Penguin Random House Ireland,
Morrison Chambers, 32 Nassau Street, Dublin D02 YH68

A CIP catalogue record for this book is available from the British Library

ISBN: 978-0-241-51439-9

Penguin Random House is committed to a sustainable future
for our business, our readers and our planet. This book is made from
Forest Stewardship Council® certified paper.

To my friend and colleague Sue MacDonald,
with thanks for many adventures.

Contents

Map	viii
Introduction: Fires in the Night	1
1. Moving to Milo	7
2. Going Round the Mountain	17
3. A Swim Through Deep Time	28
4. Dark Desert	44
5. Saro the Digger	52
6. Prediction	66
7. Festa di Sant' Agata	78
8. Treasure Beneath Their Feet	93
9. Snow Business	102
10. Into the Woods	116
11. Shepherds and Cheesemakers	127
12. City of Honey	137
13. Donkey-Milk Dairy	146
14. Soil and Society	152
15. Sicilian Emeralds	167
16. A Winemaking Revolution	179
17. Eruption!	195
Further Reading	203
Acknowledgements	207
Index	209

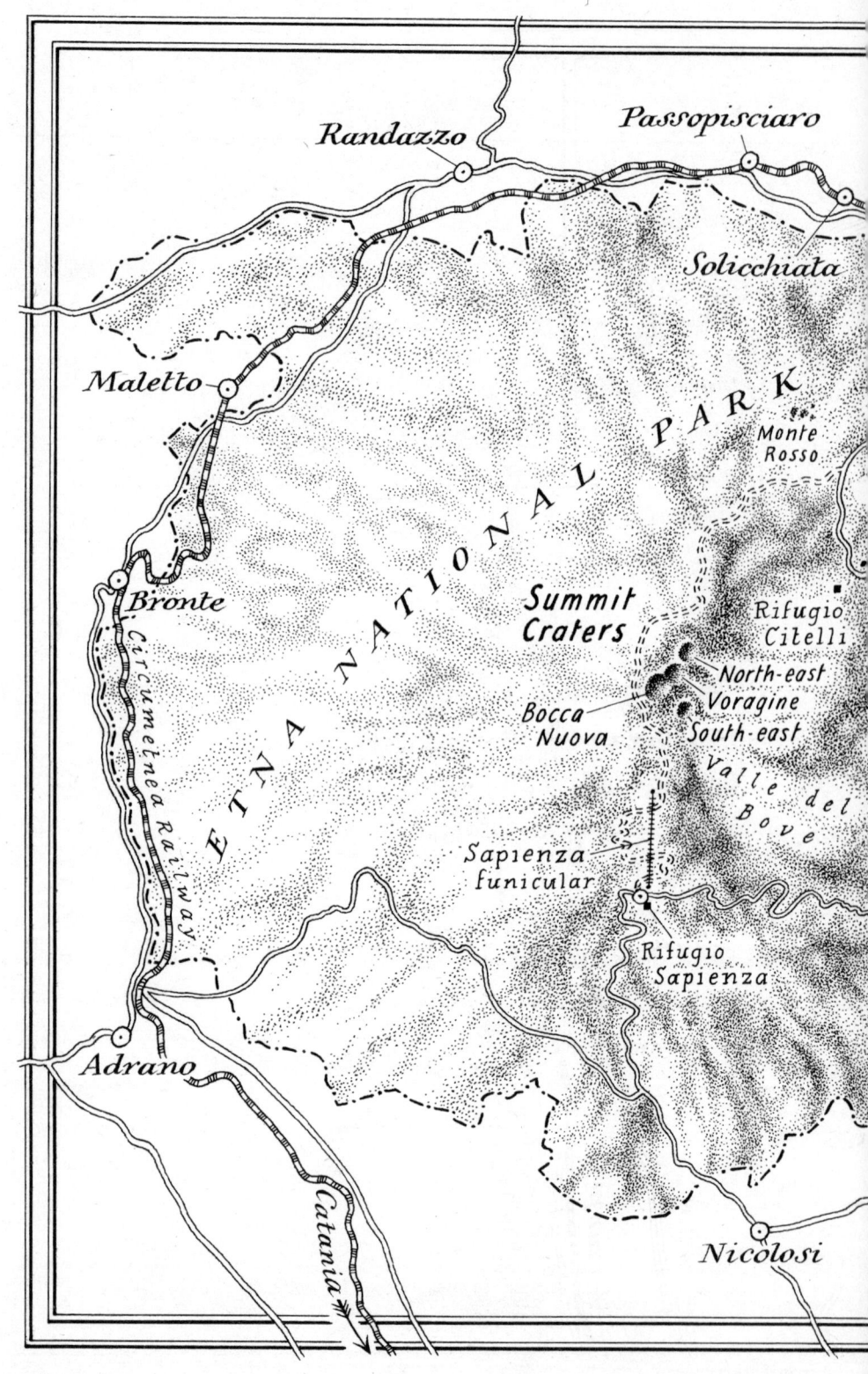

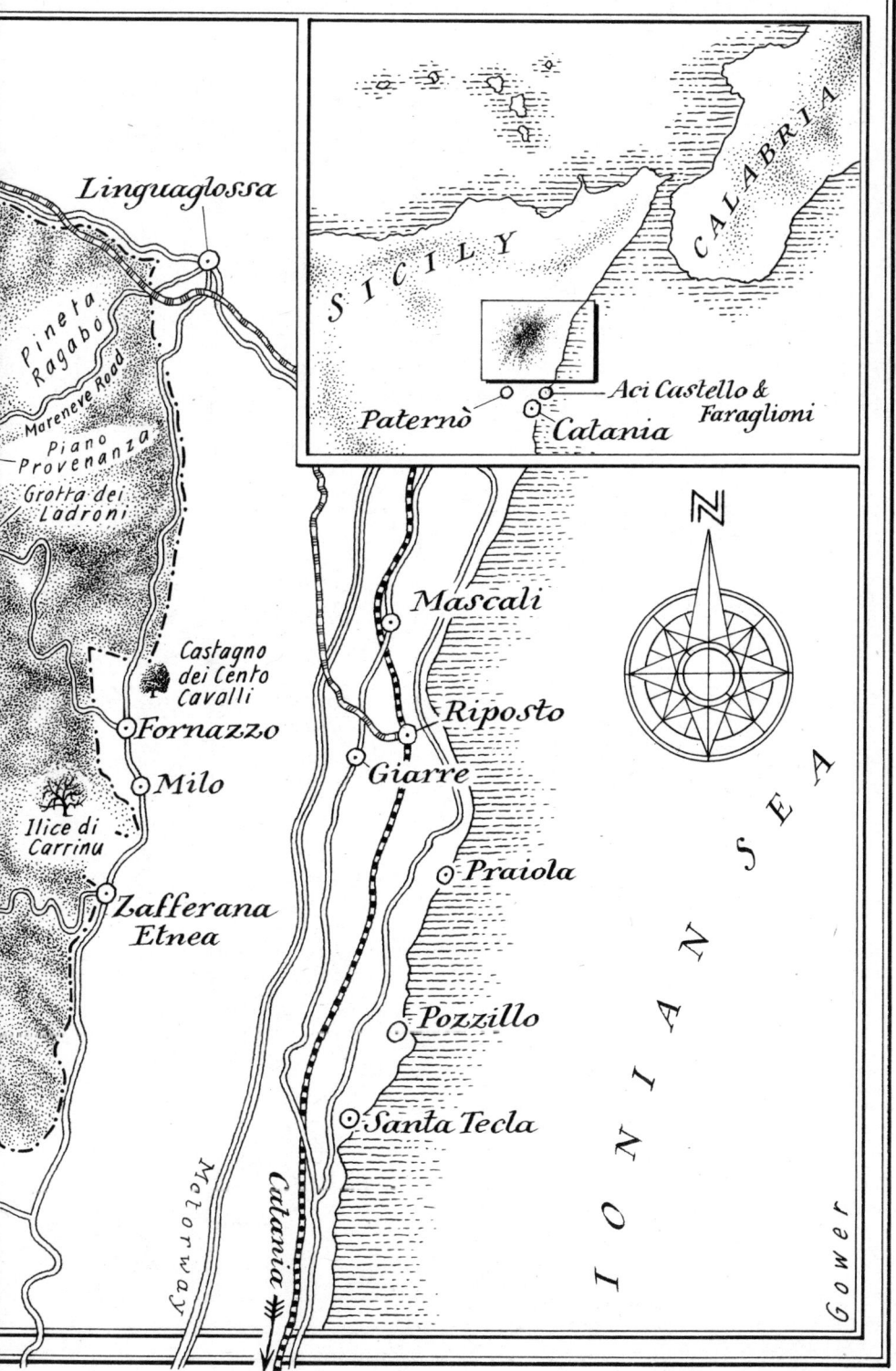

Introduction: Fires in the Night

Years ago, I checked into a hotel at the foot of Mount Etna, the shape-shifting mountain that dominates Sicily's east coast, changing height and profile from year to year, but never losing its glorious status as the biggest volcano in Europe, and one of the most active in the world.

I had been working hard all day, and yet it took me a long time to fall asleep that night because the windows in my room seemed to rattle with every passing breeze. Nevertheless, the next thing I remember is being woken in the small hours by a boom so terrifying it catapulted me out of bed, and had me running barefoot into the winter night. Outside, Etna's distant summit was erupting molten rock and fire into the sky. A full moon riding high above made the whole scene look as if it had been lifted from a Romantic painting, with me one of those tiny, silhouetted figures in the foreground. Of course, there had been nothing wrong with the windows in my room – their incessant rattling was a result of tremors caused by magma forcing its way upwards through solid rock. And as for that primal, stirring, gigantic sound, it was a voice from the depths of the earth.

That was the first eruption I had ever witnessed, but I was no stranger to Sicily that night. Nearly forty years had come and gone since 1980, when I caught a ferry from the mainland and arrived on the island for the first time. My diary, written enthusiastically for a few days and then forgotten, neatly captures the thrill of crossing the Messina Strait from Calabria. The journey takes less than half an hour, but I was startled then, as I am still, by how different everything felt on the other side of the water.

Sicily has always been a distinctive place, a place built on layer upon layer of cultural input from a weary succession of colonizers, conquerors and civilizations. All this coming and going has gifted it a culture that sets it apart from anywhere else in Italy. To go there has always been like travelling to a different country, not just an island off the coast of Calabria. When I first made the journey, politicians were talking about linking Sicily to the mainland with a bridge across the Messina Strait, and they are talking about it still. I wondered if a bridge would kill the island's distinctive culture, bringing it into line with the rest of Italy?

After getting off the ferry in Messina, I caught the slow train along the sea's edge towards Catania, the dusky city at the foot of Etna, where all the buildings are made from volcanic stone. I shared a compartment with a mother, her two leaden-faced daughters, and an old man who might have been their father. Apparently, or so my diary says, his hat was so tight that the white line it imprinted across his forehead was still visible half an hour after he took it off. Sometimes orange groves separated the railway track from the water, but more often we travelled directly along the sea's edge. The shore was crowded with brightly coloured fishing boats, and we trundled past great groups of fishermen pulling in their nets. I watched gypsies leading a yearling away from a market on the beach, where cattle were crushed into makeshift pens, and more men in hats gathered in an urgent huddle around the auctioneer. Everywhere I looked that rural landscape was busy with people at work in orchards, citrus gardens, olive groves and vegetable patches.

Work brought me back to the east coast of Sicily again and again, so that by the time I witnessed Etna erupting that night, I had long felt at home on the island. In all those years, however – and it seems odd to admit this now – I had never considered the volcano as any more than a lovely backdrop to my busy days. Seeing the eruption changed everything. In those moments, it turned background into foreground, forcing me to acknowledge the massive mystery dominating a landscape I had always pretended to know so well.

Years passed, but I was reminded of Etna every time I returned

Introduction: Fires in the Night

to Catania. Once I even glimpsed a gently smoking crater over the tilted tip of the aeroplane wing. I had seen what craters were capable of, and I was becoming ever more curious about their connection to whatever turmoil lay deep beneath the ground. Etna has almost a million inhabitants – about a quarter of the island's population – and looking down at its slopes, I also began to wonder about the people living in a landscape so turbulent that underground could become overground at any moment. How did they accommodate such vast, uncontrollable natural forces in their everyday lives? And what did the volcano give them in return for committing to its uncertain ground?

Reading about Etna's history, generally told from the perspective of outsiders, I realized that people have been trying to make this risk–reward calculation for centuries. The poet John Dryden had a son, also called John, and in 1700 he was one of the first foreigners to try to reach Etna's summit. But like so many other early visitors, he failed to consider that Etna is over 3,000 metres high, and his ascent was foiled by heavy snow. Despite this setback, he was deeply impressed by the people who dared to live on the volcano, coming to the conclusion they did so 'in continual fear and trembling', rather than forfeit 'so fruitful a soil'. He was certainly right about that rich, volcanic soil, but had he dug a little deeper, he might have discovered, as I would do, that he was very wrong indeed about the fear and trembling.

This is the story of what happened when my own curiosity got the better of me, and I decided to settle for a season on the slopes of Sicily's volcano. It had been erupting almost continuously the previous year, and I arrived like every other visitor, so pumped up with the drama of it all that I was tempted to ask the clichéd question, 'Aren't you scared?', of everyone I met. At the heart of this story is what I managed to learn about the true relationship between Etna and its inhabitants, a relationship that would prove to be much more nuanced than simply being scared or not scared.

By the time I began writing this book, every country in the world seemed to be at risk of natural disasters triggered by climate change. This made it feel urgent to find out what we might learn from people who have always had to accommodate vast, irresistible forces of Nature in their daily lives. Resilience is a word bandied about a lot in the face of the climate emergency, and I wanted to see how it translated among people so often visited by disaster. And more than that, at a time when risk analysts all over the world are begging governments to refine the early-warning systems and emergency-management plans for every kind of calamity, I was curious to find out about the work of the National Institute of Geophysics and Volcanology (INGV) in Catania, because it operates one of the most advanced early-warning systems in the world. Was there something happening on Etna we could all learn from, or at least imitate, as we faced up to our own versions of Nature's invincible power?

When I arrived at the tail-end of spring, I was surprised to find everybody, even the scientists at INGV, referring to the volcano as 'her' or 'she'. Had Etna been a *montagna*, 'mountain', there would be no confusion because that is a feminine word. However, *vulcano* is masculine, as is the nickname *Mongibello* that I also heard people using. It is formed by fusing the Latin *mons* for 'mountain' with *gibel*, which also means 'mountain', but this time in the language of Sicily's Arabic emirs. Cobbled together, they made Etna the beautiful and very masculine 'mountain mountain', or 'mountain of mountains'. Nevertheless, I got equally used to hearing it called *Idda*, which simply means 'she' in Sicilian dialect, and *la signora*, *mamma*, or even *mamma grande*, the dodgy big mamma who might nurture you tenderly for years and then suddenly dish out the brutal kind of punishment I had already witnessed from afar. Local writer and philosopher Leonardo Caffo had added to the confusion by describing Etna as a 'queer object . . . that crosses every boundary and belongs to every gender', outwitting our banal taxonomic systems, rather as the duck-billed platypus outwits the taxonomy of the animal kingdom. Nevertheless, of all the names I ever heard for Etna, the one I came to see as best at capturing her protean personality was *bruttabella*, a mashed-up version of 'beauty and the beast'. I only heard it once, from a man in his nineties, long before I came to live

Introduction: Fires in the Night

on the volcano, but it came back to me again and again as I learned more about the chimeric nature.

I paid a lot of attention to all those linguistic variations, because getting someone's name and gender right is the first thing you must do if you plan to know them better. And so, to be honest, it has been an effort to refer to the volcano as 'it' in these first few pages, because, putting Caffo aside, I long ago fell into the local habit of seeing Etna as a female presence in the landscape, so from now on I will be calling her 'she', just as the locals do.

In those early weeks on Etna, I spent time digging down into her biography, and trying to grasp the dark, chthonic processes that fuel her eruptions. I soon became fascinated by the classical myths and ancient legends baked into the local landscape. This led me to the people who have been living on Etna's slopes for thousands of years, and I began to calculate the rewards Etna has always offered to anyone willing to endure all the irritations and uncertainties that come with living on Europe's most active volcano. Of course, for many centuries most of Etna's people would have felt they had little choice about where they lived. Their outlook was transformed, however, by all the problems that festered in Sicily after it became part of a unified Italian state in 1861. Within ten years of Unification, the new government had imposed policies that toppled the island's rural economy into such deep crisis that millions of Sicilians were forced to recognize emigration as their only viable future. Nevertheless, while other rural areas on the island have never really recovered from mass emigration, Etna still attracts tens of thousands of people to live on her slopes, despite all the risks this implies.

I came to know Etna's landscape better by jumping onto a train one day that took me right around her circumference. It carried me almost at walking pace across lava flows, through pistachio orchards, cactus groves and vineyards, introducing me to many of the small towns on the volcano as it did so. Over the months, I would meet the people who worked these landscapes: Etna's shepherds, farmers, winemakers and woodsmen. It was such isolated, deeply rural territory that it was easy to assume Etna had always been a place apart. As time went on, however, I discovered that, to the contrary, her inhabitants had played their part in the political turmoil convulsing the whole island, not to mention Europe itself, throughout the first half of the nineteenth century. In time, Etna would serve as a lens through which I could view important chapters in Sicily's history.

Rural life all over Europe has changed almost beyond recognition in the past fifty years, and Etna is no exception. As weeks turned to months, I found myself talking to people who grew up in the 1960s, and first learned the skills of their trade in ways that had not changed for hundreds, or even thousands of years: making ricotta in a copper cauldron over a wood fire, perhaps, grafting pistachios onto wild terebinth saplings, using horses to extract timber from the woods, and using their own muscle to saw up ton after ton of it by hand. Ancient traditions like these are forever overlapping with contemporary life on the mountain, so it was no surprise when an old couple told me that their marriage had been arranged for them by their fathers, nor when I encountered shepherds still making cheese in much the same way as the ancient Greeks, and a man beating out metal pots as if we were still deep in the Bronze Age. Writing all this down has sometimes felt like trying to capture things on the page before they disappear forever. None of this could happen, however, until I found somewhere to live on the volcano, and this made my first return to Etna a recce trip.

1.
Moving to Milo

In the end it was word of mouth that brought me to a village called Milo, almost 800 metres above the waves lapping at Etna's coastline. I saw the house first on a dark day in winter. Unswept, the terrace was invisible beneath a pelt of black lava laid down during successive eruptions the previous year. The shutters were closed, and indoors the rooms were dark, dirty, and full of broken furniture. Except for the dining room. Dining room? Yes, a perfectly formal dining room with a marble table, a sideboard and six upholstered chairs. It is hard to remember now what made me so certain I was doing the right thing, but I came to an immediate agreement about a rent with the nuns who were to be my landladies, and then went back to Britain to prepare.

I finally arrived in Milo on 25 April, with a pile of books on volcanology and a desperate desire to see another eruption. It was Liberation Day, when the whole of Italy celebrates the end of Nazi occupation in 1945, and the fall of the Fascist regime. Sister Caterina was there to unlock the gate, and the town band played its way up the road as I carried my few possessions into the house. It looked huge and gracious now, with the terrace beautifully swept, doors and windows flung open, and every room full of wind and sunlight. Pictures of Jesus and his mother hung from every wall, and one of the Last Supper was in 3D, so that there was sure to be an apostle winking at me every time I entered the room. There were very few tables, an extraordinary number of chairs, and an unlimited supply of china and cutlery. The handsome terrazzo floors gleamed in every high-ceilinged room and corridor. The plumbing in the bathroom was eccentric, and the wiring everywhere made me anxious.

I settled like a bird in its nest, perched high above a road leading steeply down to the piazza at the centre of the village. The views from the terrace stretched over the roof of my neighbours, to the sea far below. At twilight sky and sea merged, and then ships seemed to hang in limbo. Whenever the moon rose from the water at night, I watched them sailing through the golden shaft it threw across the bay. My days were beautiful with the sounds of spring, as cuckoos called in the woods and a pigeon murmured constantly on her nest under the eaves.

Steps steep as a ladder linked my terrace to the lane below. 'Don't bother bringing your rubbish down all that way,' my neighbour Lucia told me the day after I arrived. 'Just lower it on a rope like we do. The binmen will always find it there.' Each day, I'd head down to the piazza, passing an old standpipe at the end of our lane. It gushed non-stop with mountain spring-water, and there was often a crowd beside it. People travelled miles to fill every container they owned with that bright, ice-cold supply, rich with all the minerals of Etna's volcanic soil. But not me, because the same water flowed from every tap in my house. Much of the rest of Sicily was currently so badly afflicted by drought that it was at risk of desertification, so this abundant water supply was my first experience of the very real rewards Etna could offer for living on her slopes.

Some of the people crowding around the standpipe were on their way to Fornazzo, the pretty hamlet further up the hill, where they would join the Mareneve road towards Etna's summit. My house was roughly halfway between those two places. If I walked downhill on a Saturday or Sunday, much of the traffic coming towards me was lycra-clad and on two wheels. The road was so steep that those cyclists heading for the summit often seemed to be peddling frantically just to stand still. Come evening, it was a different story. Then they glided downhill at breakneck speed, hands free, talking on their phones, and hurtling past the little shrines set into the walls of houses lining the road. Some of those dusty alcoves were neglected, but many contained candles or bunches of fresh flowers, a perpetual thanksgiving for Milo's escapes from the lava of various eruptions. Behind the houses, new leaves were showing on vines carpeting the slopes. Old barns, walls and well heads among the vineyards were all built from *basalto*. Like the water rushing from the standpipe below my house, basalt, or volcanic rock, was an infinitely sustainable supply. Here was another reward for anyone prepared to make risk their life partner, and it meant that most of the buildings on Etna's slopes looked as if they had grown unbidden from the ground.

Between my house and the piazza was a statue of Sant' Andrea, Milo's patron saint. Ever vigilant, he gazed across the roof of the village shop to Etna's summit craters, one hand held up to push back whatever they might send. You could buy anything in the shop at a price, including fresh *pecorino* cheese, made by local shepherds and cut from truckles the size of car tyres stacked behind the counter. There were local fruits and vegetables too, but you were never allowed to touch any of them to assess their weight or see if they were ripe. No, you had to wait obediently for one of the two women who ran the place to make all those judgements for you. The baker next door sold delicious, golden loaves, little biscuits as dry as archaeological artefacts, and those very thin, crunchy slices of pizza dough called *pizza secca*, all baked in a wood-fired oven out the back. No matter which loaf she slipped into a brown paper bag for me, whether a skinny *filone* or a circular *ciambella*, it had the rich, nutty flavour that comes only with dough made from Sicily's durum wheat.

Down the steep hill below the shop, Milo's main street was paved with *basalto* slabs. It may have been short, but those few shops and bars provided everything I needed. The piazza beyond them was as wide and open as the deck of an enormous ship. From the railings along its edge the sea looked like stretched cloth, lines fanning out across it from the coast some 750 metres below. The view embraced the resort town of Taormina to the north, forever bathed in sunlight on its hilltop, as if it were trying to attract yet more tourists to its narrow streets. To the south, the view stretched all the way to workaday Augusta, a town most of those tourists will never visit. Neither

Taormina nor Augusta were on Etna's territory, and yet, with all its different aspects and altitudes, the volcano was a viewpoint for the whole of Sicily. On clear spring days you could even look across the Messina Strait and see Calabria, so that although I was in a place apart, I had a sense of being at the centre of everything.

I spent my first few days settling into Milo, where the towering façade of the church dominated the piazza to one side, and I soon learned to spot its priest chatting to his congregation in the Bar Cinque Tigli on the other. *Tigli* are lime trees, and they stood in a handsome row between the church and the square, where the cold, spring evenings did nothing to dissuade men in thick coats and hats from gathering to play cards. Small children were also wrapped up warm to ride their bikes, a little pack of stray dogs following behind them or sniffing about for food. Looming over all this activity was Etna, and in those early days I began to notice how often she found her way into conversation in the bar, as if talking about the volcano's recent behaviour was as ordinary as gossiping about the neighbours.

Within a week of my arrival I had found my way uphill to Fornazzo, and turned left onto the Mareneve road. It soon delivered me to the rugged, black landscapes formed by lava flows every time Etna erupts. Some had come from eruptions of the south-east crater, some from one of the other three summit craters, and some from flank eruptions, because lava can burst through rifts and fractures anywhere on Etna. What her inhabitants dreaded most were eruptions low on Etna's flanks, because they were the ones most likely to send lava flowing into cultivated land, towns and villages.

A half-hour drive up the steep, winding Mareneve road took me to lava from an eruption in October 2002. It had engulfed the ski resort at Piano Provenzana before rampaging through a tight-knit, high-altitude pine forest called Ragabo. By now I believed there could be no such thing as silence in a place where every surface seemed to be covered by a thin layer of the volcanic debris that made walking on Etna louder than scrunching over pebbles on a beach, crunching across stubble in a corn field, or perhaps even dancing over broken china in a Greek restaurant. But Ragabo was different. Those towering pines had fostered silence for centuries by cushioning the ground beneath them with layer upon layer of fallen needles. Walking through those muffled spaces as quietly as a thief, I could hear nothing but the breeze high among their branches, and the occasional toll of distant cowbells.

The first record of Etna's august trees came with the Greeks, who used their fine, straight trunks for shipbuilding and mast timber. Even the name Ragabo is ancient, for people say it derives from *rahab*, the word Arabs used for woods and forests when they lived on the mountain between the ninth and eleventh centuries. In retrospect, I could have found nowhere better to spell out the continuity of human life on her slopes, nor chosen anywhere more likely to maximize the impact of my first real encounter with the great bolus of change, upheaval and unrest that is a lava flow.

It happened so suddenly. One moment I was in the green, twilit shade between the trees, on a path so well travelled it had worn deep into the forest floor. Next, I was out in the blazing sunlight, surrounded by a hooligan landscape of lava that had bulldozed through the forest, toppling, burning and engulfing over 200,000 trees in its path. I felt like a visitor at the scene of some terrible accident, but instead of wrecked cars, there were the charred, bleached carcasses of trees tossed on their sides in that broken landscape of contorted ridges, crests, escarpments, banks and valleys, all pitch black. Twenty years had come and gone since the eruption, and yet my surroundings were still so ravaged, raw and broken it was as if I had returned to the world's beginning, with everything yet to evolve.

I had anticipated loving all the landscapes Etna made, but the reality could not have been more surprising or less welcome, for I did not love the lava flow that had rampaged through Ragabo, and soon enough I would find myself not loving other lava landscapes too. I didn't have to go far to find them, because lava had muscled its way through the intricate, antique landscape of terraced vineyards and orchards just above Milo, a chaos of frozen energy that arrived in 1950, and now hung above the village like the snout of some grotesque and gloating animal. I would soon learn that sudden lurches from controlled domesticity to anarchy were part of the *Coltivata*, or 'cultivated zone', all over the mountain.

The flow from 1950 had already been relegated to the long history of Etna's eruptions, but her near constant activity during the year before my stay had covered the landscape in layer upon layer of fresh lava and ash that was still making every surface slippery. Out walking, I would take one step up a steep slope only to slide three steps backwards, as if the volcano were constantly trying to shrug me off. In fact, on some of those early walks I made such slow progress I wondered if something mysterious had gone wrong with my legs. Was it the altitude? Was I sickening for something? No, as it turned out, I was learning to walk on lava, while also trying to tolerate it filling my boots. When walking in Britain, I would stop to remove a single pebble from my shoe. On Etna I had to learn to endure the glassy splinters that found their way into the narrow space between my ankle and my boot, nestling there awhile before descending further to make a lava field that was mine alone, between the sole of my foot and the sole of my boot. Meanwhile, the top of my boot would continue to fill, eventually making it so difficult to bend my ankle that I would have to give in and shake it out before beginning the whole process all over again.

Flicking back through notebooks where I recorded my earliest walks on Etna's lava landscapes, 'intimidating' is the word that leaps from the page again and again. My notes record me picking my way across lava while resenting the way it denied me a handhold as I climbed steep slopes, and promised to lacerate my skin if I were ever to slip or fall. I resented the lava for filling my boots, making my skin itch and my eyes sting. I even resented some of the plants I found growing on it, because they seemed a perfect expression of the landscape's character. There is the note of my first encounter with a cushiony clump of a plant endemic to Etna called Sicilian milkvetch (*Astragalus siculus*). I knew nothing about it then, but it is one of the few plants tough enough to establish itself on the unstable, uncompacted lava after an eruption. Knowing this now, it seems appropriate that it should armour itself with the lethally sharp thorns it conceals beneath its guileless leaves. 'Typical', I thought, having tried to sit down on one before struggling on up a steep, slippery lava slope. I had come wanting to like everything Etna had to offer. Soon enough she would begin to work her magic, but for now the volcano was just too big, too bleak, too black and, above all, too sharp.

There is no end to the damage lava can do on a volcano that erupts on average twice a year. I became accustomed to the sensational sight of buildings engulfed by lava. Take the tiny chapel beside the Mareneve road. It fell victim to the flow from a flank eruption in 1979, which seemed to be heading straight for Fornazzo. However, after enfolding the tiny chapel in its fiery embrace, the lava ground to a halt, and the people of Fornazzo gave thanks for a miracle. They restored and enlarged the little building, but left the lava nudging at its walls intact. I saw other crippled buildings wherever I went. A perfectly good house cocooned in lava on the edge of the Valle del Bove on Etna's east flank, one sunk to its roofline at Piano Provenzana, and another floating on a black sea above the town of Randazzo on Etna's north flank. And these were just the visible remains. There was no trace of all the other houses, barns, and even an entire village the volcano had burnt, bulldozed or engulfed over the centuries.

Even when not destroying them, Etna's recent activity meant that she never seemed to leave houses alone. Every day I watched people climbing ladders to clear the volcanic ash blocking their gutters, or to sweep away lapilli, tiny fragments of lava so heavy they threatened to make roofs cave in. I wished I had a ladder myself, because then I could have cleared the gutter outside my kitchen window. It was so blocked with ash that water shot horizontally through a gap beneath the window frame every time it rained, and then gathered in a huge puddle in the middle of the kitchen floor. Etna was no friend to cars, either, and I often saw people driving vehicles with paintwork that had been blistered by incandescent embers. And although there hadn't been an eruption for a couple of months, the pavements of towns and villages were still crowded with piles of white sacks full of more volcanic detritus waiting for council lorries to take it away. The council sent out snow ploughs after the eruption, and the huge black piles of lava to either side of the roads looked as if they might be there forever.

These were the irritations that must be tolerated by anyone living on an active volcano, and they were impressed on me again early in my stay, when one of the summit craters put on a minor performance. I was sitting at a table outside the bar in the piazza of Zafferana Etnea, the village next door to Milo. First a thick black plume of smoke pumped into the sky above the south-east crater, then its dark edges turned to gold in the rays of the setting sun. I was transfixed, but nobody else in the piazza took any notice at all. Children carried on biking about, old men went on gazing into their drinks, and a woman continued sweeping her balcony overlooking the square. Finally, those special effects at high altitude caught a young waiter's eye, and laughing as if the whole thing were an old joke, he shouted 'The mountain is exploding!' loud enough for everyone to hear. Then they glanced nonchalantly up, just in time to see clouds of ash and vapour floating aimlessly across the sky. 'What a wonderful performance!' I said innocently as I paid for my drink at the bar. The owner's response taught me a lesson I am unlikely forget. 'It may be a *spettacolo* for tourists,' he said grimly, 'but I paid €400 to have my roof cleared the day before yesterday, and now I will have to do it all over again.' From then on, I would keep very quiet about the fascination I felt for eruptions, not to mention the hope of seeing another one, this time at close quarters.

People everywhere on Etna seemed to be constantly sweeping, and I soon discovered why, because there was always something falling from the sky onto my terrace. Generally, it was volcanic ash, a misleading word because instead of being soft and grey like wood ash, it was gritty, black and sharp. Occasionally I also wiped bright yellow sand from the table and chairs outside that had been carried across the sea from the Sahara on a Sirocco wind. Indoors, I would think I had dusted Etna's calling cards from every surface, and swept them from every terrazzo floor, but on jumping into bed at night I would often jump straight out again to sweep sharp fragments from the sheets. How they got there I never knew. Were they on the soles of my feet, or did they stow away with washing I had dried outside on the line? After throwing the shutters open each morning to sun flooding the sea far below with apricot light, it was time to get dressed and be reminded yet again that lava had a similar knack for getting inside a shirt or dress, or, worst of all, a pair of pants. I also got used to lifting and shaking my feet like some strange, sandal-wearing bird, just to dislodge the razor-sharp fragments that had found their way inside.

Again and again Etna reminded me that she was neither Italy nor Sicily as I had always known them for so long, but a place apart. Moving to Milo in late April, I had been expecting the warmth of the spring weather that was already turning the rest of the island into a southern-Mediterranean idyll. I was met instead by a bitter, north-west wind arriving like a message from lava-stained snow still covering slopes above the village, and by icy fingers reaching up from the ground each evening and driving me early to bed. April turned to May, and yet one morning I woke to cloud so dense it seemed day was hardly bothering to break. The weather became increasingly ominous that morning, with more cloud finding its way up from the sea, reaching in among the trees and drifting across my windows like smoke. Then came wind that blew my eerily squeaky gate open and shut outside. By lunchtime, it was pouring with rain, and the fog that descended was so dense I couldn't see the edge of the terrace. For days, the weather was as dark and wet as a Welsh November, the house was damp, and the cold inside it punishing. I found myself yearning to exchange Milo's mountain climate for the more familiar pleasures I knew were unfolding down on the coast, where Etna meets the sea. I imagined the air already buffered by soft cushions of perfume from wisteria flowers, lemon blossom and cut grass, and even the seaside scent of grilled fish.

Added to all these trivial concerns was a deeper anxiety. I had spent my life until then in places built on rocks formed by geological events millions of years ago, and the sense of permanence created by those ancient landscapes was a quality I had always associated with anywhere I called home. Etna was their antithesis. Her life history began a mere 15,000 years ago, and she had been extending, transforming and renewing her landscape ever since. What's more, I had learned that where I had chosen to live – on the east flank – was almost as likely to be overturned by an earthquake as it was to be engulfed by an eruption, so that I began to think of Etna as having more in common with a verb than a noun. All in all, I wondered if I would ever be able to relax around such candid displays of the Earth's deepest mechanisms, or feel at home in a landscape so lively and juvenile that everything in it still seemed to be about heat, movement, change and growth. What to do? I was there now. I could move away from it all and live down on the coast, and yet I hadn't made the long journey to Sicily only to discover more of what I already knew.

Out of this confusion came the thought that a mountain with its feet in the sea, a summit over 3,000 metres high, and flanks facing north, south, east and west must offer a dizzying diversity of landscapes, microclimates, soils, vegetation and crops. As yet, I had focused only on lava flows high on Etna's slopes, so that I knew next to nothing about any other environment the volcano might have to offer. At around this time, however, I heard about the little train that ran around the volcano's circumference, and realized that this journey would give me an overview of all the different landscapes spreading across Etna's four flanks. It would take me from sea level, apparently, to almost a thousand metres, showing me the whole of the Coltivata, and stopping at stations in some of Etna's most important towns and villages.

2.

Going Round the Mountain

The Circumetnea is a narrow-gauge railway that encircles almost the whole circumference of Etna from Catania to Giarre and Riposto. You could make the journey in under half an hour on a direct train, but it sets off in the opposite direction to its destination, going clockwise all the way round the volcano, and taking a good six hours to travel 110 dramatic kilometres through each of the Coltivata's assorted landscapes. After the line opened in 1898, Catania's city council promoted it as a tourist attraction, offering passengers 'magnificent panoramas of forests, olive groves, almond trees, vineyards, the snows of Etna and views of the Ionian Sea and Taormina', a promise that holds good to this day. Tourism was never the purpose of the Circumetnea, however, because the tiny track circumnavigating the volcano was intended to transform the economic fortunes of isolated towns, villages, and even individual farms dotted across the territory. Before its construction, most communities on the mountain were linked to Catania by what one awe-stricken nineteenth-century Englishman described as 'nothing but lava and frightful precipices'. And it was true: torturous mule tracks frequented by robbers were often the only route between rural areas and the market in Catania or the port at Riposto. The new railway line was to be both a connection to the outside world and a safe, reliable system for delivering livestock and goods of almost any kind cheaply, efficiently and in fine condition. The trains would also carry passengers and deliver mail to all the principal towns on the volcano.

The story of how the railway came to be made is a snapshot of Sicily just after the Unification of Italy. Both Palermo and Catania were full of foreigners, many of them British businessmen attracted by the opportunities that a new government might offer. However, instead of making fortunes for themselves and their own country, as they might still have done in the colonies, they married into local families and became immersed in the island economy, enriching it as well as themselves. Local entrepreneurs combined forces with these economic migrants to liberate Sicily's economy from the paralysing grip of the aristocracy. Many of the island's great estates were still in the hands of these scions of ancient dynasties, but before long the new opportunities created by a thriving economy were liberating *contadini*, peasant farmers, and *braccianti*, labourers, from the arcane, feudal obligations that so many of them still insisted on imposing.

There were already steam engines transporting passengers and connecting businesses to new markets all over Europe by the time the plan for the Circumetnea was first mooted in 1870. Nevertheless, it would take another fifteen years of bureaucratic wrangling for a consortium of local councils to sign an agreement allowing them to build, operate and maintain the Circumetnea as a public service. When the time finally came to forge ahead, however, it transpired that no one in the consortium had any experience of railway building. Britain was already well established as a pioneer in this field, and so they looked to the British community for expertise. There they found a Cornish civil engineer called Robert Trewhella. Already an entrepreneur in his own right, he owned a hotel in Palermo, a swathe of highly lucrative citrus groves nearby, and one of the sulphur mines that made so many people rich in nineteenth-century Sicily, and caused untold suffering to the people they employed. He was the ideal candidate, having worked for Isambard Kingdom Brunel in Britain, and then building railways on the Italian mainland and elsewhere in Sicily. In 1890 he signed a contract with the consortium, set up his own construction company and got to work. The enormous job of clearing and levelling the route for a line across Etna's precipitous, unstable, uneven, lava-strewn slopes would employ many tons of dynamite, and provide jobs for hundreds of unskilled labourers, not to mention the builders and stone masons who constructed bridges, viaducts, tunnels, stations, walls, platforms and engine sheds, and the mules that made it all possible.

I found it fascinating to hear some older people on Etna still referring to the Circumetnea train as the *littorina*. This was a throwback to a more recent chapter in the railway's history, when the original steam engines were replaced with six small, diesel-powered trains called *littorine*. Their driver would sit at the front as if he were driving a bus, with passengers lined up behind him on comfortable leather benches. The Fascist government had commissioned this cutting-edge design in 1937 from the best engineers at Fiat in Turin, and it was Mussolini himself who named the trains *littorine*. This was a perfect example of the Fascist Party's determination to link modern Italy with the glories of the Classical past, for *lictores* were the elite bodyguards of high-ranking magistrates in ancient Rome, who demonstrated their masters' authority by accompanying them wherever they went and carrying the *fasces*. These symbols of the magistrate's authority were made from a bundle of birch or elm rods lashed together around an axe, and would eventually become both the emblem of the Fascist party and the word from which its name derived. And if passengers on the Circumetnea still didn't get the connection between those impressively elegant, modern trains, their national government and the glories of ancient Rome, they only had to glance up as the engine approached the platform to see it proudly carrying the *fasces*, rendered in metal and soldered to its beautifully streamlined front.

Although the *littorine* were replaced long ago by a new generation of trains, I still sensed something timeless about the carriages that chugged into Borgo, the name of the first station on the line. Their red leatherette benches were soft from the sitting, and there was wood-effect Formica on the walls. After finding a seat, I realized I was the oldest passenger by fifty years or so, because all the others were children on their way home from school. They greeted each other with a kiss on the cheek before settling in to do their homework, with much highlighting and underlining of text. Meanwhile we trundled through the suburbs of Catania in the sun-filled carriage, nudging along the edges of vegetable gardens, and so close to the backs of houses that we could see the smile on the face of a woman flinging open her windows as we passed. After cutting across a stretch of land entirely covered by lava from the eruption of 1669, we were soon ambling alongside cows grazing quietly beside an aqueduct. Rolling along beneath a blue sky, we passed olive and citrus groves carpeting the fertile soil of the Catania Plain, and sometimes Etna's summit surprised us by springing up ahead, white with snow and wreathed in cloud.

Soon we were on the south-west flank, where we scraped past the prickly-pear cacti clustering up to the track. These *Opuntia ficus Indica* only arrived on the island when the Spanish brought them from Mexico in the sixteenth century, and yet postcards often feature them as if they were an essential element of any truly Sicilian landscape. And it is true that, despite their late arrival, they were very quick to spread, because when a pad detached from the parent plant it only needed to touch soil to put down roots. Soon they were making themselves indispensable on Etna, just as they did all over Sicily, where farmers harnessed the power of their fibrous roots to break down poor, compacted soil, and fed their juicy pads to sheep and goats. The fruit they wore like comical ears around the edges of those pads was soon part of the staple diet for everyone living on the volcano. This was the case all over the island, and when the British author and playwright John Galt arrived at the beginning of the nineteenth century he summed up the situation as follows:

> If a Sicilian be observed eating anything it is certainly Indian figs. If he be carrying a basket, it is full of Indian figs. Every ass that is seen coming into the city in the morning is loaded with Indian figs. Every peasant that is seen in the evening counting his copper money on a stone, is reckoning the produce of his Indian figs. If an article be bad, it is said not to be worth an Indian fig.

A century later, *fichi d'india* were still available in such quantity that the Fascist government had the ingenious idea of fermenting them to make alcohol that it then shipped to Italy's colonies to be used as fuel.

If you are used to seeing them growing wild, it comes as quite a shock to see the cacti cultivated on Etna's south-west flank corralled behind walls and high fences as if they were vicious animals. And they are vicious, because both the plants and the fruit are covered in a veil of almost invisible spines, as fine as hair and almost impossible to remove from your skin. Like many other plants now endemic to Etna, they have adapted to its conditions by developing varieties that are unique to those volcanic soils. There are three distinct varieties of *fico d'india dell'Etna* growing there today. Each one produces fruit of such a striking colour you might assume it had been treated with food colouring. Or at least I did when I first saw all three sliced in half and displayed on a market stall. Now I know that the blood-red ones come from the 'sanguigna' variety, the sulphur-yellow from 'sulfarina', and the crunchy white ones from 'muscaredda'. All three have sweet, juicy flesh that is packed with pips and has a mild, melon-like flavour. If left to themselves, they bear fruit in August. However, Etna's farmers have long specialized in a technique known as *scozzolatura*. This obliges them to don industrial gauntlets, leather aprons and goggles in May and June each year, and then strip the cacti of flowers and tiny, unripe fruit. A month later, the plants burst into flower again, and nourished by autumn rain, they produce fruit between October and December. Those winter fruits glory in the name of *bastardoni*, 'big bastards'. They are larger, sweeter, crunchier, and more succulent than the summer crop, and if the plants are carefully managed, they will be ready just in time for Christmas. All the qualities of the *fico d'India dell'Etna* have been celebrated ever since 2003 with a PDO (Protected Designation of Origin) label.

The train soon dipped underground to go screaming through modern metro stations serving the towns of Biancavilla, Santa Maria di Licodia and Adrano, before emerging on Etna's landlocked, west side. I had caught the Circumetnea to get an overview of Etna, and it was already clear that each of her flanks had a very different character. Now the landscape stretching away to either side of us seemed to have been laid down with a broader brush, the climate was clearly drier, and I could see goats and sheep wandering on slopes that were harsher, wilder and emptier. The towns and villages were set further apart as well, and even the lava flows seemed bigger and more threatening. This was especially noticeable as we began to approach the little town of Bronte, where the whole hillside had been transformed into a vast, black lava sea by eruptions during the nineteenth century. Etna has claimed very few lives over the course of her recorded history, but sixty people in Bronte were either killed or injured when lava from an eruption in 1843 flowed into a stream and exploded, sending red-hot matter high into the air, and enveloping onlookers in clouds of burning rock and lava.

When the Circumetnea first opened, engine drivers were forbidden to exceed 15 mph, and breaking the speed limit meant instant dismissal. Maybe this is still the case, because outside the windows everything was moving at such languid speed that I was able to watch a man picking greens in a field next to the track, and then laboriously tying them into a tight bundle with string. But even at this slow pace we were making progress, and soon enough we were deep in the lava landscape between Adrano and Bronte, where pistachios have made an ideal territory for themselves among those benighted lava fields. They were probably introduced much longer ago than prickly pear, and like them they have evolved into a unique variety called the Pistacchio Verde di Bronte, Bronte's emerald-green pistachio. The track climbed along the perimeters of their fields, and I was able to look straight down into the intimate arrangements they made with the lava, their contorted trunks happily emerging from it, their branches touching it with a fingertip caress. There were so many of them that they seemed to steal colour from the landscape, turning every slope the same neutral shade as their bark. The only change of palette came with men in faded blue overalls working among the trees, waving and whistling as we chugged slowly past.

We had been climbing gradually higher ever since leaving

Catania, and the warm spring weather by the sea. It was sunny still, but now people getting onto the train were wearing scarves, and sometimes even woolly hats. The highest point of the track came above Bronte. As we worked our way laboriously towards that 967-metre pinnacle, I was struck again by the extraordinary challenges met by the hundreds of men and boys who cleared and levelled a route across such precipitous, unstable terrain. They must have struggled to find a path across the lava flow that lay just outside town, because after continuing confidently to the north, the track turned abruptly back on itself. Almost at once we began to descend the mountain's west face, and suddenly I could see the train's other carriages snaking away ahead of mine across the precipitous slope.

Maletto was the next stop. The village sat high above the line, set at 1,000 metres against the snowy backdrop of the mountain. There have always been entrepreneurs on Etna and, unlikely as it sounds, Maletto was the first place to grow strawberries commercially in Sicily. During the 1950s, farmers there dug strawberry beds between rows of vines, and planted a variety called 'Madame Moutot'. It flourished, as most things do in Etna's rich soils, but it was a variety bred in an innocent time, when plants weren't expected to work so hard, and fresh produce was eaten close to home. Nobody minded then that it bore its sweet, succulent fruit for only a month, and they forgave that fruit for needing to be eaten on the day it was picked. Needless to say, very few people grow 'Madame Moutot' in Maletto today, and during the strawberry festival the town organizes each summer, the stalls are piled high with more commercial varieties.

We had to change trains in the lava-black town of Randazzo on Etna's north face. I would come to know it later for Bar Musumeci, a place I returned to again and again for the best granita I have ever tasted. It was also in Randazzo that I saw one of Etna's indigenous dogs for the first time. Just like the local varieties of plants and trees, there are several breeds of animal unique to Etna. The Cirneco dell'Etna is a sleek, sinewy sight hound that has been chasing game across her slopes ever since it arrived on Sicily with the Phoenicians in about 500 BC. Narrow-faced and cock-eared, it looks like a version of the Egyptian dog-deity Anubis, so it's no wonder the Greeks chose to emblazon its noble profile on coins. I am told *Cirnechi* have the kind of steely strength tailor-made for Etna's punishing territory, so they can bound across the razor-sharp surface of any lava flow, hunt for hours under blazing sun, and do without food, shade or water all day. I was familiar with all these impressive facts before I sighted my first Cirneco shambling down a backstreet in Randazzo. He was a disappointment, to be honest, with his grizzled, antique face and bandy legs. However, his Tuscan owners told me he perked up a bit on Etna's black, volcanic beaches, so perhaps there was an atavistic sense of origin somewhere beneath those wonky ears.

There was an hour to wait in Randazzo before the connection to Giarre and Riposto arrived. This was plenty of time to walk into town, where I found a bar selling a pastry made with Bronte's unique variety of pistachios. It was topped with a glistening pile of nuts under a glaze of sugar icing. The whole thing, no bigger than a golf ball, was a miniature masterpiece shot through with the unmistakable flavour of local pistachios, a blend of rosewater, sap, and subtle sweetness.

Changing trains had come upon me like an interval after the first half of a very long film. Now we launched into the second half, and although the main character was the same, the scenery unscrolling outside the windows was completely different. Had I made the same journey only two or three decades sooner, most of the farms on this north-facing side of Etna would have lain abandoned. Then the terraced vineyards on slopes all around them would have been derelict and overgrown, but now we were trundling through the immaculate vineyards at the heart of an ongoing wine-making renaissance.

The vines lining up beside the track had all been neatly pruned and tied with white string. This had turned the fields into a *festa* of waving white flags, and the journey into a demonstration of best vine-pruning practices. Everywhere I looked, lava cleared from the land had been built into bizarre little towers that resembled abstract sculptures on the edges of the vineyards. Some had grown so large that they looked like ziggurats, or the leavings of some past civilization.

The perspective from Etna's north face made it easy to see how her slopes were divided into three distinct regions. We were still in the Coltivata, but some vineyards were at such high altitude they seemed almost to overlap with the *Boscosa*, *Selvosa*, or *Nemorosa* region immediately above it. This 'woody', 'sylvan', or 'shady' area encircles Etna's midriff from approximately 900 to 2,000 metres, and has gone by all these names over the centuries, each one more literal than the last. The treeline is somewhere between 2,000 and 2,300 metres, and above that comes the *Deserta*, a volcanic desert covering the whole of the mountain from an altitude of roughly 3,000 metres.

Local mapmaker Giuseppe Gemmellaro spent his whole life on the volcano, and published *A Historical, Topographical Map of the Eruptions of Etna from the Era of the Sicani to the Year 1824*. He made its three regions look very uniform, but of course nothing on Etna is either as simple or as clear cut as it looks on his beautiful nineteenth-century map. For example, temperatures on the north flank can be ten degrees lower than those on the coast where the sea laps at Etna's east face, and rainfall varies enormously from flank to flank. This gifts each face of the volcano its own microclimate, as well as soils with a huge variety of mineral contents. And as if this astonishing range of growing conditions were not enough to grasp, each one of the three regions spans hundreds of metres in altitude, so that the climate from bottom to top of the mountain ranges from southern Mediterranean on the coast to Alpine on the summit.

Our next stop on the Circumetnea was Linguaglossa, the town that serves the ski resort of Piano Provenzana. Later I would learn that nobody gave skiing a thought on Etna until after the Second World War, when men from Linguaglossa were sent to Piemonte in Italy's far north to do military service. They brought the skiing habit home with them and passed it on to their friends. Soon, carpenters in Linguaglossa were making wooden skis, and people from Catania were careering down the slopes above the town. In

1971 the enterprising mayor raised funds to build a small ski resort with a hotel, restaurant and ski lift at Piano Provenzana. He also persuaded four instructors to come down from Piemonte and start a ski school. This changed the fortunes of Linguaglossa, prompting its transformation from a typical agricultural town to a centre for ski tourism.

We had been trundling progressively downhill, and as the train rounded the mountain we entered the gentle landscape low on the east flank. We were approaching the sea now, with the sunny coast of Calabria clearly visible on the other side of the Messina Strait, and my home in Milo above us. There were lemon trees laden with fruit to either side of the track, a sight that always makes me think of Eugenio Montale's poem 'I Limoni', where he describes the sight of the fruit as 'a golden roar of sunlight'. Perhaps the picnicking tourists in my carriage were inspired too, because at that moment one of them began peeling an orange, filling the carriage with its scent. I returned fire by pulling one of the last plump, loose-skinned *Tarocco* blood oranges of the season from my bag, countering the volley of essential oils released by the skin of their orange by peeling my own. The exchange seemed a perfect marriage of season and place, for we were all eating oranges that grew only there and only then, all enjoying sweetness tempered by sharpness, as if the taste had been designed to serve as an ideal metaphor for what I was learning about Etna's character. As spring had turned to summer during my stay on Etna, I had become used to seeing people selling local mangoes, avocados and papayas, all of them grown on trees that thrived in the same soft, damp, semi-tropical warmth as citrus at the base of Etna's east flank.

After the wide, sparsely populated landscapes of the west and north faces, I was surprised by the sheer number of small farms and farmhouses packed side by side on the seaward side of the mountain, where the steep slopes were cut into terraces supported by retaining walls made from rough blocks of lava. It was already late afternoon by the time we pulled into the station they call Giarre-Riposto. Riposto was once a thriving port for ships that would set off from it carrying a medley of precious produce from the volcano.

Going Round the Mountain

This was the final stop on the Circumetnea line, and so the guard told us all to get off. If we wanted to return to Catania, he said, we had to walk to the mainline station. We set off in a bemused crocodile, and after a few minutes I turned around to ask the three people behind me if they knew where we were going. 'No!' they said, 'we're following you.' We fell into step, and at the station we spurned the express and chose the local train that would leave an hour later for less than half the price. An hour in Giarre. What to do? The two brothers among my new friends headed, like eighteenth-century travellers, straight for Finnocchiaro Cioccolatteria, the chocolate house. And like eighteenth-century travellers again, they knew exactly what to order in that dark, wood-panelled interior: *cioccolato classico finnochiaro*. It came in cappuccino cups, as thick as custard and spiced with chilli, cinnamon and cloves that tingled in the mouth and on the lips. In its glow, Cosimo, the older of the two, told me they had left Sicily as children and lived their whole lives in Milan. 'Nevertheless,' he said, 'I have always felt something extraordinary for Etna.'

I envied Cosimo the extraordinary something he felt for the volcano, but I could never have it because it came only as part and parcel of a lifelong connection to the place. Nevertheless, viewing almost the entire circumference of Etna from the train did turn out to be a shortcut to building a deeper and more satisfying relationship with my surroundings. After that journey, you see, I had to admit that I had never encountered a place demanding so insistently that I understand how it had been made, and how the extraordinary events leading to its creation had come about, not once, but over and over again. Answering that call would be my route to the deeper connection with Etna I craved, because it obliged me to unpick both her geological and human histories back to their very beginnings.

3.

A Swim Through Deep Time

Travelling back to the roots of Etna's history meant driving down to the chaotic beaches that she and a whole series of her angry ancestors had been littering with debris over hundreds of thousands of years. This was no hardship. A drop of a hundred metres saw me turning off the car heater, another hundred and I was opening the windows to warm air thickened with the joyful scents of early summer. I could even stop on the way to buy strawberries from a van by the side of the road, delicious, dark fruit that filled the car with a lingering smell of caramel long after I had eaten it.

There were lots of small ports along the rugged Ionian coastline, places with black lava shores, where the sun shone reliably all summer on lazy days punctuated by swims, lemon granita, and the chiming of a church clock. Fishing boats were always pulled up on those beaches, or anchored along the harbour walls, so I had to pick a path among mooring ropes if I wanted to swim out through water that lay warm between basalt breakwaters. There was often a slick of engine oil across its surface, and a smell of fish hanging over the boats, but it was lovely to look back at the village above the little beach, with Etna's south-east crater towering over it. Below me a palimpsest of maritime history was spelt out in ancient anchors, lost mooring ropes and boat parts on the seabed. And one of my earrings, unfortunately, somewhere off the coast of Etna, where I know it to be both perpetually lost and there forever.

Lava from Etna's eruptions has only reached that coast four times in recorded history, once in 396 BC and again in 1030, 1160 and 1669. The first and last of these events were the most dramatic in human terms. With perfect timing, lava from the eruption of 396 BC blocked the advance of Carthaginian troops marching on Catania. According to the ancient Greek historian Diodorus Siculus, their general had intended to make them invincible by sending them down the coast from Naxos in step with the fleet. But Etna foiled his plan by flooding the coastline with burning lava just before the troops arrived, forcing them to take the more arduous route down the volcano's west flank. And as for the eruption of 1669, Etna had never before achieved such devastation in human history and, thankfully, has never done so again. The 400 years that have elapsed since then count for nothing in geological time, and so it is only by looking much, much deeper into her past ancestry that volcanologists can hope to understand whether she might erupt with equal violence in the future.

Wind and water have eroded some of the lava deposited by Etna and her predecessors on the coast, but much of it is still as rugged and inhospitable as the day it arrived. Go to that volcanic riviera in early summer and you will find it ringing with a cacophony of drills, hammers and saws. This is the sound of local clubs, bars and lidos defying the lava's challenges by erecting temporary decking over it, and then sinking the short ladders their members can use to climb down into the sea. I belonged to none of those organizations, and at first the locals would look pityingly at me as I wobbled my way to the water. I only had to watch them, however, to learn their near invisible routes across sharp volcanic clinker to the shore. But those beaches were no place for cissies, and it didn't seem to matter how often any of us made that journey: it was always the same teetering, tottering, inelegant process. We didn't care. We were happy to wobble back from the water and cast ourselves onto any flat surface we could find.

Aci Castello was one of the small places where a few fishermen gathered on the dock each day to sell their catch, and the beach was an unholy mess of lava. There was a waiter in a restaurant on the front who always wore a sailor's hat. On my first visit he lured me inside with stories from his life in 1970s London, and promises of fish cooked *alla brace*, 'over embers'. The view from the tables was of the Faraglioni, lava stacks that rose from the water offshore roughly half a million years ago. They were the root of Etna's family tree, the first symptom of the volcanic energy that would eventually create the volcano that has come to obsess me.

Ever since they first rose from the water, the Faraglioni have been weathered by the elements, so that seen from the shore they resemble *arancini*, those deep-fried balls of rice you find in every local bar. Or to be more precise, they resemble *arancini* as they are made here on the east coast, where they are nearly always cone shaped, as if each one were a homage to Mount Etna. The analogy wouldn't work at all on the island's west coast, where the shape of an *arancino* is more likely to be true to its name, 'little orange'.

The Sicani – one of Sicily's indigenous tribes – had been living on Etna long before the Greeks arrived, but it is Greek voices that call across millennia from the beginning of Etna's written history, and Greek imaginations that peopled Etna's slopes with a *millefois* of mythical figures. These associations were so enduring that eighteenth- and nineteenth-century travellers couldn't see Etna without a miasma of classical associations hanging over her like sea mist, or the smoke from her craters. As if to sum up this impression, the late-eighteenth-century Scottish writer and traveller Patrick Brydone described the volcano as simply 'the great mother of monsters'. Gazing at the Faraglioni from my table outside the restaurant, it struck me that whether they had just arrived like me, or pitched up on her shore thousands of years ago, any stranger coming to live on Etna must wrestle with the same mysteries and misgivings, and what's more, she has the geomythology to prove it.

The Greeks laid down the first layer of this geomythology by imagining a world inside the volcano peopled mostly by monsters. Virgil named one of them Enceladus in the *Aeneid*. He was a gigantic typhon, a hundred-headed, fire-breathing hellraiser, with huge leathery wings and coiled serpents instead of legs. His hideous head brushed the stars, and his vast bulk was scorched and scarred by thunderbolts thrown at him during the Gigantomachy, a battle between gods and giants for control of the cosmos. After being taken captive in combat, Enceladus was imprisoned for eternity beneath the mighty weight of Etna, and by throwing himself against the walls of his prison he caused the earthquakes that have always dogged the region. As for eruptions, they occurred whenever his furious, fiery breath melted rock, sending it exploding high into the sky and coursing down Etna's flanks.

Even at the quietest times, smoke drifts from Etna's summit, and the Greeks attributed this gentler form of communication *de profundis* to Hephaestus, God of Fire, who had a forge in the bowels of the volcano. According to Hesiod, three industrious cyclopes called Brontes, Arges and Steropes worked for him there, stoking the furnace and beating out the lightning and thunderbolts Zeus would use to slaughter his enemies.

A mural of the huge, grizzled face of Polyphemus, another cyclops, glares out from the wall of Aci Castello's community centre, a single eye in the centre of his craggy forehead. Ovid had Polyphemus falling in love with the water nymph Galatea in his *Metamorphoses*. Tiny, fragile and perpetually young, she spurned his lumbering courtship, his gnarled old body and frightening face in favour of Acis, a beautiful shepherd much closer to her in age and stature. Of course she did. When Polyphemus caught sight of them together on a beach, he hurled rocks at Acis, and despite a brave attempt to swim away, the poor boy was spatchcocked. Acis' memory is perpetuated in the name of Aci Castello, and that of eight other local towns, all with Aci as their prefix – another of the indelible marks made by the Greeks on Etna's landscape.

There has never been any doubt among Etna's inhabitants that Polyphemus' disastrous encounter with Odysseus took place on Etna. This episode in Homer's *Odyssey* makes sense of two mysteries specific to the volcano and her surroundings, explaining both the existence of the Faraglioni, and that of gigantic, fossilized bones still lying just beneath the surface of the ground all over Sicily. Legend has the cyclopes living between Etna, Catania and the town of Lentini on the Catania Plain. This area may well correspond to places where those vast, unintelligible bones were exhumed by

Greek farmers cultivating land at the foot of Etna, or by erosion, rain, floods and earthquakes.

The Greeks were our first palaeontologists, and they recorded those fossilized bones and displayed them in their museums and temples. But what were they to think when they found skulls twice or even three times the size of their own, with holes in the centre of their foreheads? We know now that these bizarre bones belonged to the descendants of elephants that strolled across to Sicily from Calabria when sea levels dropped during one of the great ice ages. After the water level rose again they were trapped on the island, poor things, struggling to move their enormous bodies across its rough terrain, and rarely finding enough to eat or drink. Before long, however, they had begun to adapt to the island's environment by getting smaller with every generation. Eventually they were no bigger than large dogs. Fat, knee-high dogs that weighed nearly 115 kilos apiece and lived on or near Etna's territory between 6 million and 250,000 years ago.

They keep an *Elephas falconieri* skeleton in Room 120 of the University of Catania's geological museum, and its thickset, yellowed bones and gigantic tusks convey a vivid impression of an animal both small in stature and immensely large in volume. Looking at its skull, it is easy to understand how Greeks – who might never have seen an elephant – could mistake the oval cavity where the trunk was once attached for the socket of an enormous, single eye. And their conviction that those vast, misshapen skulls belonged to gigantic humans would only have been confirmed when they found elephant femur bones, because they looked like gigantic versions of human thigh bones, and the same went for shoulder blades and teeth. In the glass cabinets lining the walls of the same room in the museum are the bones of other local creatures just as well suited to living in that mythical, upside-down volcanic landscape: dormice the size of rabbits, gigantic turtles, oversized swans and miniature hippos. Best not go too close though, for there is a professor of palaeontology haunting Room 120 who will shout '*Non toccare!*' despite the glass between you and the collection. Perhaps she has shared her prehistoric zoo too often with local schoolchildren.

So much for elephants, but what of the Faraglioni? The Greeks would have passed the extraordinary sight of them emerging from the sea again and again as they sailed in and out of Naxos, their first colony on the island, founded close to the foot of Etna in around 735 BC. They would have demanded explanation then just as they do today, and here it comes. Do you know the story of Odysseus and the cyclops Polyphemus? The one where Polyphemus devours a few of Odysseus' shipmates, and then Odysseus blinds him with a wooden stake? It is still alive and well on Etna, where a young man told me he had met people who didn't think Homer was a real person. And even if they did, they said he had never set foot on Sicily. 'But I don't agree,' the young man said, 'because he seems to have known everything about our Pinzirita sheep.' These elegant, long-woolled, long-faced sheep are native to Etna, and although they have thick ringlets of wool hanging right down their sides, their stomachs are completely bare. This was the young man's point, because Odysseus and his men could never have escaped from Polyphemus if they hadn't been able to conceal themselves beneath his ewes' bare bellies, and remain suspended there by clinging on to the woollen ringlets hanging down on either side.

Back on board his ship, the hold now full of Polyphemus' finest animals, Odysseus presents as more pirate than hero. He could still see the cyclops blundering blindly about on the mountainside, and from the safety of the deck he began to taunt him and shout abuse. Maddened by pain and humiliation, Polyphemus responded by ripping the peaks from towering crags all around him, and flinging them towards the sound of Odysseus' voice. One after another they landed in the water, creating huge tidal waves, and there they remain to this day in the form of the Faraglioni, and a scattering of smaller rocks.

All that said, we should not forget that alongside those mythical justifications for Etna's landscapes and behaviours, there were the explanations of early scientists among the island's Greek settlers.

Their deductions may not always have been scientific in the sense of the word today, and yet they were as deeply concerned as we are with finding rational explanations for the mysteries of the universe. One was Empedocles, who lived on Etna early in the fifth century BC and invented the immensely influential theory that all matter consists of four elements: fire, earth, air and water. He named each of them after a different god. However, living on Etna, he knew full well that fire was as creative as it was destructive, and therefore he referred to it both as Hades, the annihilating god of the Underworld, and Hephaestus, the blacksmith god hard at work in the bowels of the volcano.

I often returned to Aci Castello, where there was always an artist selling local views from the esplanade. They all showed the same thing: the Faraglioni and Isola Lachea, the tiny island next to them. Looking at them as that painter did from the coast was about as satisfying as viewing sculptures in a gallery on the other side of the road, and one day I decided to put this right by setting off like Odysseus from the shore. Had I been alone, I might have chosen to hire a kayak or a paddleboard, but summer had delivered the first raft of visitors to fill my roomy eyrie in Milo. We hired a pedalo from the backstreet boys, the ones whose battered craft were moored in an awkward, rocky inlet beyond the fish market. There were four of us in the crew. Four adults, solid and well grown, and only one pedalo left in dock. It's true that it had four seats impressed into its moulded-plastic deck, but with its scuffed edges and faded hull it looked a frail vehicle for such a substantial load.

Nevertheless, off we went, pursued by shouts of 'left, then right' as, hopelessly incompetent, we veered towards billowing lumps of lava just beneath the dazzling surface of the water. By pedalling frantically to find traction on a choppy sea and tugging at the tiller, we eventually headed straight for the Faraglioni. It took half an hour to make the journey, half an hour across the bumpy wakes of speedboats, and as the shore receded and the waves whipped up, I was struck by the absurdity of treating a pedalo as a geological survey ship, or even a seagoing vessel at all. I can't promise that all my companions were still on message by the time we arrived, but to my mind the crossing had neatly transported us across 500,000 years to the first signs of volcanic activity here, and the very beginning of Etna's history.

The deep, underground events that birthed the Faraglioni are part of the same processes that would eventually result in the formation of Etna, just as they have resulted in many other volcanos all over the world. Like them, the Faraglioni are made from lava that poured through fissures in the floor of a shallow, primordial sea we call the pre-Etnean Gulf. Its waters once submerged the coastline we had just pedalled out from, as well as the entire area now occupied by Etna.

Here, on the starting line of Etna's history, seems a good place to remember what lava is, and why it might suddenly come bursting through the Earth's surface. To do this we must plumb the depths beneath a landscape where, untold millions of years ago, the African and Eurasian tectonic plates collided. Their impact was slow, but so powerful that the rocky African plate was pushed beneath the Eurasian one. It would have been descending into the Earth's mantle when the Faraglioni were formed, and it is still grinding down into it as I write these words today. This never-ending collision created such inordinate amounts of heat and pressure, miles beneath the bed of that primordial sea, that together they drove water from cracks and crevices in the African plate. The same pressures then forced it and the seawater it had dragged down with it to percolate into the rock of the mantle. This altered the mantle's chemistry, causing fragments to melt and form magma, or liquid rock.

As it was less dense than the solid rock surrounding it, the magma began to rise through the mantle towards the Earth's surface, eventually finding somewhere just below the seabed to pool and accumulate. It might have stayed there for millennia, but those tectonic plates were never at ease, and the tensions they created were forever tearing the Earth's crust apart. This made it inevitable that magma would eventually find its way through a weakness on the Earth's surface, just as it does today. And whenever this happens, it changes its name from magma to lava. And what with all the minerals, volatile gases and liquids that have escaped from it in transit, it is a very different brew to the original melt that set off on that long journey.

After the Faraglioni were first formed by lava bursting through fissures in the sea floor, they were hidden deep beneath the surface of the water. But as those tectonic forces continued to exert their pressures, the seabed beneath them was gradually crumpled and raised, pushing the tops of the stacks above the waterline, and depositing shells of prehistoric molluscs and sea snails on land that now forms the flanks of Etna. And there the Faraglioni are to this day, a blatant statement of the connection between this uneasy landscape and the invisible world deep beneath the Earth's surface, where extreme processes with unthinkable outcomes account for the existence of Etna and all her predecessors.

There were plenty of other people visiting the Faraglioni on the same day as us. Some were paddling frenetically around the rocks in kayaks, while others surveyed them imperiously from paddleboards. There was a temporary mooring for inflatables and yachts, a party place where boatloads of boys blasted the air with music. Speedboats made their roaring passage slightly too close to our precarious pedalo, fishing boats chugged past on their way to open water, and super-yachts sent their wakes crashing against the Faraglioni like pernicious memories, returning again and again to the same place. In the middle of all this traffic action was a man sunbathing at the base of the Faraglione Grande. He didn't seem to have a paddleboard or a pedalo, and yet there he lay, complacently reading a paperback and smoking a cigarette, two things that depend entirely for their success on being dry. The stack above him was made from a fabulous mosaic of columnar basalt.

Of all the wonderful shapes lava can make, those hexagonal cylinders are my favourite. They would have formed as the surface of the lava bursting from the seabed began to cool, then to contract and crack. At first the cracks would have been superficial, but then they would have spread downwards, cutting the lava into perfectly formed, hexagonal columns. Half a million years of weathering had undercut their sharp regularity, so now the Faraglioni looked as if they were clad in the peeling scales of some vast, prehistoric reptile.

We launched ourselves awkwardly into the water from the slippery metal ladder at the pedalo's stern. Beneath its blue-black surface, all was undulation, quietness and blur, a shimmering, shifting theatre of light and dark around the flanks of the Faraglione Grande. Seen at close quarters, its ridged and crenellated sides were a high-rise housing project for crabs, sea urchins and fish of every size, startling stripe and colour. Normally, I would expect fish to flick away as I approached, but where Etna meets the sea is a marine park, and to make any progress at all I had to push through shoals as fearless as creatures of the Galapagos. Below them the sea floor was strewn with the puffy shapes of pillow lava – a form that lava took as it continued to emerge from the seabed thousands of years after the Faraglioni were formed. This time it responded to the cooling effect of the water by billowing into rounded shapes enclosed by a glassy rind. And still the lava erupted, pumping up those pillows from the inside until their rinds ruptured, releasing hot lava from their cores and sending more and more pillows spreading across the seabed.

The slightest kick took me back through the glittering surface of the water to the clamouring world of waves, music, motors, laughter and shouting, and yet I will always associate the beginning of Etna's history with that underwater world. And casting my mind back by half a million years I will also recall the old hunting dog bobbing along beside us on our return journey. He sat insouciantly on the back of his owner's paddleboard, and trailed his tail in the water like a rudder. With his solemn face, long ears, and the wrinkle of skin across his poor old back, he seemed to embody the antiquity of the landscape all around us.

Caught between mythology and volcanology, the Faraglioni may seem to belong to a distant and unrepeatable past. However, we should never forget those seething energies underground, or the possibility that something similar could explode from the seabed at any time. For example, it is less than 200 years since fishermen found shoals of boiled fish floating on the surface of the sea south of Sicily. The stink of sulphur was so strong that some of them passed out. A few days later, on 10 July 1831, a volcanic crater burst from the water overnight, and spat fire, ash and lava for the rest of the month. By August a new island had been formed. It was not even a kilometre in diameter, and rose to only 60 metres above the waves, but nevertheless many people believed they were witnessing the birth of a new continent. Ferdinandea, as the Sicilians called it in honour of their king, was strategically placed for international shipping routes. Needless to say, Italy, France and Britain instantly laid claim to it. International negotiations had solved nothing by the time the island sank back below the water, only five months after it first appeared.

Etna is the product of geological events that unfolded over hundreds of thousands of years. Long after the Faraglioni were formed, prodigious quantities of lava went on spewing from fissures in the bottom of the pre-Etnean Gulf, and spread far across the seabed. In fact, it wasn't until about 200,000 years ago that any volcanos broke the surface to appear above water. A little later, volcanic activity began to move inland from the coast, so that each new volcano seemed to march a little closer to the territory now occupied by Etna. Instead of running from horizontal fissures, lava was now erupting from conduits in the centre of these volcanos. That is how Trifoglietto was formed 80,000 years ago, and Ellittico 20,000 years later. Their remains would form the foundations for the new summit that began to grow only 15,000 years ago, and eventually formed the volcano we call Etna, or Mongibello Recente.

The east flank of the new Etna volcano was built on top of the remains of Trifoglietto, which stood in turn on the ancient clay bed of that pre-Etnean Gulf. Over millennia, rain seeped in through the lava of its flank and lubricated the impermeable clay of the ancient seabed, rendering both it and the surfaces of the volcano slippery. There are several theories about the shock that set them moving 8,000 years ago. Whether it was a violent eruption or an earthquake, something made the whole of the east side of Etna collapse and slide towards the sea. Look back at her east face today and you can clearly see the horse-shoe-shaped chunk missing from it. They call this the Valle del Bove, and it has been acting as an invaluable receptacle for lava from Etna's summit eruptions ever since, often preventing it from flowing on down the slopes and into the fields, towns and villages below.

At the time, however, the collapse sent a catastrophic avalanche of lava from Etna and her ancient predecessors tumbling down the east flank, picking up speed, soil, rocks, mud and vegetation as it went, and engulfing streams and snow until it became a lethal, rolling slurry hurtling towards the coast. The soil in Milo was made from this unique mix of ancient lavas, and Giarre, Riposto, numerous other towns and villages, and even a section of the motorway, are built on top of debris left by the landslide as it came crashing down the mountain. Still more of it tumbled into the sea, and as if to demonstrate that Etna's powers were international, it triggered a tsunami that engulfed and destroyed coastlines as far away as Greece and North Africa.

The tail end of that momentous landslide formed a cliff that runs along the coast from Pozzillo to Riposto. They call it the Chiancone, and at first glance it looks like any old cliff running behind the houses, and then swerving towards the sea on the beach at Praiola. Waves have been gnawing at its frayed and crumbling base where the beach runs out, but still it rises for 30 impressive metres from the sea. Looking at it closely, you can distinguish distinct layers of lava and alluvial mud. Were I a geologist or a volcanologist, I could read this mix like a book about Etna's history, making a mine of information from the textures and colours of all those fragments of ancient lava.

Etna had already been drawn into the first stirrings of scientific thinking by the ancient Greeks, and in the eighteenth century she became even more deeply entwined in human thought during the debate about the history of the Earth that raged all over Europe. According to conventional Christian belief, the Earth had been formed in a single frenzied week of creation, had never changed, and was less than 6,000 years old. The first person to challenge this orthodoxy was a British philosopher and priest called Thomas Burnet. Stepping away from convention, he began to envisage a longer past – a deep history – for landscape. The book he published in 1681 was called *Telluris theoria sacra* and was translated in 1684 as *The Sacred Theory of the Earth, Containing an Account of the Original of the Earth, and of all the General Changes Which It Hath Already Undergone, or is to Undergo, till the CONSUMMATION of all Things.* Burnet's book triggered a storm of controversy. Even its title was bound to upset a lot of people, but as so often happens, attempts to discredit Burnet's ideas sparked a debate that served only to make them common knowledge. And within a hundred years, travellers on Etna were collecting scientific data and questioning the significance of everything they saw.

Quite unlike Vesuvius, which had long made Naples a necessary stop on every eighteenth-century Grand Tour, Etna was rarely seen by foreigners before Patrick Brydone's ascent of the volcano in 1773. When his *Tour Through Sicily And Malta* became a bestseller, however, it brought Etna to the attention of a whole generation of would-be travellers, transforming it in their minds from a mythical place to a destination that would soon become the southernmost point on many a Grand Tour. Tourists often brought a copy of Brydone's book with them, and some, like Samuel Taylor Coleridge, used it as their guide for climbing the mountain. Not an entirely happy experience in Coleridge's case, as looking down into the obscurity of the summit crater reminded him of the 'impenetrable darkness' of his opium addiction. Meanwhile, the same ascent was inspiring other Romantic poets to link the depth of Etna's summit crater with the interior landscape of the mind in ways so repetitive that Byron, who described poetry as 'the lava of the imagination', would declare in 'Don Juan':

> I hate to hunt down a tired metaphor,
> So let the often used volcano go.
> Poor thing! How frequently, by me and others,
> It hath been stirred up until its smoke quite smothers!

One of those tired tropes was undoubtedly the widespread use of volcanic eruption as a metaphor for political ferment. Both Etna and Vesuvius had erupted repeatedly during the French Revolution, and there was an irresistible analogy to be drawn between lava altering the structure of the natural landscape and revolution changing the structure of society. Incandescent lava coursing down their flanks was also a potent metaphor for the revolutionary crowds surging through the streets of Paris. Untameable, impossibly powerful, both they and the eruptions were seen as simultaneously destructive and creative, because having sterilized the social and physical landscape, they transformed it forever.

Brydone's local guide to Etna and her territory was Canon Giuseppe Recupero, a Catholic priest he named Etna's 'historiographer'. Recupero was eager to share what Etna had revealed to him about the age of the Earth, and he acted as guide to many other foreign visitors, including that pioneer of volcanology, Sir William Hamilton. Recupero took Brydone first to Santa Tecla, and showed him a mighty lava flow plunging into the sea. Afterwards, Brydone wrote, 'This lava I imagined from its bareness, for it is yet covered with a very scanty soil, had run from the mountain only a few ages ago . . .' Wrong, for 'this very lava is mentioned by Diodorus Siculus . . .' in connection with the Carthaginian army in 396 BC.

The following day, Recupero accompanied Brydone on another field trip, this time to see a well that had been cut through layers of lava. Each layer was exposed, as was the generous layer of soil that covered it. The flow at Santa Tecla had revealed that it took over 2,000 years for even the scantiest layer of soil to form on top of lava. Consequently, Brydone reported, Recupero considered the well proof of 'the great antiquity of the eruptions of his mountain'. Elsewhere, he had dug down through seven distinct layers of lava, 'one under the other', each covered in 'a thick bed of rich earth'. By his calculation, this made the lowest layer at least 14,000 years old. He told Brydone he was 'exceedingly embarrassed' by these discoveries, so that:

Moses hangs like a dead weight upon him, and blunts all his zeal for inquiry; for he has really not the conscience to make his mountain so young as that prophet makes the world.

He was already in trouble with his bishop, who had warned him 'not to pretend to be a better natural historian than Moses'. Ouch! Nevertheless, the Church could not prevent Recupero's nephew from publishing his uncle's research posthumously in 1815, calling it the *Storia naturale e generale dell'Etna, del Canonico Giuseppe Recupero – opera postuma.*

Brydone had no such misgivings, and from the summit of Etna he looked down her flanks to hollow craters 'now filled with stately oaks, and covered to a great depth with the richest soil'. As if still thrilled by Recupero's revelations, he remarked 'What an idea does not this give of the amazing antiquity of the mountain!' For geologists like James Hutton, at work in the same period, Brydone's account of Etna was another argument for the existence of Deep Time.

My own sense of time and place was beginning to alter. Until now, Etna's geological past had been no more to me than a shimmering succession of colossal numbers that I failed again and again to retain. Having seen her history embedded in the coastal landscape, however, I was finding it easier to grasp. Going to Santa Tecla just over 250 years after Brydone, I encountered the same chaos of lava that he described. It lay beside the sea as if it had only just cooled into a frozen cascade of vast and unrepentant blocks, their crushing weight conflicting with the waves dancing at their feet. And underwater the lava landscape stretched on and on, clothed now in seaweeds, red and green.

Learning a little about Etna's past made me feel more embedded on her slopes in the present day. My new life in Milo was also beginning to take shape, and I liked everything about it. I liked the long-distance chats with my neighbour Lucia across the chasm between my terrace and hers. We talked about chores, about wild asparagus growing in the woods, and visits from our children. I had begun to feel an unfamiliar enthusiasm for cleaning in my sparsely furnished home, for running a mop over its shiny terrazzo floors, and polishing the windows to preserve the crystalline views. The houses to either side belonged to the convent as well. The same two families from Catania had been taking a summer's lease on them for years. At first, they came only at weekends to prepare for their stay. 'But from 6th June we will be here full time,' said one of them, over the fence that divided us, 'and then it will be a continuous party.'

I liked that idea, and I liked the walk down to the Cinque Tigli bar for breakfast on Saturdays, because now that short journey unfolded in a chain of friendly waves from passing cars, and conversations with more distant neighbours. I liked to see the *barista* starting to make my cappuccino as I walked through the door, and I appreciated the breakthrough when he stopped asking, as *baristi* must of strangers, whether I wanted *crema* or *marmellata* inside the flaky pastry of my breakfast *cornetto*. The bar filled with cyclists on those early summer mornings, clip-clopping inside in their special cycling shoes. I had noticed that people talked almost as much about the weather in Sicily as they did in Britain, and because Etna's behaviour had so much influence on whether clouds deposited their rain or drifted on by, the *signora* at the till usually had something to say about her. And when I eventually walked back up the steep hill to the house, the gaggle of stray dogs outside the gate rushed to greet me as if we had been best friends for years.

Yes, I was settling down in Milo and feeling more at home there every day. So what next? It was staring me in the face every time I looked up from Milo at the *Deserta* surrounding Etna's summit. The time had come to reckon with all the ambiguous feelings that Etna's austere, black landscapes still provoked by confronting the ultimate lava landscape head on.

4.

Dark Desert

It is easy enough to get up to the volcanic desert surrounding Etna's south-east crater these days, but spare a thought for tourists trying to reach her summit in 1900. *Baedeker's* guide gave them detailed instructions about going first to Nicolosi to hire the licensed guides, apprentice guides, porters and mules they would need to make the expedition, and buy the correct quantity of candles for the final approach in the small hours before dawn. Among the provisions recommended for the journey were bottles of strong coffee, wine, cold meat, bread and salt. 'Even in hot weather,' Baedeker went on to advise, 'the traveller should not fail to be provided with an overcoat or plaid, as the wind on the mountain is often bitterly cold. In winter or spring, when the snow is still unmelted, a veil or coloured spectacles will be found useful . . . warm gloves, woollen stockings and strong shoes are of course indispensable.'

The ascent from Nicolosi to the first refuge ever built on Etna took seven hours by mule (assuming, of course, you knew how to ride a mule). This stopover was actually a small observatory built in 1804 by mapmaker Giuseppe Gemmellaro's brother, Mario, who was one of Europe's first volcanologists. Only a few years later the Royal Navy, then posted in Sicily to mount a blockade against the French, contributed the necessary money to extend the building. Thereafter, British travellers had the satisfaction of staying in a modest stone hut known to all as the Casa degli Inglesi. Baedeker promised them 'several hours of repose' there, although they had to set off again at 2.30 a.m. to make the last ascent to the summit. The plan was to arrive in time to watch the sun rise from the sea far below, and then see the volcano casting 'a colossal isosceles triangle' across the west side of the island. That done, they returned to Nicolosi the same day.

My own ascent began by driving up a peaceful road out of Zafferana Etnea, first through the gentle shade of chestnut woods, and then around spectacular bends leading up the volcano's south face to Rifugio Sapienza. The refuge sits at almost 2,000 metres, which is as high as you can get on Etna by car. It is the biggest building of its kind on the mountain, and in its enormous restaurant they serve good, solid rewards for days well spent on the summit. That is where I met Fabrizio. Compact and wiry, his head shaved smooth, as if he thought hair might slow him down, he was one of the 'Gruppo Guide Vulcanologiche Etna Nord' in Linguaglossa. Like all the guides in that close-knit clan, he was intimate with the volcano in ways that came from clambering about on her slopes since childhood. They all knew about volcanology, of course, but were also expert in the volcano's folklore and mythology, plants and trees, not to mention mountain rescue and first aid. More important still, they were privy to the current state of Etna's activity, and were able to calculate the risks she posed on any particular day. The volcano works hard to ensure that hiking maps are never accurate for long, but the guides knew about any change to her morphology as soon as it occurred.

We had chosen to reach the summit in the easiest possible way that day, and so into the funicular we went, like sardines into a tin. With a sudden, lurching acceleration it took us high above the south flank, and then spat us out into blazing sunshine, blustery wind, and the parched volcanic desert that was the apotheosis of all I had come to dread. Cartographers have spent centuries choosing words to encapsulate the nature of that sun-dazzled, primordial world. *Discoperta*, 'uncovered', is one, *Nuda* and *Deserta*, 'nude' and 'desert' or even 'deserted' are others. Any one of them fitted the landscape I found myself in. We were 500 metres above the tree line, too high for any living thing, however hardy, to take root. Without the background scents of plants and trees, the air all around us felt vast and empty.

The south-east crater was our horizon. When those tourists had laboured up Etna in 1900, she still had only one, central crater on her summit. Today there are four summit craters and about three hundred lateral craters. Those lateral craters burst from Etna's flanks whenever magma rising towards the surface finds a weak spot in the Earth's crust. Sometimes successive eruptions occur along the same fault line or fissure, and then cones of lava and ash spring up in the straight line that Italians refer to as a *bottoniera*, like the buttons on a shirt.

The north-east crater was the first new crater to be formed on Etna's summit in 1911. The next was Voragine, which sprang up inside the old central crater in 1945. Then came Bocca Nuova in 1968. Over time, each of those twentieth-century craters has developed a character all its own, and some semblance of a pattern of behaviour. Consequently, I've heard local people refer to the south-east crater birthed in 1971 as 'the wicked boy', or even 'nasty brat'. I would have loved to climb to the top of it, but that would have been much too dangerous. By erupting almost continuously between 2021 and 2022, it had doubled its volume and added 30 unstable metres to its height, so that Etna's summit was now 3,357 metres above sea level – higher than it had ever been before. This could have been cause for celebration, had all that extra height and weight not been resting on such a steep, unstable slope. Everything about the south-east crater was precarious now, and one side of it had been riven in two by a large fracture. Parts of its flank had already collapsed and triggered landslides. None had caused much damage, but no one could predict how big the next one might be, or where it might go.

Everything that lay before us was black, except for the synthetic jackets of a few other walkers strung out like colourful beads against the dark backdrop. Nothing but an innocuous wisp of smoke rose from the south-east crater that day, but Fabrizio reminded me that even when she appeared inactive, you never knew when Etna might throw out a casual shower of bits and pieces that could kill you if they landed on your head. And that is just one of many eventualities. People still talk about an unexpected catastrophe in March 2017. Ten people were injured while visiting that summit landscape, when a burning lava flow from the south-east crater ran into snow at the base of the cone, creating a violent explosion. It is impossible to predict an event like this, so all Fabrizio could do was equip me with a hard hat.

Coming up to high altitude with Fabrizio as my guide gave me a first glimpse of the kind of relationship that can be forged with Etna's lava landscapes. While I could see nothing but lava and lava flows stretching ahead of us like a series of insurmountable barriers, Fabrizio seemed to confront the landscape like a puzzle to be solved, and soon he had picked out the hint of a path to lead me uphill. We climbed steadily on the whisper of ways that were the only logical route across the *Deserta*'s fragmented territory. And as he led the way through each lava puzzle, I noticed that, far from being empty, the air around us was full of ladybirds. They settled like bright red jewels all over the ground, on my T-shirt, my hands, my hair. Kidnapped by currents of warm air, they had been carried to a place of no escape, and Fabrizio told me they couldn't hope to survive the sharp drop in temperature overnight.

We were surrounded by broken lava boulders and sharp clinker. Some people like to crack the same joke again and again, saying that the technical term for this kind of lava is *'a'ā*, because that is the noise you would make if you tried to cross it in bare feet. In reality, *'a'ā* is one of many Hawaiian words baked into the international language of volcanology. *'A'ā* flows are the most common kind on Etna, and they are formed when thick, pasty lava fragments into random, jagged shapes as it runs down her steep slopes. I saw now that the lava formed by this process was very much more varied than I had realized.

Etna produces enormous quantities of lava every time she erupts. Its temperature can be anything from 950 to 1,200 degrees Celsius, and no matter what form it takes, all her output goes by the generic name 'tephra'. Tephra fragments are classified by size. At the finest end comes volcanic ash. You might think someone so given to complaining about ash in her boots was making a fuss about nothing, but think again. The great, dark plumes of ash that rise from Etna's summit are made from tiny, broken fragments of abrasive rock, minerals and sharp volcanic glass. An ash cloud can drift for miles on the wind, and people live in dread of it depositing its cargo on their village, house, farm or garden. Large amounts of ash cause car accidents, block roads, clog sewage systems, damage buildings and suffocate garden plants and crops. There are three airports within a hundred kilometres of Etna, and ash has the power to close them all for fear of blocked runways, and even aeroplane engine failure. Exposure to ash can also cause respiratory disease, and during long eruptions the authorities sometimes distribute masks to the island's inhabitants, in a bid to protect them from inhaling too much of it.

If the rock fragments now nestling between my ankle and my boot measured between 2 and 64 millimetres they would be categorized as 'lapilli'. The word derives from *lappilus*, Latin for pebble or small stone. Lapilli are made from molten or semi-molten lava that has cooled mid-air. Anything larger than 64 millimetres is categorized as a 'bomb'. Volcanic bombs are made when, instead of fragmenting like ash or lapilli, lava coalesces mid-air. Imagine that. An incandescent bomb flying through the air and then hurtling randomly down Etna's slopes. Nine tourists lost their lives to bombs during a sudden explosion of the north-east crater in 1979.

When I first looked around at the *Deserta*, I saw nothing but a landscape cobbled together from expressions of the Earth's unrest. Whether it was formed from lava flows, cones or craters, it had all been birthed by forces too mighty to properly comprehend. When Fabrizio looked around, he saw a place as dear and familiar to him as his own back garden. It was engraved with memories from a lifetime of exploring. Here was the place, for example, where he and his friends used to skate every spring. Their rink was a little lake at the bottom of a slight incline known as the Piano del Lago. But the *Deserta* is landscape in fast motion, where building or destruction that might take millions of years elsewhere can happen overnight. And so it was in 2001, when a brand-new lateral crater burst through the middle of their skating rink. It was christened Laghetto, little lake, in memory of what had been there before.

Lateral craters can pop up anywhere on Etna, even in the Coltivata, where you will sometimes find them nestling among fields, roads and houses. Clothed now in orchards and vineyards, they look like wild creatures tamed. Some people have even built houses on them, and although this may sound like madness to us, they are safe in the knowledge that lateral craters are like monocarpic plants that only blossom once before they die. Etna's four summit craters, on the other hand, are constantly connected to her magma chamber, and this means they can erupt again and again. As we passed the flow from an eruption by the south-east crater only two weeks before, Fabrizio told me not to step on it because it would melt my boots. I would soon discover that boots never last long on Etna, what with the heat of fresh lava and its super-abrasive qualities when cold.

We stopped again at the base of another lateral crater, named Barbagallo after one of the oldest families to work as guides on Etna, passing their job on from father to son for almost 200 years. Steam was belching from a cleft in the rocks at its base. 'Put your head inside,' Fabrizio ordered, as if this new marvel were the most ordinary thing in the world. I pressed my face right into that hot, damp cavity, as if committing to some expensive spa treatment.

We were climbing still higher now, high enough to feel the cool edge of the breeze, high enough to find a slippery layer of snow beneath the lava as we walked. In a shallow dip ahead of us I saw the ground in cross section, with alternating layers of snow and lava neatly piled one on top of the other in an arrangement Fabrizio described as a *tiramisù*. I would have expected lava to melt snow, but nothing on Etna was as expected, and Fabrizio explained that lava acts instead as insulation to preserve it. Snow and lava, ice and fire, white and black, fertility and sterility, breaking and making, beauty and horror; people have been writing about these contradictions on Etna for centuries. One of the first was Patrick Brydone, who described the juxtaposition of fire, 'forever existing in the midst of snows which it has no power to melt', and snow and ice surrounding fire 'which they have no power to extinguish'.

Nearing the end of our walk now, we ran down a long, soft, deep lava slope, pushing our feet outwards as if we were still able to skate on the icy Piano del Lago. The cliff at the bottom overlooked the Valle del Bove and the glinting expanse of sea far below. About 8,000 years had come and gone since Etna lost that enormous bite of land from her side. In the meantime, lava from untold numbers of eruptions has built so many fanciful structures, so many ridges, escarpments, cones and valleys that my brain could hardly compute their variety, or the technicolour tricks played by the sun with all those different shapes and their shadows. All of it felt very recent, very immediate, as if I were visiting the factory floor to see landscape being made there and then, and in plain sight. Among all the emotions this provoked, the one that dominated was no longer intimidation, but awe.

I am not going to pretend I had an epiphany up there in the *Deserta*. I am also happy to admit to my sense of relief as the great open spaces of the air filled again with the rich scents of leaf mould and growing things as I descended the mountain. Nevertheless, thanks to Fabrizio, I came away with a new way to approach Etna and the challenges she posed. The first revelation had been the path I'd seen him pick out across that maze of lava flows. Walking alone again, I began to seek out those elusive routes across lava landscapes for myself. Before long I realized that unless they were brand new, most of Etna's flows had been domesticated in this way by the footfall of shepherds and their flocks, by foresters, farmers and other walkers. Sometimes their subtle routes were marked with the tiny stone towers they call *omini*, little men, and sometimes with the painted red stripes of an official footpath.

The second lesson concerned the lava itself, for now, instead of seeing it as one fearful fabric, I began to scrutinize it for different qualities. In some flows I found it creating shapes as delicate as icing piped from a bag. In others it rose in folds like neat seams across the surface of a lava boulder, rippled like currents in frozen water, or waves in a frozen sea. Beautiful effects like these were all the product of *pahoehoe* lava, another Hawaiian word. It is formed when fluid lava flows slowly enough for a thin, glassy skin to form on its surface. Meanwhile, the hot, molten lava inside the flow continues to move beneath that superficial skin, dragging it into all those sculptural shapes. In time, all these new insights would transform me from a helpless onlooker to someone with the proper tools to appreciate, and eventually even admire, Etna's starkest landscapes.

5.
Saro the Digger

I had arrived in Milo in the wake of such an extraordinary spate of volcanic activity that eruptions were always in people's minds. If I let on what I was doing there, it was never long before someone whipped out a mobile to show me extraordinary photographs of the south-east crater erupting immediately above the village. The last summer had been 'worse than winter', they told me, because when the council snow ploughs came to clear lapilli and ash from the roads, their gates were blocked by great mounds of detritus, so that they were effectively snowed in.

Those were the stories of the immediate past, but I came to understand that any lava flow that descends the volcano far enough to penetrate the Coltivata has a human story attached to it, a story made unforgettable by being forever embodied in the landscape it has created. Of all these stories, the one set in 1669 is the most dramatic, because no eruption before or since has had such a devastating impact on Etna's inhabitants. Only two other eruptions seem to be so deeply engraved in the inherited memory of Etna's people. The first was in 1928, and it was one of the few times she succeeded in destroying an entire town. Spotting an opportunity for propaganda, the Fascist government rebuilt it as part of the first modern disaster-management plan the volcano's inhabitants had ever seen. The second was in 1991, close to my home in Milo. It stands out for being the longest eruption for 200 years, and for eliciting the most sustained attempt ever made to divert a lava flow. Reading about these three eruptions at my kitchen table, I found myself marvelling at the extraordinary resilience, ingenuity and determination of every generation of Etna's inhabitants.

Sicily had been a Spanish possession for 200 years by the time Etna erupted so catastrophically in 1669. It caused no deaths, but by laying claim to great swathes of rich farmland, bulldozing multiple towns and villages, dramatically altering the lie of the rural landscape, and even entering Catania itself, the eruption rendered thousands of people destitute, and made an enduring impact on the history and economic development of Etna's south-east flank.

The action began with a whirlwind ravaging Etna's slopes. Then the mountain shook with such violent earthquakes that the poor town of Nicolosi on her south flank was reduced to ruins before the eruption had even begun. Earthquakes often herald a flank eruption on Etna, and so it was that on 11 March a long fissure opened between 950 and 700 metres on the south side of the volcano. It was only six feet wide, but no one could tell how deep it was, and a terrifyingly bright and eery light shone out from inside it. It began emitting such quantities of lava that it soon generated the cinder cone of ash and lapilli that people would name Monte Ruina (Mountain of Ruin) because of all the damage it did. Before long the *monte* became *monti*, two cones that were later renamed Monti Rossi in an attempt to expunge the inherited memory of that dreadful time. The tale of what happened next is best told by people who were actually there, and able to observe the lava's progress. There are plenty of sources, because this was the first time in history that one of Etna's eruptions became international news. In fact, it is sometimes cited as one of the first ever 'international media events'.

One vividly evocative description comes from some *'Inquisitive English Merchants now residing in Sicily'*, who sent their first-hand account of the eruption to the Royal Society in London. For fifty-four days of the eruption's 122-day duration, they saw neither the sun nor the stars, watched a vast pillar of ash 'which exceeded twice the bigness of Paul's Steeple in London' shooting into the sky, and suffered a terrifying roaring from Etna that could be heard as far away as Messina. They watched lava 'overwhelm in the upland country some 14 Towns and villages, wherof some were of good note, containing 3 or 4 thousand inhabitants'. Among those unfortunate places were La Guardia and Malpasso, Mascalucia, and Camporotondo, all on Etna's south face. 'As to the matter, which thus ran,' the merchants said:

> it was nothing else but divers kinds of Metals and Minerals, rendered liquid by the fierceness of the Fire in the Bowels of the Earth, boyling up and gushing forth, like the water does at the head of some great River.

This torrent would bring its full weight down on any building it encountered, 'burning whatever was combustible' and crushing the rest. During the first three weeks of the eruption it engulfed some of the richest land on Etna, destroying Misterbianco, and every other town, village and hamlet in its path, so that 'only the Church and Steeple of one of them, which stood on high ground, does still appear'. Those inquisitive merchants also watched an entire vineyard floating past them on the surface of the lava flow just outside Catania. A vision from a dream. Towns that escaped inundation were nevertheless destroyed by layers of ash and lapilli that caused roofs to collapse and buildings to cave in. In the countryside all this detritus suffocated plants and trees, and smothered pasture so effectively that grazing animals had to be evacuated. After weeks of these surreal conditions, it was inevitable that the whole area should begin to add food shortages to the list of its woes.

According to Patrick Brydone, nearly 30,000 people were 'reduced to beggary'. Over the course of just a few weeks 20,000 of them poured into Catania, convinced it was too far from Monte Ruina to be at risk. This sudden influx of the destitute almost doubled the city's population. According to another eyewitness report, however, this time from a British observer called Heneage Finch, all the *catanesi*, from the most humble to the Bishop of Catania himself, as well as other 'persons of quality and estate', 'opened their doors and filled their houses with as many distressed people as they could possibly receive'. What with housing evacuees, gathering in their multitudes to carry the relics of Agata, their patron saint, through the streets, and 'mortifying themselves with Whips and other signs of penance', the *catanesi* were too distracted to notice that bands of brigands and thieves had arrived in their city. These villains made 'prey of the already distressed people, and . . . they had murthered several of them for their goods'. Conditions continued to deteriorate very quickly, and within three weeks of the beginning of the eruption the authorities had completely lost control, the whole city had descended into panic, riots and looting, and the streets were so dangerous that people were afraid to leave home. The situation was only resolved when the viceroy representing Sicily's Spanish government called up the cavalry. It met violence with violence, setting up three new sets of gallows, arresting the perpetrators of unrest and hanging them without trial.

All this drama and more had been triggered by Etna by the time lava reached Catania's city walls. Now those anonymous merchants described people trying to protect themselves against the oncoming flow. They pulled down buildings and barricaded the ends of streets with their debris. Many of Catania's tradesmen fled the city. This added to the troubles of the remaining population by causing the economy to collapse.

What happened next is captured in a painting by Giacinto Platania, made in 1675, and hanging now in the sacristy of Catania's duomo. Platania had very particular qualifications for making that painting: he had been among the men from Pedara who attempted to save Catania by diverting the course of the lava. Until then, people on Etna had always accepted eruptions as a form of divine retribution, hence the self-scourging during the eruption on the streets of Catania. This makes it all the more radical that the first ever attempt to fight back against one of Etna's eruptions should have been led by the local priest, Diego Pappalardo. Dressed in animal skins soaked with water, Pappalardo, Platania and a few companions climbed high on the mountain and attacked the eastern edge of the flow with sledgehammers and pickaxes. After several hours' work, the lava overflowed through the channel they had made with such force they were nearly burnt alive. Undeterred, they continued their work until a broad stream of lava was pouring away to the east of the flow. According to an account published that year, their plan to save Catania would have succeeded had it not been for the arrival of 500 furious men from Paternò, convinced that lava was being deliberately diverted straight towards their town. Hugely outnumbered, Pappalardo and his team had no choice but to abandon their work and flee for home.

This first-hand experience enabled Platania to create an accurate bird's-eye view of the lava's three-pronged attack. He painted Etna's summit smoking innocuously above the Coltivata, where the beautiful landscape untouched by lava is scattered with peaceful villages and lovely villas. He showed Catania as it was before the earthquake of 1693 would raze it to the ground. Medieval houses crowd together along narrow streets, and the lofty tower of the ancient cathedral overshadows them all. Castello Ursino looks much as it does today, and the huge Benedictine monastery of San Nicolò l'Arena backs onto the city wall to the north. We could be looking at a fresco depicting the landscape surrounding a beautiful Tuscan town, were it not for Monte Ruina belching lava that tumbles across the benign landscape above Catania, the monks and nuns escaping by boat from the harbour, and the wealthy families loading their possessions into carriages. More dramatic still, the painting shows how lava built up against the city wall behind the monastery until it was so high that it had to overflow. Go there today, and you will see just what Platania depicts: a formidable lava front poised like a ravenous beast about to pounce on the building. According to those anonymous British merchants, however, the walls of the monastery were so strong that although 'all were driven in, whole and entire, almost a foot', they did not collapse, despite 'the rising of the tyles in the midst of the floor, and bending of the Iron-bars that went across above'.

Over the following months lava did destroy parts of the city's southern and north-west quarters, but the city walls saved Catania by diverting most of the flow around it towards the sea. You can still see the lava that flowed down one side of the moat surrounding

Castello Ursino. Looking at that thirteenth-century monolith now, it is astonishing to think that it originally stood on a rocky promontory overlooking the sea. It is almost impossible to imagine the quantity of lava that must have plunged into the water in front of it, for it extended the shoreline by almost a kilometre into the waves, relocating the castle forever inland.

It was as if a curtain had been twitched back during the eruption, revealing another Etna hovering behind the beautiful mountain. This was her alter-ego, and its remorseless power was truly monstrous. Eight towns and twenty-four villages had been devastated. Almost everyone living in those stricken places and the countryside surrounding them had depended on land for their survival, so it's no wonder Privitera, derived from *privo di terra*, 'without land', is still a common surname on Etna. And the message Etna sent by scaling the walls of Catania is still there to see. Like a big beast in the wild, she had made it clear she would tolerate humanity's presence in her landscape, but only for as long as it suited her.

Etna has always been a place of contrasts and opposites, however, and it was fitting that both the city council and the Spanish government should have turned disaster into an opportunity to boost the economy by restructuring the port and building an entirely new neighbourhood. Of course, *basalto* was the building material they used, for just as magma changes its name to lava when it reaches the Earth's surface, the lava that cools and compresses inside a flow becomes 'lava rock' or 'basalt'. Stonemasons all over the volcano were kept busy extracting it from just below the surface of any accessible lava flow, where it was porous and easily worked with the simple tools they would have used to knock out rough blocks for paving roads and building walls.

Nothing to rival that eruption has ever occurred again, and yet Etna has certainly flexed her muscles since then. Almost 250 years later, an eruption razed the densely populated town of Mascali, on Etna's east face, to the ground. It was lived in largely by peasant farmers and labourers who left home each morning to cultivate some of the finest land on the mountain. Etna's activity began benignly enough on 2 November 1928 with an eruption from the north-east crater lasting little more than an hour. The next day there was a flank eruption lower down the slopes, but it was over by the end of the day. On 4 November, however, another flank eruption began at an altitude of only 1,200 metres, and unfortunately the lava flow found its way into an old riverbed. This is one of the worst things that can happen during an eruption, because the smooth, waterworn surface of a riverbed enables lava to move faster. In this case it covered six kilometres in twelve hours, burying a couple of small villages in its path. In 1669, lava had overlain a much simpler landscape of terraced fields and houses. In 1928 the eruption also erased the infrastructure of modern life, severing both the Circumetnea and the main railway line so that transport all over eastern Sicily was paralysed; it also blocked roads, toppled telephone poles and power lines, and cut off the water supply to several villages.

By the morning of 6 November the lava front had arrived in Mascali, where the sheer force of the flow destroyed 700 houses, and damaged another fifty. It took Etna only four days to make approximately 5,000 people homeless. She was back, the chimera, the monster forever lurking alongside Mongibello, the beautiful mountain.

In the past, Etna had received very little attention on the mainland, and until the Fascist government came to power in 1922, no government leader had ever bothered to travel to Sicily in the wake of an eruption. It is often said that Mussolini's greatest political strength was his ability to turn any event into an opportunity for propaganda. And so it was that, during the eruption of June 1923, he went straight to the scene of destruction in the company of King Vittorio Emanuele III. Naturally, he made sure that there was excellent press coverage of his visit, and of the emergency response delivered by soldiers, policemen and other state employees. Mussolini was so successful at being centre stage throughout the whole undertaking that a pro-Fascist newspaper in Catania suggested that his mere presence had brought the eruption to a speedy conclusion, as if he were the Messiah himself.

The Fascist propaganda machine also extracted maximum political advantage from the eruption of 1928. It was the first eruption ever to be filmed, so that thousands of people crowding into cinemas on the mainland were able to track the terrifying progress of the lava. Those grainy Pathé newsreels also captured firefighters, municipal guards and soldiers helping people to empty their homes of possessions and pile them onto army lorries parked in the narrow streets. Some could be seen stripping the tiles from their roofs and the boards from their floors as the lava front came bearing down on them. It is a pathetic sight, and yet the film left no one in any doubt that the evacuation of Mascali had been well handled by the state. Its reaction was the watershed between fragmented, pre-industrial responses to eruption and modern disaster management.

As well as supporting Mascali's inhabitants in the immediate aftermath of the eruption, the government undertook the rebuilding of the town to a design that would broadcast Fascist ideology in perpetuity. Mascali was originally an *agro-town*, one of those impoverished, downtrodden places where *contadini* and *braccianti* took shelter each night, and then tramped out each morning to work in the surrounding countryside. There were similar places all over Sicily and southern Italy, with streets that were mostly dark and narrow, and too many people crammed into small houses that lacked either plumbing or running water. New Mascali was built at enormous speed, and workers were soon rehoused in rows of cottages with modern bathrooms and running water. Although it is a little dusty and dishevelled now, the town's layout, proportions and public buildings still convey their message loud and clear. Each of the three piazzas at its heart is big enough to satisfy the needs of a modest city. An enormous town hall dominates the central piazza. Made all the more imposing by a completely unnecessary flight of steps, it can have left Mascali's inhabitants in no doubt of the power of government. The architect reinforced this message on the façade of a church as big and grandiose as a small cathedral, where the Fascist torch takes pride of place above Christ himself. A large primary school and nursery dominate the other two piazzas. The nursery is dedicated to Mussolini's mother, and you can still just make out her name above the door. The size and prominence of those two buildings were surely intended to remind Mascali's inhabitants of one of Mussolini's favourite policies, the so-called Battle for Births, aimed at making Italy war-ready by increasing the population from 40 to 60 million. In side streets between those gigantic *piazze* are glamorous houses, each one as remarkable as it is unique. Some are built in the same Rationalist style as the town hall, but others are Art Nouveau or strictly Modernist. However, they all had something in common with each other and with the rows of cottages where *braccianti* and *contadini* lived, and that was the running water coursing from their taps. And who wouldn't support Fascism, when they had been used to carrying water from a communal well?

The third eruption forever ingrained in local memory unfolded very close to my home in Milo. It began on 14 December 1991, and for an astonishing fifteen months lava flowed from the south-east crater like a lunatic motorway designed to link it straight to the Coltivata. It was the longest eruption in two centuries, and by threatening the town of Zafferana Etnea it triggered the most determined attempt ever made in modern times to divert a lava flow. This turned the volcano's east flank into a battlefield, where humans grappled with lava in the most visceral way possible.

Until 1991 there was an exceptionally beautiful valley called the Val Calanna above Zafferana. Of course, loss is bound to make people remember it more fondly, but some still speak of climbing the steep lane out of town to get their fruit and vegetables from farms in the valley. It was also a lovely place for walks, in the woods, or among nut groves, vineyards, orchards, and fields cultivated by the same families for generations. There were stories of camping trips too, and memories of the sweet spring water piped from the valley to their taps. However, everything this gentle, generous landscape had to give was lost to the burning chaos of 1991.

I went to Val Calanna for the first time in early summer. The long, narrow valley stretching away from me was now a lava circus of balancing acts, a tumble of turrets, shields, sheets, shattered slabs and boulders that had once marched across the landscape like an invincible, incandescent army, burning and toppling everything in their path. The air above me teamed with Etna's trademark opposites: butterflies as white as snow, and high above them lava-black swifts. Etna seemed to specialize in these striking, two-colour combinations, and a little higher up the flow the pink flowers of valerian blazed against black lava as far as the eye could see.

Val Calanna used to be skirted by chestnut woods, but the only woodland surviving there now is in a little green island at the top of the valley that is surrounded by lava on all sides. Those green oases in a lava flow are known as *dagale*, a word that comes from *dag allah* in Arabic, 'saved by God'. That particular *dagala* was formed from quaking aspens (*Populus tremuloides*), quite the wrong trees to have suffered such a narrow escape, because their leaves were still shuddering and whispering as if they hadn't yet recovered from the trauma of it all. Shedding branches had left oval marks on their trunks, marks that looked like startled, eery, khol-lined eyes, staring straight back at me. An ancient shepherd's hut at the trees' edge had been repaired and turned into a tiny refuge. Inside were the bare essentials, wood for the fire, a saw, a bent spoon, a knife, a candle, and a broom so you could sweep lava and ash from the floor and leave the place cleaner than you found it. The hut with its sparse comforts reminded me of people like Fabrizio, who want nothing more than to spend time in as close proximity as possible to Etna and her lava landscapes. On that beautiful day in the Val Calanna, with the whispering aspens and the swathes of pink valerian, I thought I might be beginning to understand them.

The eruption started high above the *dagala* in 1991, when fractures opened in both the north and east sides of the south-east crater. At first lava flowed harmlessly into the Valle del Bove, that great repository for all output on the east-facing side of the mountain. Hard to believe when you see it now, but until the eruption of 1991 one side of the valley was still covered in grass, and in summer people did indeed bring cattle – *bovini* – up there to graze. There was a small refuge there too, where skiing competitions were held every winter. However, lava buried the slopes and the refuge, and accumulated to a depth of a hundred metres in places. It might have stopped right there in the Valle del Bove, as it had done so often before, but this time it nosed its way into an old lava tube. Lava tubes, or caves, form when lava at the edges of a flow begins to cool and thicken. As it solidifies the lava forms banks to either side of the flow that grow steadily higher and more solid until they eventually meet in the middle to form the roof. This subterranean architecture remains in place long after an eruption finishes, and when fresh lava happens to find its way into an old tube, as it did in 1991, it can spell catastrophe. Instead of cooling as it might otherwise have done, and then grinding to a gradual halt, the lava gushing through the insulated tube stays hot and travels swiftly over surfaces already polished by previous flows.

In this case, the lava did not re-emerge until it had reached the far side of the Valle del Bove, where it formed an incandescent, braided flow straight down the steep slope towards the Val Calanna. When farmers in the valley looked up and saw tongues of fire approaching, they knew it would only be a matter of hours before the lava arrived, and they set about saving all they could. This meant felling fruit and nut trees for timber rather than sacrificing them to the volcano, and covering precious springs and water pipes with earth and logs as if that could save the springs that supplied Zafferana's water.

Soon enough, the lava reached the valley and headed straight for Zafferana, triggering the biggest ever, full-on, people-against-volcano campaign, directed by the National Volcanology Group (GNV), the National Research Council and the Major Risks Commission. It began with dozens of digger and bulldozer drivers trying to corral the lava flow at the far end of the valley. Working day and night, they built an earth dyke 200 metres long and 20 metres high. This kept the lava at bay for a month, but when the dyke gave way the flow rushed forwards, full of pent-up energy. People still talk about coming to Val Calanna at dusk to see the lava making its way relentlessly towards them. Sometimes it seemed to pause, they say, but then with a creaking clatter and a hiss it would inch forwards again, toppling and burning trees as it moved ever closer to town.

Operation 'Volcano Buster' was the next phase of the campaign against Etna, a name that was surely dreamt up by the US marines stationed nearby. They collaborated with Italian marines, launching the full force of their munitions against Etna. First they blasted through the roof of the lava tube in the Valle del Bove, and then they attempted to stop the flow with reinforced-concrete blocks dropped into it from American military helicopters. There are videos of those huge helicopters hovering against the ash-black sky, of men in army jumpers stumbling about near the surface of the lava, and others grappling with vast concrete blocks and chains. It was an ingenious, ambitious, heroic attempt, and yet a journalist on the scene compared the entire endeavour to dropping rusks into hot milk and watching them dissolve.

Meanwhile, the lava continued to burn its way down the valley towards Zafferana like a crusty black monster, its glowing proboscis now 5 metres high and at least 30 metres wide. It edged its way towards the end of the valley and approached the first house in a hamlet called Piano dell'Acqua. Bowing to the inevitable, its owner painted the bitter words *Grazie Governo* on the wall, as if more government resources might have stopped the lava in time to save his home. Then he put a table on the terrace outside, covered it with a clean cloth and set out a loaf of bread, a glass and a flask of red wine. 'Who for?' people asked. They were for Etna, he replied, who would surely arrive hungry and thirsty after all her hard work.

The final chapter in this astonishing campaign against the unbridled forces of Nature saw an old Fiat excavator with caterpillar tracks picking its way between the crazy contours of the Valle del Bove, virgin territory for vehicles of any kind. Salvatore di Carlo was driving it, although everyone knew him as Saro Ruspa – 'Saro the Digger'. It took him two days to lumber eight kilometres across the Valle del Bove, a journey that burned out the excavator's engine and destroyed one of the caterpillar tracks. But never mind that, he stood by until a helicopter could deliver replacements from Turin, did the repairs himself and laboured on. When he finally reached the site of the hole in the lava tube, it must have looked like an abandoned operating theatre, the wound still gaping, lava flowing like blood, and the ugly debris from earlier operations scattered all around.

Saro focused on the lava tube, just as the marines had done. Working on advice from experts at the GNV, he dug a canal below it that would divert lava back into its original course through the Valle del Bove, and starve the flow towards Zafferana Etnea. That done, he spent days selecting huge boulders and bulldozing them and piles of lava rubble into the tube. There are plenty of videos of him, in his bobble hat and mountain jacket, working at an altitude of 2,000 metres in the thick of an ongoing eruption. His digger looked like a toy as he manoeuvred it expertly through that colossal landscape. He was constantly surrounded by a haze of ash, and so close to boiling lava that he must have been continuously inhaling its burning fumes and dust.

At the end of each day Saro was airlifted off the mountain by helicopter and delivered to Rifugio Sapienza. His son worked as chef in a restaurant there, and so he was able to pick him up and drive him home just like any other commuter. After two weeks he succeeded in diverting the flow back into its harmless course through the Valle del Bove. Denied nourishment, the lava front finally creaked to a halt on 30 March 1993. It had endured for 456 days, and the flow stopped only just before reaching the second house in Piano dell' Aqua, a mere 700 metres from the centre of town. The local priest had led his congregation up to the lava front in a procession just moments before the lava came to a stop. They had taken the Madonna with them from the mother church, as if to put Heaven and Earth together to fight it out in the ring. When locals told me this story, they talked about witnessing a miracle. All this happened over thirty years ago, and yet one friend told me that even the thought of what he witnessed that day still makes the hairs stand up on the back of his neck.

People in Zafferana Etnea seem unable to forget their narrow escape, and on the first weekend of June each year they acknowledge it with a pilgrimage to the point where the lava stopped in Piano dell' Aqua. There is a steady build-up of dignitaries of every stripe on the steps outside the church long before the procession sets off, threaded through with swarms of small scouts in thick corduroy shorts, and choirboys sweltering inside cassocks and surplices. The town's brass band mills about in the piazza below until it is time to leave. Then everybody follows the choirboy tasked with carrying a mighty crucifix and leading the procession uphill. There was quite a crowd of us when I went. First came priests and a retired bishop wearing fuchsia pink, then families with small children and babies in pushchairs, adolescents in big trainers, old ladies in high heels, young couples holding hands, firemen and policemen. We made our way slowly up narrow roads between the houses, where people had gathered on balconies and doorsteps to wave at us as we passed. And then we were among vineyards on a country lane that seemed to be heading straight for the south-east crater. It was such a steep climb that you wouldn't think it possible to go on playing any wind instrument, let alone a trumpet, while walking up it, but the band played steadily on. When we finally arrived, there was an altar against the end of the lava flow covered in a snow-white cloth, surrounded by an enormous crowd of people. Parked cars lined the road, and the rows of chairs on the grass were all taken. Although there has been a decline in church attendance all over Europe, ceremonies of thanksgiving for narrow escapes on Etna seemed always to attract a good crowd.

These are the stories of just three of the lava flows that have breached the Coltivata in the past, but of course there have been many others, and there will be many more. This will always make prediction the most effective weapon in the armoury of our defence.

6.
Prediction

Etna is kept under 24-hour surveillance by automatic instruments permanently stationed on her flanks, and by volcanologists and other scientists using hand-operated devices. The nerve centre for all this information is a handsome palazzo in the centre of Catania, where data from over 400 different sources flows into the control room of the National Institute of Geology and Volcanology (INGV). I had made an appointment with Giuseppe Salerno, Director of Volcanology at the institute, to find out more about the system for predicting major eruptions. But spending time in the control room also had the unexpected side effect of making me feel as if I were digging down at last into the processes at the root of Etna's behaviours. These were the things that gave Etna her character, made her unique, and distinguished her from Vesuvius and Stromboli, two more live volcanos on Italian soil that were also being monitored by flashing screens in the control room. I already had a sense of Etna's underground dimension, but that day the astonishing pressures, unimaginable heat and perpetual movement of that subterranean world came alive for me, as if overground and underground were finally linked in my imagination, and, like Patrick Brydone, I was sensible at last to 'the hell with all its terrors immediately under our feet'.

There are all kinds of scientists working at the INGV at any one time – volcanologists (obviously) but also geophysicists, geochemists, geologists, physicists and computer scientists, and together they monitor Etna as closely as a patient in intensive care. There is an anthropomorphic aspect to some of the data they garner. For example, just as a doctor might monitor a patient's respiration, automatic stations on Etna monitor the fluctuations in the gases she exhales as if she too were breathing. These gases are one of the keys to predicting eruptions, but only if you understand the vital, three-way relationship between magma, gas and eruption. Deep beneath the ground, the weight of overlying rock exerts so much pressure on magma that the gases it carries with it are reduced to liquids in the magma's molten mess. However, as the magma forces its way upwards, the weight of downward pressure decreases, and those gases are able to form bubbles, tiny at first, but gradually expanding as the pressure inside them builds. Bubbles are magma's motor, making it more buoyant than the rock surrounding it, and dragging it upwards as they try to escape its constraint. The viscosity of magma depends on the amount of silica it contains. There isn't much silica in Etna's magma. This makes it quite runny, so it is relatively easy for gas bubbles to break free. They find their own way to the surface, where they seep from craters, fissures and even the soil itself.

To scientists in the control room, gases rising from the deep are like direct messages from the magma. They can monitor their fluctuations to learn how far it is beneath the ground, how much magma there is, and how much pressure has built up inside it. More literal still, magma makes sounds as it moves, and although these are at frequencies too low for us to hear, they are captured by infrasonic sensors on the mountain slopes. Close observation has shown scientists that Etna's deep mutterings settle into a predictable pattern just before eruption, making this data vitally important to the prediction process. Eruptions happen when gases that still remain in the magma are finally able to explode into the air, dragging lava, rocks and ash with them. The violence of the explosion depends on the amount of gas the magma still contains when it reaches the surface. It is this that defines the nature of an eruption.

When it comes to violence, Vesuvius is the outright winner of the three live volcanos on Italian soil. It has a history of brooding in silence on its grievances for decades, centuries even, before releasing all its anger in one lethal event. This is partly because it is fed by magma containing such high levels of silica that it is as viscous as treacle. Unable to escape from that sticky mess, the gas bubbles build up such enormous amounts of pressure that Vesuvius' eventual eruptions will be fierce and explosive. So much better to have Etna as your neighbour. She was forever grumbling, forever sending something from the craters on her summit, as if she wanted to engage us in constant, one-sided conversation. I had got used to this, living in Milo, directly beneath the south-east crater, and glancing up at it as often as you might glance at a clock on the kitchen wall. Sometimes its degassing muddied a sunset with dense clouds of dark brown ash, sometimes it was no more than a whisp of water vapour rising gently into the sky, and very occasionally it formed perfect smoke rings blown insouciantly, as smoke rings must be, by a crater. All these displays were powered by gases being released benignly from magma still deep beneath the ground, so that her eruptions are generally termed effusive rather than explosive, meaning that although they produce enormous quantities of lava, they are relatively benign. In fact, as far as we know, Etna has killed only seventy-seven people in her recorded history. Compare that to Vesuvius. A single eruption in AD 79 killed approximately 2,000 people in Pompeii. More important still, Etna does not go in for the same asphyxiating avalanches of incandescent rock fragments, gas and ash, those blood-boiling, lung-vaporizing pyroclastic flows that were the death of them. Pompeii is a treasure trove for classicists and archaeologists, a thriving tourist business and an outright wonder today, but deep down the citizens of Naples must ask themselves when something equally catastrophic is going to happen.

I had already learned that it was flank eruptions low on the slopes that people on Etna fear, because they are most likely to send lava into the inhabited areas where it can cause terrible damage. And yet at the INGV I learned that flank eruptions are also the most difficult to predict. They come from cracks that open without warning, so the landscape looks the same as ever immediately before they occur. This is why, like a patient once more in intensive care, Etna must also have her temperature taken. The INGV uses thermal-imaging cameras to highlight areas on her flanks where the temperature of the rocks is higher than that of the surrounding landscape. This reveals the stealthy surging of magma underground, already gifting its incandescent heat to the overlying landscape.

Etna trembles when magma carving its route to the surface triggers movement in one of her underlying faults. This is another symptom of an impending flank eruption, this time picked up by seismometers on her slopes. Those seismic tremors are generally quite shallow, and not nearly as powerful as the tectonic earthquakes that sometimes occur along the big faults running beneath the Messina Strait.

In the days leading up to a flank eruption, when the pressure underground mounts to bursting point, Etna's magical landscape can swell up like a bruise, or stretch and wrinkle like a length of elastic. These gymnastics are captured by GPS monitors and satellite images. The monitors are kept especially busy on Etna's east flank. There, perpetual, thrusting subterranean forces deform her sides so much that she is making a slow but continuous march towards the sea, a process she can reverse as suddenly as someone exercising her core muscles.

Etna's inhabitants have every reason to trust the INGV to pass on information that will enable the Department of Civil Protection to give them adequate warning if they ever need to evacuate. That said, a long-standing member of the INGV team once told me that all the signals he and his colleagues captured so carefully with their instruments were part of Etna's language, which he liked to describe as a very ancient form of Sicilian dialect. 'But unfortunately, it's a polysemic language,' he went on to say, 'and so the signals don't always mean the same thing,' which was another way of explaining that risk can never be entirely eradicated.

INGV scientists can usually give the Department of Civil Protection two to three hours' warning of a major eruption, which is enough time to organize an evacuation. Nevertheless, these scientists are forever on the lookout for other forms of prediction that might help them to improve on this figure. The search has taken some of them to the mud volcanos known as *salinelle*, because of the crusts of mineral-rich salt (*sale*) deposited around the base of their sloppy cones. There are only three sites on Etna where *salinelle* can be seen. One is on the edge of Paternò, an ancient town on the south-west flank, where a dented sign attached to a rusty, collapsing fence declares the place a nature reserve. Beyond it are the crazed mudflats where miniature volcanos emit warm burps of mud into shallow pools that overflow into a great grey expanse of their own making. The silence is broken only by the noise of gas gulping and golloping out of tepid, mineral-rich mud. This is another of Etna's many voices, another way of making sure we never forgot that we are on her territory and in her presence.

Those muddy creatures are known as *vulcani* because they erupt, but instead of magma, they are fed by gases mixed with the watery fluids and mud they drag along with them as they rise to the surface of the Earth. Volcanologists take particular interest in Paternò's *salinelle* because the cocktail of gases they emit is so unusual. Methane from primordial vegetation decaying just below the Earth's surface is the dominant gas emitted by mud volcanos everywhere else in the world, but not in Paternò. There they exhale carbon dioxide rising from magma reserves that may be as many as 10 kilometres deep beneath Etna.

Living close to that warm, moist nest of miniature volcanos, where salt and tepid water were always there for the taking, was once considered a convenience, and local people have been finding uses for the *salinelle* ever since the Bronze Age. In fact, Late Neolithic pottery found nearby wears a bright red slip glaze made from the iron deposits bubbling up through the mud. When the artist Jean-Pierre Houël published *Voyage pittoresque des isles de Sicile, de Malta et de Lipari* at the end of the eighteenth century, he depicted the same wide, watery, benighted landscape busy with people peering into muddy craters, kneeling down to collect the salt from their edges, steadying themselves on sticks as they gazed across that slippery territory, or crossing it on horseback. The taste of Paternò's home cooking must have had a very special meaning in those days, because the salt they scraped from the edges of the *salinelle* came in a mix of iron oxides, carbonates, sulphates, other chlorides, sulphides and hydroxides. Nevertheless, Houël had no qualms about sprinkling salt on his food, and pronounced it to be of *bonne qualité*.

Houël was both author and illustrator of his *Voyage pittoresque*, such a mighty book it had to be delivered to me on a trolley in the British Library. There was plenty of space on its huge pages for close detail, and Houël explained that although all the pools were quite close together, each held water of a different quality. Some was viscous and muddy, and some smelt 'distinctly of bitumen'. This is no surprise because the water would have had to pass through hydrocarbon reserves in the Earth's crust. However, there was at least one pool full of water so deliciously fresh and clear that local people drank nothing else. Another contained ochre-coloured pigment useful for dyeing cloth. Men in Houël's watercolour image gather around the most curious pool of all, where a substance that reminded him of milk curds floats on the surface. Although he could see it still when he plunged a hand into the water, there was nothing to get hold of there. It was, a bystander told him, flowers of sulphur, and a terrible smell hung over the pool.

People went on using the *salinelle*'s warm mud to treat their arthritis until the beginning of the twentieth century, as well as slathering it onto sprains and strains in horses' legs. But nowadays Paternò seems to do its best to ignore the primordial landscape lapping at its edge. A football stadium covers part of the site, and the rest is barred behind that rusty fence. These are futile gestures, for every so often the *salinelle* remind Paternò never to turn its back on them by overflowing, and then sending a slurry of mud through streets and into houses. And as if that weren't dramatic enough, a new *salinella* will sometimes grab the town's attention by bursting up through the floor of someone's garage, or in the middle of their garden.

There is some doubt now about the wisdom of living close to such rogue phenomena and their noxious gases. However, by observing the *salinelle* over an extended period, researchers at the INGV have realized that when the mud volcanoes are very active, it is a sign that huge amounts of gas must have accumulated beneath the volcano, and this in turn means there must be quantities of fresh magma available for eruption. On these occasions the temperature of the fluids they gargle can shoot up, and taken together these symptoms often presage a true eruption by Etna herself. The *salinelle* can never be trusted to predict its precise timing, but they are now considered a valuable addition to data provided by more technical equipment.

The INGV also harnesses animals' powers of prediction through a project called International Cooperation for Animal Research Using Space, ICARUS, that was originally conceived by Martin Wikelski, director of the Max Planck Institute of Animal Behaviour in Germany. He has always been interested in the way animals seem able to sense natural disasters like tsunami, earthquakes and eruptions before they occur. 'We call this animals' "sixth sense",' he said in an interview. 'There's nothing magic about it. It is simply collective behaviour, the swarm intelligence of animals.' Helped by local people and farmers, Wikelski and his team have harnessed the natural intuition of animals, birds and insects all over the world by fitting them with featherlight, solar-powered transmitters and tracking devices. He calls this 'giving them a microphone, so they can tell us what they know'. This knowledge takes the form of a constant stream of data about their movements and condition, and the temperature and air pressure of their surroundings. Those mini transmitters send all this information to the international space station, which transmits it in turn to a ground station, and from there it is sent to Wikelski and his teams of researchers, who monitor it in real time.

He has been enrolling animals on Etna into the ICARUS project ever since 2011, when farmers on the north flank insisted that their goats could predict eruptions. He and his team responded to their claim by replacing a few of the goats' bells with sensors. They then recorded their movements for over two years, and compared them to Etna's activity. The results confirmed the farmers' claim, for they showed that the animals had moved frantically across the slopes of the volcano, and then hidden themselves deep in undergrowth a good six hours before the major eruption of January 2012. Over time, other data has revealed that goats only react in this way to the prospect of a large eruption, but on those important occasions they can be relied on to pre-empt the predictions of the INGV's most sophisticated equipment by several hours.

In 2022 Wikelski extended the project on Etna to a group of donkeys in Milo, and a handful of the stray dogs living in Fornazzo. I had expected the donkeys to take their role as citizen scientists seriously, but after speaking to their owner, I realized that I could not have been more wrong. Apparently two of the four project participants managed to remove their expensive new collars within a couple of days. One collar was never found again, despite its GPS sensor supposedly giving an accurate account of where it should have been. They put a collar back onto the other donkey, only to find it had managed to remove it again after a few days. The two remaining donkeys doubled down on this message by removing their own collars a couple of weeks later, 'and at that point', their owner told me, 'we didn't insist'.

After this disappointment the Icarus Project must depend on Randazzo's goats and Milo's stray dogs. There were plenty of dogs in Milo. The flocks of sheep and goats had their guardians of course, with shifty eyes and matted, verminous coats, but while they worked, other dogs paced out their lives on balconies and flat roofs, barked between the bars of locked gates, or flung themselves dramatically from the ends of short chains. And then there were the city dogs that occasionally arrived in Milo for a holiday or a weekend visit, wearing coats perhaps, or sitting on people's laps to lick ice cream from a spoon.

Of all the dogs in the village, it was the strays that made the most impression. There are stray dogs all over Sicily, or *cani liberi* (free dogs) as some like to call them. People treated them so kindly on Etna, organizing rotas to feed them, taking them to the vet at their own expense, that I found it hard to imagine the brutes who had abandoned them in the first place. In Milo and Fornazzo most were large, handsome dogs. They spent their days trotting nonchalantly about in pairs or even small packs, cantering joyfully after cars, soaking up morning sun in the middle of the road, and sleeping in the shade. All day they were polite, restrained and unfailingly friendly, but darkness transformed them. By standing on their back legs they could reach the sacks of rubbish we all lowered from our balconies at night, and left dangling for the binmen to collect next day. They eviscerated them and, that done, were frequently beset by all the losses and traumas of their pasts. Then they gathered below my bedroom window to howl out their sorrows to the moon. When you saw them scratching a hard-to-reach itch, or rifling through a rubbish bag, it was hard to believe that some of those rogues were now enrolled with ICARUS, and contributing data to Wikelski and his team. By monitoring it in real time day by day, those scientists were building up an even more intimate picture of their habits than I had while living among them in Milo. Only time will tell whether they have the same powers of prediction as Randazzo's goats.

Information transmitted by 'sentient sensors' all over the world is being collated into what Wikelski calls an 'internet of animals'. He believes that this vast pool of data will have the potential to change our understanding of the planet as radically as the human-genome project deepened our understanding of human DNA.

The INGV's role as interpreter of Etna's language sees it take part in regular meetings convened by the government's Department of Civil Protection. Staff there will use the information they provide to issue alert levels corresponding to the current state of the volcano. The INGV's report will also underpin any decision to send a warning to the mayors of local towns that are likely to be affected by a potential eruption. Town councils will then issue orders restricting access to the volcano. These orders are a relatively recent thing, for in the past no one would have stopped you from climbing the mountain in order to get very close indeed to a lava front. First-hand descriptions paint a vivid picture of the chaos that broke out during the eruption of 1971, when thousands of people came to see the lava threatening to engulf Fornazzo. They arrived with children, babies and elderly relations, abandoning their cars at random in the narrow lanes above the village, and creating such congestion that even the local *carabinieri* were at a loss as to how to resolve it. You have to admire the enterprising people who set up stalls at the edges of the flow, selling pizza, beer and soft drinks. Some even took to fishing out incandescent lumps of the lava flowing from the mouths of new fractures, and beating them into ashtrays and other souvenirs for sale.

When Etna was made a National Park in 1987, it became possible for the park authorities to limit access to the summit or other dangerous areas by making them restricted zones. No one is allowed to climb above 2,800 metres today without a licensed guide. No one except the team at the INGV, of course, who quarter the volcano's slopes in their battered white Land Rovers, and are always first on the scene of a new eruption.

Volcanos fall into patterns of behaviour, rather as we do ourselves. These play out across geological timescales so vast that scrutiny of Etna's current behaviours cannot be hoped to give adequate insight into what she is capable of, or what she might do in future. However, debris from past eruptions tells us that she used to be much more violently explosive, ejecting enormous quantities of ash and gas. Might she revert? Nobody knows, and the INGV make a point of stressing on their website that 'sudden, even completely unexpected changes in volcanic activity are always possible'. There are hazard maps now, delineating areas most likely to be affected by future eruptions, but anything is possible.

I had gone to the INGV with a question at the back of my mind. Was there anything its work could teach us as we face up to our own versions of natural disaster triggered by climate change? I came away believing that a reliable system for predicting disasters and a robust one for issuing early warnings would always be our best defence.

Visiting the INGV had been reassuring to an extent, but like every other outsider on Etna, I was still uncertain how people tolerated the ever-present possibility of becoming a part of the next indelible story on her flanks by losing everything they had. This is the question that Leonardo Mercatanti, a geographer from the University of Palermo, has spent several years trying to answer by pinning down elements of what he calls the 'deep', 'paradoxical' and even 'incomprehensible' local attitudes to Etna. In 2013 he made Nicolosi, a town often threatened by earthquakes and eruptions, the focus for this research. He distributed a questionnaire to 400 people there during a period of frequent eruptions. In one of the multiple-choice questions, he asked them to tick the box that best described their most powerful feeling about the volcano. The majority ignored 'indifferent' and 'frightened' in favour of 'respectful'. Mercatanti went on to interpret this respect as a two-way phenomenon. On one side were the locals who held Etna in 'a kind of reverence', treating her like a neighbour whose moods could make or break their day. On the other was Etna herself, whose eruptions had caused so few deaths in recorded history that Mercatanti suggests she might even be described as respecting her inhabitants.

People living on Etna must build a unique relationship with landscape. Elsewhere, we humans tend to shape our natural surroundings to meet our needs. Not on Etna, where the eruptions of 1669, 1928 and 1991 all demonstrated that there is never any guarantee of our pathetic, human infrastructure surviving in a place where the Earth has so many ways of flexing its muscles. What if, instead of being shaped by them, Etna shapes the people who live there? Every landscape does this to some extent, but I had begun to suspect that Etna did it in spades. Mercatanti, who was also interested in this question, went so far as to say that instead of being shaped and dominated by its people, Etna's landscape was itself 'a cultural producer', capable of moulding the 'character, personality, culture, skills and way of thinking' of people living there. This fascinated me at a time when I was just getting to know those people, and to observe their relationship with Etna at close quarters. I was already convinced that the young John Dryden had made a lazy assumption when he described Etna's inhabitants in 1700 as living

Prediction

'in continual fear and trembling', and as I learned more about them, they surprised me in unexpected ways. For example, I had assumed living on the biggest and most active volcano in Europe would make my friends and neighbours even more serious about insurance than we are in Britain, where we habitually insure lives, journeys, houses and cars, as if the policies alone could protect them and us from harm. Of course, everybody in Italy is obliged to insure their car, but when it came to house insurance on that live volcano, well, some of my friends seemed quite mystified by the idea. However, as the summer season for religious festivals and saints' day celebrations got underway, I began to think that thousands of people on the mountain were choosing instead to put their trust in a kind of spiritual underwriting that dates back to the age of saints and early Christian martyrs.

7.
Festa di Sant' Agata

Etna's glorious saints' days had me standing by as saintly effigies and relics were wheeled out of churches all over the volcano. They saw me startled again and again by mortar shots, firecrackers, fireworks, clamouring bells, frenzied cheering, explosions of custom-made confetti showering from the sky, and shouts of *Viva Sant' Alfio!* or *Andrea*, or any one of a panoply of other local saints. I watched barefoot pilgrims pouring into villages, many of them carrying yellow beeswax candles almost as tall as they were themselves. I processed around narrow streets, uphill and downhill, behind a golden palanquin, or *fercolo*, carrying all those sacred objects and the local priest in his feast-day finery. I saw nuns almost crushed by crowds, pilgrims and policemen lining up for photographs like guests at a wedding, I came close to fainting during a long sermon in the midday sun, watched crying babies lifted up to be blessed, and listened to choirs singing their rousing local songs accompanied by wild brass bands and drums.

I soon discovered that many elements of those celebrations dated back to the third century AD, when Etna's people began to adopt elements of Christianity into the panoply of ancestral rites and traditions that had always shaped their relationship with the volcano and her eruptions. For them, paganism was an ensemble of customs and beliefs bolted together over the centuries to broker the best possible relationship with their risk-laden environment. At first, they treated Christianity as a new and more powerful brand of magic that they could adapt to their own needs. It also provided them with another understanding of Etna's eruptions. Now, instead of believing them to be the expression of angry or industrious monsters living inside the volcano, people gradually began to perceive eruptions as punishments visited on them by one God living in a realm high above its summit. And instead of being the entrance to the classical underworld, dark caves and smoking craters became gates to the ultimate place of punishment, a Christian hell.

People elsewhere might have responded to the omnipresent threat of damnation by begging Christ to protect them and intercede on their behalf. Not on Etna, where they put all their faith in whichever local saint their town or village had adopted as its patron. Many of these saints were early Christians martyrs like Agata, patron saint of Catania, and the three brothers Alfio, Filadelfo and Cirino. Over time, the beliefs of people on the mountain came together in a very local and distinctive form of popular Catholicism that still incorporated elements of pre-Christian folk religion, and turned the usual hierarchy of Christian heaven on its head. Christ was considered more powerful than God, the Madonna more powerful than Christ, and the particular saint belonging to your own town or village more powerful than God, Christ, Mary and all the other saints put together.

Etna's people were not unique in shaping Christianity to suit their circumstances. The Church in many other places in Medieval Europe was at the heart of a similar *bricolage* of beliefs, evolved over time to address the particular anxieties of its community's collective life. On Etna, for example, there was a timeless tradition of processing to the lava front during eruptions, often carrying relics, saintly images, and other sacred objects thought to be invested with supernatural powers of protection. These rituals had been evolving for many centuries by the time the Council of Trent made its painstaking review of Catholic doctrine in the mid-sixteenth century, and then declared them inconsistent with current dogma. It also pronounced upon the relics and other sacred objects in which people invested so much trust, deeming them idolatrous. That these new rules had little effect on Etna comes as no surprise, when circumstances there were so extreme, and the sense of protection they brought so important.

Indeed, even in the late eighteenth century, chatty Patrick Brydone found it 'curious to consider, how small is the deviation in almost every article of their present rites from those of the ancients'. By the time he was writing, patron saints had such entrenched local connections on the volcano that they would have become essential to the identity of the towns and villages where they were worshipped. You only have to live on Etna for a short time today to realize that this is still the case. It is also clear that some of the traditions and many of the relics the Church was trying to outlaw almost 500 years ago are still firmly in place in the twenty-first century.

Am I suggesting Etna's people belong to some strange, old-fashioned community bound by arcane superstition? No, not that – something much more nuanced and interesting. They are thoroughly modern people deliberately preserving rituals that have been comforting and reassuring the volcano's inhabitants for over 2,000 years. Saints' days and other religious festivals in towns and villages all over the volcano are also perfect occasions for fostering cooperation and close social connections. Research by the Lloyds Register Foundation for its Resilience Index has shown that communities bound together by strong connections like these are better able to survive, rebuild and perhaps even thrive after a disaster. This makes me wonder whether those ancient rituals go some way towards explaining how Etna's population manages to recover again and again in the aftermath of the eruptions and earthquakes that have always been a feature of life on the volcano.

The quintessential saintly celebration on Etna is the Festa di Sant' Agata, and it takes place each year at the beginning of February. Every Catholic growing up in Catania would have been fed the story of Agata's life with their first solid food, and her blond-haired image was likely to be as familiar to them as their best friend's face. But what a brutal story for Catania's children to digest. I had watched it being re-enacted years before, as a play in a church in Catania. That is where I too learned that Agata, the epitome of youth, determination and intelligence, was an early convert to Christianity. So early, in fact, that an edict was still in force obliging everyone in the

Roman Empire to continue making animal sacrifices to the traditional pantheon of gods. However, Agata refused to follow ancient rituals belonging to gods she no longer believed in. She was, as she told us again and again, 'the bride of Christ'. And well she might, for Quinziano, the emperor's representative, made every attempt to seduce her, while simultaneously prosecuting her for defying the edict on sacrifice. Things went downhill very fast on the steps at the front of San Francesco di Paolo. Before we knew it, Agata was being tried then tortured, in ways you can easily discover without me dirtying these pages by glorifying an ancient and attenuated act of femicide. However, if you are to understand anything at all in Catania during the *festa*, you do need to know that all this took place in about AD 250, and one of those acts of sadism was the removal of her breasts with red-hot pliers.

The aftermath of her murder was marked by a violent eruption. She had only been dead for a year or so, but the citizens of Catania's first instinct was to grab the veil she once wore and process with it up to the lava front. The combined force of that holy object and their prayers seemed to stop the lava in its tracks, and Agata was canonized soon afterwards. The faithful in Catania believe she has given the city the same protection during fifteen eruptions over the last eighteen centuries, and even when lava scaled the city walls during the catastrophic eruption of 1669, they thanked her for diverting it around the castle moat and into the sea.

Catania has a population of just over 300,000, and yet so many tourists and pilgrims pour into the city to celebrate Agata each February that more than a million people crowd the streets over the three days of the festival. February was long gone by the time I moved to Etna. However, I returned for the *festa* the following year, deciding to beat the crowds by arriving in Catania a few days before it began on 3 February. Nevertheless, the build-up was already underway, and every night the streets and squares were brimful of jubilation and crazy fairground tunes played by a very secular combination of drums, cymbals and trumpets. All the action at this point revolved around the *candelore*. The clue is in the name, for those mighty wooden structures were made in the shape of candles. If you can visualize three metres of gilded wood carved with differing combinations of baby-faced cherubs and golden lions, scrolls, herms, eagles and other elaborate baroque and rococo decorations, if you can deck it with electric candles, chandeliers, teardrop crystals and three-dimensional scenes from Sant' Agata's life, and finally crown it with banners, flags and a globe of flowers, you will have some idea of what a *candelora* is.

The *Catanesi* have been processing around their streets with *candelore* every February since the end of the fifth century. When those gigantic candles first appeared in Catania, they were perpetuating the pagan tradition of offering lit candles to the gods of the underworld in early February each year, a level of continuity that must surely have been building the *Catanesi*'s sense of community for the best part of two millennia. And yet, as if to counteract this atavistic memory, each *candelora* has always been dedicated to one of the many stolid and reliable trades practised in the city. The pasta makers have always had one, and so have the bakers, cheesemongers, tavern keepers, grocers, greengrocers, wine merchants and florists. The number of *candelore* is always changing. There were twenty-eight in 1674, but what with the demise of carters and other redundant trades, they have dwindled to eleven today, each with its own distinctive decorations. The greengrocers hang a wreath of plastic fruit and flowers on theirs, and a smiling cherub holding Agata's breasts on a plate. A garland of blue flowers encircles the fishmongers' *candelora*, and orange starfish bob in that blue sea as it moves. Butchers have never been squeamish, and the cherub on their *candelora* is grasping the red-hot pincers used to remove Agata's breasts. Of course, this theatrical celebration of Catania's most important trades must always have reinforced yet again a sense of identity and belonging among that element of the city's population.

As for the children in Piazza del Duomo that night, dancing around the *candelore* to the sound of wild music, it struck me that the excitement of dancing in the dark for Sant' Agata might just be embedded in their memories for life. The *candelore* danced too, although not for long because they were immensely heavy. In fact, the biggest weighed 900 kilos, and it took twelve men to hoist it onto their shoulders like an enormous sedan chair. There was something strangely suggestive about a *candelora* dancing, something elemental about its undulating movement that seemed to befit its pagan connection. Needless to say, those strongman acts were highly competitive, and as the *festa* got underway the *cannaluristi* (people leading the *candelore*) would challenge each other to endurance tests by seeing who could dance for longest.

A party atmosphere infiltrated every quarter of the city centre at night. Sweet sellers had already set up their stalls in Piazza dell' Università, and the air smelt of nothing but spun sugar and roasting nuts. Meanwhile, it was time for families living in the city's old working-class quarters to come out and stroll along Via Plebiscito. I had already seen enough saints' days on Etna to know how important they were to the inhabitants of her towns and villages, and on the streets that night the sense of community was so strong it felt almost tangible. Horse meat is part of Catania's culinary identity, and a particular speciality in that part of town, where steaks and kebabs were sizzling on charcoal grills outside a string of restaurants. As soon as they were cooked they would be spritzed with lemon juice and oil, then stuffed into a *panino* to be eaten on the go. *Polpette di cavallo catanesi*, horse-meat rissoles, were another speciality, made from mince bound together by egg, breadcrumbs, cheese, garlic and chopped parsley. Iron-rich and tender, they are often eaten by pregnant women and fed to children.

Despite being caught up in the party spirit, I had no appetite for horse, and I sought out a restaurant with fish on the grill outside. There were paper cloths and plastic glasses on the tables, and a serve-yourself buffet of vegetables, roasted, stewed or fried in batter. It was a place where everybody seemed to belong, and the rushed-off-her-feet waitress made me feel part of that festive, local community even as I waited at mysterious length for what she always referred to as my tiny little fillet of swordfish. 'Sta arrivando' ('It's on its way') she would say every time she sailed past, giving a quick touch to my arm. I spent half an hour or so watching a father trying to teach his young son to wink. And then, 'You haven't got any toothpicks have you?' said a querulous old man at the table next to mine. Treating all of us with the absolute attention of a good nurse, rushed-off-her-feet pulled a packet of toothpicks from her apron before sweeping on. Eventually I ate the whole of my enormous, tiny little swordfish fillet, just to please her. And was it exactly what I wanted? 'Yes signora, yes, yes, yes.'

Although I walked away alone along smoky streets, the camaraderie of *festa* was everywhere, as was the horse meat, still being served every which way on stalls by the road. I saw whole horse legs folded onto themselves and into galvanized dustbins, as the scent of burnt flesh rose steadily heavenwards. All in all, it seemed a lot of beasts to burn in celebration of a saint so resolutely opposed to animal sacrifices. There would be plenty of other things to eat during the *festa*, of course, things that spelled home for every *catanese*, and sometimes, more specifically, spelled Sant' Agata herself. By this I mean, of course, *the minne* or *minnuzze di Sant' Agata*, Agata's breasts sold in every bar and *pasticceria*. There's nothing odd about going into a bar in Catania during the festa and shouting *una minna per favore* ('a breast please'). That very local treat is built upon a base of airy sponge, then comes the *cassata* made from creamed ricotta, a punch of sheepy milkiness that I found a bit unnerving in this context. On top of the ricotta comes a thin layer of marzipan tinted green by the addition of a tiny bit of fine pistachio flour, and then a pale glow of saintly icing. Though I balked at eating the glacé-cherry on top, it's a mistake to be squeamish about Agata's breast cakes, because they are integral to being in Catania for the celebrations.

The *catanesi* have always turned to Agata for protection during eruptions, but over the centuries her gruesome form of martyrdom has also made her the patron saint of wet nurses, breast-cancer patients, and even the victims of rape. But, for all the cohesion and community spirit on display on the eve of the *festa*, I thought it unlikely that young people in Catania would still identify with such a macabre story. Not so, for later that evening I got talking to the *barista* in a side-street bar and asked him what he thought about the story of Agata. 'We were talking about her just the other day,' he said, as if she were always cropping up. 'There was this girl walking down the street who was dressed very provocatively. I mean,' he said, 'I don't mind, that's up to her, but to think she was showing off her breasts to look good, and Sant' Agata had hers cut off.' My Lord, I thought, Agata is as real now as she ever was, and present in the present day. I remembered then how often it's said that even atheists in southern Italy are quite capable of believing in their local saint.

The first day of the *festa* dawned bright and cold, and they were doing brisk business in the bar on Via Plebiscito, where Nino the barman was caught up in an ongoing dance of coffee-making, kissing, chatting, pastry-serving and polishing. One after the other, the regulars came in for their take-aways, handing over an empty bottle for him to fill. There is nothing that shouts 'home' or 'belonging' more loudly than a barman who knows what you want before you have even opened your mouth. And that is how it was in the bar on Via Plebiscito, where Nino's customers had been repeating the same instructions for so long they no longer had to say a thing. First came a single *espresso* followed by a *lungo* with five sugars, poured into empty beer bottles, given new plastic caps and wrapped in coloured paper like presents. A *caffè latte* in a plastic cup, wrapped, ditto an *espresso*, wrapped. Mine was a cappuccino and I was staying put. I had a *cornetto* with it, a huge pastry that looked as if it might have been fried and then slightly run over. Eating it was a real undertaking of oily, flaky deliciousness, all over the floor, the bar, myself. 'When will I ever learn?' I said, glancing down at my feet. 'Oh, it's impossible to eat those without making a mess,' Nino replied, tactfully flicking stray crumbs from the shiny surface of the bar. Just then a corpulent child burst in and he passed her a square of kitchen roll as if this, too, was something that happened every day. Then she barrelled into the loo, coming out again moments later and giving me a joyful, cross-eyed grin as she ran for the door.

Outside, traffic was surging along Via Plebiscito, and the owner of the religious artefacts store was refreshing the red balloons around his door by bursting the deflated ones underfoot. I could have bought model *candelore* from him built to any scale, from matchbox sized to a metre high, plates for a dolls' house laden with Sant' Agata's breasts, Sant' Agata rosaries, or canvases and cushions emblazoned with her face. A man came tearing up to him as I walked past that morning, like someone caught up in an accident. 'Have you got any *sacchi* left?' he gasped. 'No,' said artefacts man, 'the only one left is for a baby.' But he was gone before he had finished his sentence, leaving nothing but troubled air behind him. The *sacco* he wanted was the uniform identifying all Agata's devotees throughout the *festa* and, like it or not, few things bring a greater sense of belonging than a uniform. This one was a white, calf-length tunic, bound at the waist with a cord and worn with a black velvet beret and white gloves.

The shopkeeper took his time explaining that each element was laden with symbolism. At one level the outfit simply recalled the return of Sant' Agata's relics after they were stolen in 1040 and taken to Constantinople. After stealing them back nearly a hundred years later, two Sicilian brothers delivered them to Aci Castello by boat in the dead of night. News of Sant' Agata's return spread rapidly so that soon everyone in town was jumping out of bed and running down to the beach. And that's the significance of the *sacco* – the shirt and beret are a simple commemoration of the nightshirts and nightcaps they all wore. Apparently, though, other layers of symbolism have been added to the outfit over the centuries, making those white tunics spell penitence, the cord belt spell chastity, and the black velvet beret, ashes.

I had been to enough festivals in Italy over the years to know how important it is to spend time with someone who can explain the scenes unfolding on the streets. I had put all my faith in this respect in a local historian and self-professed expert on the *festa*. We met that morning outside Catania's famous Bellini Gardens and walked together to Piazza Stesicoro. The crowds were already dense by the time we arrived, and *candelore* were processing down Via Etnea, glinting and bobbing in the midday sun. Each had its own band of drums and trumpets competing to play the loudest, while children backed them up on plastic instruments bought from toy sellers now roaming the streets. We were standing on the edge of a group of volunteers from a local charity called the Lions Club, and as each *candelora* arrived in the square it paid tribute by surging towards them in a great bow, while the police blew their whistles and pushed back the crowd. In the midst of all the pushing and cacophony local historian recounted his great tumbling mix of information, a plethora of facts about Agata and the festival that I often couldn't hear. Afterwards, he fell into conversation with a friend, because after all, meeting up with old friends is a big part of saints' days everywhere.

When the procession began to move off down Via Etna, local historian beckoned me to fall in with the Lions Club volunteers as they delivered their votive candles to the cathedral. The street ahead had been cleared, the silent crowds held back behind barriers, and a sermon was being broadcast at deafening volume over loudspeakers. Unlike the others, I had no candle in my hand and no hi-vis jacket on my back, and yet there I was, suddenly walking quietly down the centre of Catania's main street, dropped as if by magic into the heart of both the community and the *festa*. Inside the cathedral our party merged with the slow-moving inundation of pilgrims, children, babies in their buggies, and even a bobbing helium balloon in the shape of Micky Mouse, floating up towards the ceiling high above.

The duomo was blazing with candles already, and the first day of the *festa* is the best day of the year for wax workshops all over the city. Some people go straight to source for the candle they will offer to Sant' Agata, selecting it from among hordes of others pilloried by their strings from metal frames, or lying in tawny, scented piles on the floor. Traditionally, the size and weight of the candles Agata's *devoti* carry depends either on the blessing they have received or the one they are ardently praying for. Some still honour the tradition of choosing a candle the same height or weight as the person carrying it. Catania's young men must have had much to ask or much to be thankful for, because many of them struggled through the streets with candles weighing 75, 80, or sometimes even an insane 120 kilos balanced across shoulders carefully padded with lumps of foam.

As I made my way downhill towards the duomo on the second morning of the *festa*, a few tired figures wearing *sacchi* were making their way uphill. They had already been to dawn mass in the duomo, and then seen the effigy of Sant' Agata and the various caskets and reliquaries containing her relics loaded onto the silver-plated *fercolo*, a mobile shrine, and brought outside. Some had already shed both beret and gloves as they climbed the hill, hoisting their white tunics up and tucking them, workmanlike, into their trousers.

When I caught up with the *fercolo* I saw that it was built like a temple on Corinthian columns, and decorated with scenes from Sant' Agata's martyrdom. But now she rode in glory, her pink-cheeked, smiling face topped with a golden crown. She had a sweet, homespun look, and yet her torso was so exotically decorated with jewels, crosses, chains, necklaces and other ornaments given as offerings over the centuries that it seemed to belong to another creature altogether. Even her fingers had four jewel-encrusted rings apiece. Glorious and glittering, her *fercolo* was also so ornate that – as the local historian had made a point of telling me – it weighed nearly 2,000 kilos. And that was without the priest riding on it in his fuschia pink cape and dark glasses, without his helpers and the master of the *fercolo*, without the enormous candles offered up by the crowd, the coins exchanged for prayer cards, the babies and young children lifted aboard to kiss the saint, or even the carpet of carnations decorating the front and sides. You might think such a hefty contraption needed a good, solid engine, but it depended entirely on Agata's *devoti* to haul it along with thick ropes. So, there Sant' Agata was again, building the fabric of resilience by unifying her followers, this time through gargantuan effort and teamwork. In front of the *fercolo* came the lurching procession of *candelore*, and in its wake was a retinue of ambulances interspersed with balloon sellers holding tight to a menagerie of bobbing unicorns and teddy bears. Pushing their way through all this mayhem were mobile toy stalls loaded with enough plastic swords and guns to keep children armed throughout the festival. And of course, but for an act of ancient Roman violence, none of it would have been happening at all.

Agata's devoted faced their greatest challenge as darkness fell, for that's when they had to pull the massive *fercolo* and all its passengers up the steep slope from Piazza Stesicoro, past the Roman amphitheatre and three churches dedicated to the memory of Agata's trial and martyrdom. Eventually they hauled it up onto Via Plebiscito, where winter darkness had already fallen, and I fell in with the crowd surging alongside it. Pushing their way through the throng were roving street sellers with shopping trollies full of fizzy drinks, and their smallest children hitching a ride. The pavements were cluttered with sweet stalls, and smoke from braziers cooking yet more horse meat made everything hazy and dreamlike. Ahead of the *fercolo*, the *candelore* filled the street with their rich colours, flags and banners, golden baroque carvings and light from their electric candles and chandeliers. Each one had policemen in attendance, and there was a frantic blowing of whistles to clear the street before any of the *candelore* could dance forwards, looking for all the world like someone dancing awkwardly in a tight skirt. And no wonder, because once in motion, no *candelore* could possibly have made an emergency stop.

I had been attending the *festa* each day like the guest at the birthday party of someone I didn't know, dipping in and out of proceedings as I pleased, and following the *fercolo* as it tracked backwards and forwards past an unfolding frieze of handsome palaces, past shrines to the saint piled with flowers, and through the scent of lilies hanging heavy above dirty streets. And wherever I went, Etna was overlooking the proceedings, lined up with the Via Etnea, in glimpsed views across rubbish-strewn car parks, or at the far end of inconsequential little streets. I remember taking the winding stairs to the cupola of the Badia di Sant' Agata at sunset one evening. Seen from that perspective, her snowy mass dwarfed the tiled roofs and church towers of the city, making me feel as if I had blundered inside the frame of one of those bird's-eye engravings so popular in the eighteenth century.

People have always bled the wax from their votive candles onto the ground to give the *fercolo* a smoother surface to travel over, and by the last night of the *festa* the streets were slippery with yellow candle wax. On that final night, people stood in silent, pensive groups, doing just that on almost every street. Their candles were rugged now with drips and runnels of wax as they tipped them towards the ground. That done, they leaned them, still blazing, against the wall below one of Agata's shrines, or handed them over to be tossed into a skip at the collection point near Porta Uzeda. Nothing would be wasted, for all the wax was going to be recycled to make candles for Sant' Agata the following year.

Sant' Agata's fireworks astonished me. I had slipped away from the crowds in the main square to the streets between the railway arches and the fish market. I noticed an old man there as soon as I arrived, standing beside a table spread with plates of sliced citron, the lemon's knobbly ancestor. I have never been able to resist Sicily's citrus fruit, and I gave him some coins, sprinkled a few slices with salt from the bowl on the table and began to eat. We stood side by side, the citron seller and me, as the sky above us filled with chrysanthemums, and then carpets of falling stars, layer upon layer of fireworks below a full moon. Towards the end of the show he tore a thick strip of kitchen paper from a roll on the table. 'It's going to get even louder now,' he said during a momentary pause, 'and I would hate you to hurt your ears.' Obediently, I stuffed my ears with wads of kitchen paper for a finale so loud it reverberated in my chest. When it was over, we both freed up our hearing, clasped hands, and looked deep into each other's joyful faces. 'Thank you for your company,' I said, and as I walked away it struck me, as it often had before, that there was never any need to be lonely on Etna's territory, because conversation was always there to be had.

I was convinced now that saints and their celebrations nurtured resilience in villages, towns and cities all over the mountain. And what's more, saints' days were also a huge get-together, an opportunity for families and old friends to reunite and, above all, a time to revel in a deep sense of belonging to your community, with all the hugging and kissing and embodied well-being that involves. It delights me to imagine the writer D. H. Lawrence enduring any of those occasions while he was living in Taormina, because he made such a point of deploring public shows of affection. 'They never leave off being amorously friendly with almost everybody,' he said of Etna's inhabitants, 'emitting a relentless physical familiarity that is quite bewildering to one not brought up near a volcano.'

I had experienced all this at first hand in the tight-knit village community of Milo, where the austere ladies running the village shop had soon begun to be friendlier, and when I didn't have enough change for the baker, she would just shrug and say, 'Pah, signora, you will pay me back one day.' If I took my car to the garage, the mechanic would glance up from under a bonnet and mutter, 'Now what?' as if I had been there for years, and the ironmonger knew where to deliver a new bottle of gas for my cooker without me telling him. Neighbours invited me to pick wild asparagus with them in the woods in spring, and pick grapes with them come autumn. They invited me to village events, gave me jars of home-made jam and wobbling towers of fresh ricotta. In summer the holiday houses to either side of mine began to fill up with the families who had rented them every summer for years without fail. We sometimes coincided in the lane outside, or in the village shop, but more often we were shadows on either side of the fence dividing us, living each other's lives vicariously. The rumble of their conversation, the gales of laughter and the sudden rounds of applause were the background music for my own quiet meals on the terrace, and the sound of their children weathering another interminable summer afternoon became the soundtrack of my own summer.

As I got to know more people on the mountain, I began to notice the same phrase cropping up again and again, as if it were the catch-all justification for anything the volcano might do. Sometimes said thoughtfully, sometimes defiantly, 'Etna gives so much more than she takes away.' There it was at last, the contract underpinning Etna's relationship with all those patient people, a *quid pro quo* of glorious returns for any inconvenience, or indeed suffering, her eruptions might impose. But what were they? I supposed that almost everyone working in Etna's rural landscape must know what she had to give, because their jobs had always depended on her resources. And so, as the season slipped into high summer, I made a point of trying to meet people who had found ways of reaping those returns.

8.

Treasure Beneath Their Feet

Deep inside every substantial lava flow is basalt, a smooth, grey rock made from compressed lava. This seemed a good starting point for any investigation into Etna's natural resources, because everything on the volcano, from Catania to the smallest hamlet, is built from this infinitely sustainable material, and today it is also at the heart of a prosperous, international business.

When I say Catania is built from basalt, I don't just mean the buildings themselves. Look around you on those eighteenth-century streets, and you will realize that steps, walls, fountains, pavements, roads, kerbstones, arches are all made from Etna's leavings, brought up with no human effort from miles below the surface of the Earth. Look more closely, and you will see that each of those paving slabs has been arduously worked over with a hammer and chisel to pit its surface, a traditional technique that has always been used to prevent it becoming slippery when wet. Look more closely still, and as often as not, there will be fresh falls of volcanic ash in the cracks between the basalt paving at your feet, as if Etna could not stop signing her name over and over again on the same territory.

The layout of Catania today dates back to the aftermath of its destruction by the most severe earthquake Sicily has ever known, before or since. It came in 1693, only twenty-four years after the worst eruption in Etna's recorded history. Rough basalt blocks had been used for rebuilding houses, roads and walls after the 1669 eruption, but the earthquake soon made a mockery of all this hard work by reducing any building between Catania and Siracusa to rubble, and killing over 50,000 people in the process. In Catania, all the medieval buildings that had survived the eruption were razed to the ground. The earthquake also triggered a tsunami that sent waves crashing through the streets for 350 metres inland. According to contemporary records, 16,000 of Catania's 20,000 citizens were killed, many as they tried to escape those narrow, medieval streets that were now either flooded or blocked by the debris from fallen buildings. The city descended into anarchy just as it had a quarter of a century earlier, and thieves took every opportunity to loot homes, businesses and workshops.

Many people thought Catania had been hit too badly this time to rise again. By the middle of the following year, however, a committee formed by surviving members of the Church and aristocracy had decided to rebuild the city to a new plan. They managed to do this at lightning speed by giving themselves power to sell properties that had been abandoned, reducing property prices by a third, and standardizing the price of building land. Although the roomy, basalt-built piazzas and broad, basalt-paved streets of the new city look like a gesture towards grandeur today, they were actually built with an ulterior motive, because those spacious streets and piazzas would make it easier to escape in the event of another earthquake. The whole project was eventually so successful that by the middle of the eighteenth century Catania had become a favourite destination among affluent tourists, who described it again and again as one of the most beautiful modern cities in Europe.

The most important palaces and squares in that new city had been designed by Giovanni Battista Vaccarini, a flamboyantly baroque architect who was born in Palermo but trained in Rome. Many were built from basalt picked from ruined buildings in the medieval streets of the old city. When it came to decorating the spectacular fountain at the nucleus of the new layout, Vaccarini was also able to reuse a sculpture that had already been at the heart of the city's identity for hundreds of years. It was the huge, basalt elephant that still tops the fountain in front of the duomo to this day. No one knows exactly how old it is, but according to one of the Arabic geographers who wrote about Sicily in the tenth century, it was already being used as a symbol of the city. Everyone calls the elephant *u liotru*, the dialect version of the name Eliodoro. No one is really sure who Eliodoro was. Some say he was a magician living at the foot of Etna, who brought the elephant to life and rode it through the streets at night, and some that he was a sculptor who fashioned the elephant from incandescent lava. To this day, it is one of the city's best-known landmarks. It is a useful landmark, too, and when the piazza was packed with people during the Festa di Sant' Agata, I overheard somebody on their mobile saying, 'Yes, you'll find me easily, I'm just behind the elephant's bum.'

The same rebuilding process unfolded all over the earthquake-stricken mountain. Walking through the quiet back streets of the town of Acireale on Etna's east flank is like visiting an exhibition devoted to the work of a family of stone carvers called the Flavetta. In street after street, the handsome, basalt-built palaces and houses have frowning masks, plumes of feathers, acanthus leaves or shields with coats of arms carved into the basalt keystones of the arches over their magnificent front doors. The door frames are also decorated with leaves, branches and imaginary animals. Most have balconies on the first floor, and the brackets supporting them display an even more entertaining menagerie of fantastical creatures, and comically grotesque, semi-human faces, all made from *basalto*. Among many reasons to visit Acireale, this always struck me as the most pressing, for those creatures were so lively they looked as if they might just have moved on before I came again.

Nothing in those elegant streets suggested what would happen next, but soon enough the fashion for elaborately carved decorations died out, and as a result basalt fell out of fashion and was soon demoted to being no more than a cheap construction material. In the twentieth century people began to balk at the brutal process of quarrying it for such small returns, and by the 1970s the industry built around Etna's most copious gift had virtually died out. However, in the 1990s two local brothers called Salvo and Raimondo Lizzio began to investigate the potential for relaunching basalt as a high-end material. They had grown up in a family of sculptors and stonemasons, and they knew that working any kind of stone in the past had always depended largely on brute strength. However, as Raimondo explained, they were also aware of a whole new generation of machinery invented in the 1980s for extracting and processing granite. They realized that with only a little adjustment, those new machines could transform the beleaguered basalt industry by enabling them to extract large blocks of basalt intact. The machines would also do all the heavy work, Raimondo said, freeing people up to be artisans. There was a powerful new kind of excavator, for example, that would be able to extract the best stone from deep beneath a lava flow, and then lift and transport vast blocks of it with ease. There were gargantuan circular saws, too, with diamond blades capable of cutting basalt into such thin slices they could make tiles, work surfaces and beautiful flagstones for floors and terraces.

This vision for basalt's new future was all very well, but everybody else in Italy still thought of it as a material best suited to making cement, roads and walls. Or, as Raimondo put it to me, 'nobody recognized the treasure beneath their feet'. His first step towards relaunching it as ornamental stone was to make himself basalt's ambassador at trade fairs all over the world. There was a lot to tell potential customers about the qualities of the stone lying beneath the surface of a lava flow. For example, it could be polished until it 'turned to velvet' (Salvo's words) and revealed a phenomenal array of patterns and colours. Unlike marble, it was tough enough to withstand rapid temperature changes without cracking. In fact, basalt tiles could be made virtually indestructible with the application of a ceramic glaze fired at such high temperature that glaze and stone melded together.

Getting up before dawn, and making my way to the Lizzio brothers' basalt quarry low on the volcano's south side, was an expedition to another world. Up in Milo, and almost everywhere else within the 50,000 acres of the Etna National Park, we lived cleanly and tidily in our beautiful surroundings, as mountain people so often do. And yet, as I crossed the park's boundary and drove down to those lower slopes, I was reminded that Etna could also be a hell hole of broken roads, abandoned buildings, and the fly-tipping that infected both cities and countryside like a disease. I could have re-furnished my house over and over again with the stained sofas and blistered coffee tables, sagging beds and slightly broken chairs left strewn across the sides of country lanes. Some people even fly-tipped beneath the very signs that declared it illegal. Why didn't they just put their rubbish out for the binmen who collected my waste so efficiently every day except Sunday? Because, I soon learned, over half of Etna's inhabitants were either unable or unwilling to pay the addition to their council tax that would cover rubbish collection, and local councils would not enforce payment for fear of losing votes at the next election. Added to this problem was the fact that just three rubbish tips served Etna and her hinterland. Worse still, all of them belonged to *malavita*, meaning they were either controlled by or collaborating with the Mafia. Their owners had consistently refused to invest in modern waste-treatment facilities, preferring to earn thousands of euros a year by illegally selling some of the rubbish from their local communities. This meant that as well as being full, the old tips were now obsolete. The true purpose of their owners' business was laid bare in 2020, when the police raided a tip in a town on the plain extending from Etna's south and south-west flanks. They uncovered plastic cannisters buried deep beneath the rubbish. Inside them were 116 million euros of very dirty money linking Etna to networks of organized crime that extended far, far beyond her territory.

Extraordinary though it seems, the flow the Lizzio brothers are quarrying so profitably today was formed during the devastating eruption of 1669, when it robbed countless people of their liveli-hoods. Layer upon layer of lava were added to that mighty flow over the space of four months, so that the towering walls of the quarry were over 30 metres high. The surface of the flow was still all mess and mayhem, but looking at in cross section from the quarry floor, I could see where the lava had been compressed to form basalt as smooth as syrup and full of wonderful, subtle colours. At the base of the quarry walls there was a bright-orange streak of colour where the first fiery layer of lava from the eruption had seared the soil like a steak. Lower still in that geological sandwich was a seam of primordial rock pre-dating Etna's very existence by millions of years.

The quarry was a vast, sunbaked arena, where gargantuan blocks of basalt lay about like beached whales on the dusty ground, their curvaceous flanks so smooth that I couldn't resist running my hand over them. Most other kinds of rock compact over millions of years, and this makes them resilient enough to be cut straight from the wall of a quarry without shattering. The basalt in the quarry was a geological baby compared to them, because it was formed from lava less than 500 years old. When it finally stopped moving, the surface of the flow cooled first, shrinking and cracking like dry mud into myriad prismatic shapes. It took much longer for the lava deep inside the flow to cool, but as it did, the cracks on the surface would have extended progressively downwards, cutting through the new rock to create rough columns. Had Salvo Lizzio tried to cut those convenient blocks of stone out using heavy machinery, they would simply have shattered like glass. Instead, he was obliged to unsettle them in ways that would persuade them to fall from the quarry wall almost of their own accord.

Salvo and his small team of *pirriaturi* (quarrymen) had spent the past three weeks bothering one of those columns. It was about 25 metres broad and 30 metres tall, a gargantuan thing that they were trying to convince to extract itself from the quarry wall. 'All we need do,' Salvo explained, 'is separate joins that are already there.' He spoke as if dividing one colossal basalt block from the next were as easy as pulling perforated paper apart, but in reality there was still much gruelling, dusty work to be done beneath a pitiless midsummer sun. He pointed out the section of the quarry wall they had been working on, and the long, vertical crack they had already induced to form down one side of it. Now a battered yellow digger entered stage left. Dwarfed by its surroundings, it trundled slowly towards us across the quarry floor. The driver squared it up beneath the block, heedless of the vast, fractured weight towering above him. There was nothing subtle about his arts of persuasion, for now the digger took huge bites from rubble immediately below the crack in the rock wall. Salvo stood by, hands clasped firmly behind his back. He was flawlessly turned out in white trainers and pristine shorts and T-shirt, and even when he disappeared behind whirling curtains of dust, I could still hear the piercing whistle he used to direct the driver. They shared a perfect understanding, so that after whistling to attract his attention Salvo needed only the slightest hand movement to tell the driver to make a hasty retreat as rivulets of shattered rock ricocheted onto the ground all around him. Sometimes the driver climbed down and the two of them stood side by side beneath the block, gazing up as if to gauge what it might intend to do now.

The next machine to arrive on that battleground was more brutal. With a huge chisel on the front of it attached to an articulated arm, it seemed to have its own intelligence, pecking and scraping away at the base of the block like a long-necked bird. On and on it went, rummaging and prodding, as if after three weeks of gentle persuasion the time had come at last for straight talking. However, despite this new sense of urgency, everything had to be done slowly and thoughtfully, for quarries are dangerous places, and Salvo told me someone had been killed in another local quarry only the previous week. 'So, we mustn't rush,' he said. 'After all, it's not as if we were working in a restaurant.' After fossicking through the block's support system for half an hour or so, Salvo decided it was time to stand back and see if it would collapse of its own accord. I took this opportunity to jump into the back of a car going up to ground level where I would be able see the situation from another angle. That viewpoint revealed such huge cracks between the block and the quarry wall that it was hard to understand how it was still standing.

I have been told again and again that hospitality is sacred on Etna, but of all the places I have experienced it, that quarry was surely the strangest. I was back on the quarry floor when the digger driver strolled over, grasping a plastic garden chair in his gnarled hand, pale dust filling every deeply corrugated line on his face. He set the chair down gently in the shade, reassuring me that nothing serious would happen yet, despite the showers of rubble falling from the block. Someone else appeared then, a complete stranger carrying espresso, warm and sweet, in a plastic bottle. 'And these *biscotti* are for you, too,' he said, pulling pink paper and delicate, golden ribbons off a tray of freshly baked biscuits. We set all those good things out on the bonnet of his car, sipped coffee, and chatted about the quarry business. 'The heat, the cold, the dust, the danger, young people today want none of it,' he said, which didn't seem unreasonable.

The block had already been given every chance to surrender, and now it was time for decisive action. I returned to my seat and perched there as if I were a spectator at the races, although the digger progressed at snail's pace as it chugged up to the surface of the flow. Salvo strolled across to tell me that I could do 'absolutely anything' I liked, as long as it didn't involve moving a single centimetre from my allotted place. I didn't need telling twice, for now the digger driver had reached the top of the flow, and he was pushing and hammering the block with such force from behind that the long arm of the digger squealed with effort. Cloud after cloud of dust exploded into the air before the block finally collapsed with a roar of shattering stone. I couldn't see a thing through the dust, but when Salvo stepped from the dusty clouds like a miracle, he was as clean as ever, his shoes still mysteriously gleaming white. (He told me later his skin was immaculate too, on account of constant exfoliation by lava dust. 'But you wouldn't want to see the inside of my lungs.') And there on the ground beside him that basalt colossus lay felled at last.

A huge articulated lorry had been waiting for hours to load up another block lying in the dust. Somewhere, someone was waiting for its arrival, because companies supplying a high-end customer base of interior designers, architectural practices, tile and flooring manufactures often select and buy blocks in situ, long before they are felled. This one was shaped like a gigantic femur. Inside it had the aerated texture of ancient bone, but outside its planes and surfaces were as smooth as butter. Toppling a block is one thing, but lifting it again onto the back of a lorry demands different procedures and another set of skills. Now Salvo jumped up onto a mighty machine and manoeuvred the heavy block onto a forklift. If you consider that a sheet of basalt only 2 centimetres thick weighs 60 kilos per square metre, you begin to appreciate the challenges involved in transporting those behemoths to their destinations. Added to that, their shapes were always so irregular that they could never sit squarely on the flat bed of a lorry. The lorry driver had been busy making a framework of worn, wooden props for that stone femur to rest on. There was a bit of crunching and shifting when Salvo eventually lowered it into place, but the driver's work held good. He was no advert for a job in the stone industry, however, with the brace he wore to support an injured leg, and another formidable brace strapped over his jaunty T-shirt to support his back. Wedging and roping the block in place, he said cheerfully, 'It's so heavy that it will still fall off if it wants to.' What a thought. Eventually, the lorry set off at walking pace, the suspension creaking ominously as it began the journey that would transform basalt from being an element of chaos and destruction in the landscape, to a tame, beautiful and highly valued material that now fed wealth into the local economy.

9
Snow Business

Spring had come late to the mountain, but now we were in high summer, that great succession of days undone by heat. Little wonder then that I should become so fascinated by a trade long devoted to softening the impact of scorching Mediterranean summers.

What could be more wonderfully unlikely than building a business around something that could simply disappear before your eyes? And yet, from the sixteenth century until the beginning of the twentieth century, Etna's abundant snow supply put her at the heart of an international trade so improbable and deeply difficult it seems almost unbelievable today. Imagine transporting snow at a snail's pace through the heat of high summer, when rough tracks and tiny paths were the only routes across the slopes of a fiery volcano. And what about loading snow and ice onto boats, and sending it across the Mediterranean to Malta in soaring heat? Every aspect of the snow trade sounds as fantastical as the challenges set for the heroes of myths or folk tales, and yet the long tradition of 'cultivating' snow, harvesting, storing, preserving, selling and distributing it, endured on Etna until the middle of the twentieth century. That is a long time ago now, but not long enough to be forgotten, and the trade makes its presence felt on Etna to this day. You can still walk the steep tracks to high-altitude lava caves, ravines, gorges and man-made structures that were used as snow stores, and you can still find Via Neve in Catania, and in other towns and cities all over the island. Until the twentieth century these 'snow streets' would have been lined with shops that stayed open day and night to sell snow and ice. An even more tangible connection to the trade's long history comes each summer in the form of noisy little granita vans catering for a population with tastes first inspired and then shaped over many centuries by the snow trade. I met them hurtling between towns and villages all over the mountain, and saw them screeching to a halt alongside beaches as if they were responding to an emergency. Just to add to this impression of urgency, the driver constantly sounded a whistle with as many decibels as a siren, jolting sunbathers awake and sending their children into a frenzy of excitement.

You should be ashamed to be seen drinking a cappuccino after eleven in the morning anywhere in Italy, but there really is no wrong time to eat granita in a place that has prized chilled and frozen foods ever since the Greeks first brought the idea of preserving snow to Sicily. Ancient Greek poet Simonides' delightful description of this habit was 'burying snow alive so that it could live on and soften the summer'. The Romans were just as keen on chilled wine as the Greeks, and Seneca fulminated against all the fashionable young men in Rome 'tossing bits [of snow or ice] into their glasses lest they become too warm merely through the time taken in drinking'. He seemed equally angry about the sheer number of warehouses and shops dedicated to storing and selling the stuff, and all the horsepower employed to carry it into the city. Nevertheless, chilling food and drinks became so fashionable among the Romans that snow often cost more than the food or wine it was used to cool. Pliny the Younger made this abundantly clear in a furious letter to a friend who stood him up for dinner: 'I will certainly send you a sizeable bill for the snow,' he wrote, 'for it was ruined in the serving.'

Cold drinks and chilled foods enjoyed by Greeks and Romans were only the precursor to Sicily's happy addiction to snow. The next significant moment in an ice-bound history of the island came in the ninth century, when Arabic settlers pulled their boats ashore in Mazara del Vallo, a crumbling Phoenician settlement near Trapani on the north coast. Of course, the real story here is the beginning of a campaign that would eventually make Sicily part of the Islamic Caliphate, but within the narrow ambit of a nascent snow trade there are other, more important things to consider. For example, the Arabs introduced Sicily's population to iced sherbets – or *sharbat*.

These drinks were made by boiling sugar and water to make a syrup, flavouring it with fruit juice, spices and flowers, and chilling it in a container sunk deep into the snow. Any history of the snow trade on Etna is bound to involve granita, and these iced sherbets would eventually turn out to be its true ancestors, just as granita is ancestor to ice cream.

Sicily had been part of the Caliphate for barely 200 years when the Normans invaded in the eleventh century, making Gran Conte Ruggero the new ruler of Sicily. One of his first tasks was to re-establish Catholicism as the official religion. This might not seem to have much to do with the history of the snow trade, but when he re-established the Bishopric of Catania in 1092, Ruggero included a sizeable share in Etna's snow fields, on the condition that the bishop would supply Catania in perpetuity with the snow its population now depended on to chill their drinks.

Etna was not the only snowy mountain in Sicily, but although snow was also harvested on the Peloritani, the Madonie, and mountains near Palermo, Enna and Agrigento, none could rival Etna. As the highest mountain on the island, her snows were the most abundant, and she retained snow on her slopes throughout the year. The density of the population on her lower slopes meant that snow traders could always find people to harvest and transport the snow. And finally, the volcano's east flank ran straight down to the sea, where there were several ports, and boats to carry the snow to towns and cities on the coast, or across the sea to Malta. Consequently, the snow trade grew, and by the sixteenth century it had taken on the formal structures it would retain, more or less unchanged, until the middle of the twentieth century.

This wasn't an easy business at any level. Labourers shovelling snow on the mountain were at one end of the trade, and at the other were bishops, princes and landowners who inherited rights to snow as strange and inalienable as English monarchs' ownership of swans. In between these two extremes were tens of thousands of producers and consumers, an intricate and finely tuned network of labourers, muleteers, agents, shopkeepers, customs officials and tax inspectors, not to mention doctors and the patients they treated with ice and snow, the confectioners and chefs who made ice cream and granita, and the people who ate it, the households, great and small, using snow and ice to preserve meat and fish, the skippers and crews of boats that ferried snow up and down the east coast of Sicily and took four or five thousand tons of it over the sea to Malta once a fortnight. This eccentric business propelled the vast, untameable landscape of Etna into the heart of domestic life in Sicily and Malta, made a handful of snow lords very rich, ensured a comfortable living for others, and earned many more just enough money to survive.

Those who earned least from the snow trade worked at the highest altitudes. They were *nevaioli*, or 'snowmen'. A typical day's work in winter would see them getting up before dawn to climb up Etna's slopes to the snowfields. Their job was to harvest snow and pack it away in a *neviera*, or snow store. This could be a natural hollow or crevasse in the ground, one of Etna's many caves, or a purpose-built structure. One of the most famous snow caves is known as Grotta dei Ladroni, 'robber's cave', because like so many other caves on Etna, bandits were supposed to have used it as their hiding place. The date 1776 is scratched into the wall at its entrance, and this is probably when it was converted into a *neviera* by knocking the two circular holes in the roof that would have made it easier to fill with snow. A precipitous flight of steps leads down into the depths of the cave, where you can still see your breath in midsummer. In Jean-Pierre Houël's *Voyage pittoresque des isles de Sicile, de Malta et de Lipari*, I learned that in the eighteenth century the Grotta dei Ladroni was on a long lease to the Knights of Malta. Much of the snow sent to their sun-struck, rocky island was gathered by the Bishop of Catania's snow merchants from a large tract of land set aside solely for this purpose. To ensure an uninterrupted supply, however, they rented private *neviere* like the Grotta dei Ladroni and employed their own team of *nevaioli* to work there. They used a brigantine, the fastest sailing ship of the era, to ship the snow to Malta.

At lower altitudes snow was often stored in purpose-built *neviere*. These relics of the snow industry are scattered all over the Boscosa. Their altitude on the mountain throws a harsh light on our changing climate, for it would never be possible to conserve snow at such modest heights today. They are extraordinary, quasi-industrial buildings, often built in natural hollows that their owners dug out further, levelled, and then lined with blocks of basalt. Originally, the ground all around them would have been kept clear, but those that survive are generally lost among trees or swamped in undergrowth.

The methods for gathering the snow and carrying it depended on the lie of the land. When working on a steep slope, for example, the *nevaioli* could just make a gigantic snowball and roll it straight to the store. Otherwise, they might pile it onto a canvas sheet or into wicker baskets and carry it there like that. As the snow level inside the *neviera* rose, a few members of the team known as the *pisaturi* (tramplers) strapped clean wooden boards to their feet, climbed down onto the snow, and began systematically tamping it down until it formed a level layer only 30 centimetres thick. They divided one layer of snow from the next with leaves, dry grass or ferns, as this would make it easier to cut each one into neat blocks when the time came to extract it in summer. As they trampled down layer after layer, the lower layers of compacted snow began to turn into *neve ghiacciata*, 'icy snow', which kept better and was easier to transport than fresh snow. When the *neviera* was full at last, the *pisaturi* insulated the top of their snowy lasagna with a thick layer of clean fern leaves, broom branches, dry grass, or anything else that might protect and preserve it until summer.

Tucked away like an animal in hibernation, the snow was supposed to lie undisturbed until the heat rose in late spring. It was vulnerable lying there, and merchants were often forced to pay protection money to bandits who threatened to destroy their crop by tipping barrels of oil over it. Theft was another worry: the snow in isolated *neviere* was kept under lock and key as if it were money in a safe. And these were not the only risks faced by anyone committed to trading in a product so perishable it made fish or vegetables look like cast-iron investments. For instance, unseasonable rain might wreck the snow, the snow store could be engulfed by lava, an unexpected blizzard could halt the caravans of mules, and storms at sea could keep a ship at anchor until its precious cargo was no more than a puddle in the hold. Notwithstanding all these fearful possibilities, snow merchants were obliged to sign tightly worded contracts detailing punitive fines that would be imposed if the snow supply should ever be interrupted. In the case of the bishops of Catania, this meant they often paid for the harvesting, storing and transporting of snow at no profit to the bishopric. No wonder they tried to liberate themselves from the ambiguous implications of Gran Conte Ruggero's gift, but that was a fool's game, and they were unable to make their escape until the twentieth century.

As spring turned to summer, Etna's snow merchants assembled new teams, this time made up of muleteers – *bordonari* – and their animals, and *nevaioli* who specialized in cutting snow and ice. These specialists changed into clean leather slippers before they clambered down into the *neviera*, where the temperature still hovered below freezing. First, they had to clear away the insulating branches and hack their way through an icy crust to expose the surface of the store. Advertisements for Etna snow always focused on its whiteness and purity, so this was a make or break moment. Had the snow been insulated well enough that winter? Was it clean? Did the uppermost layers have the soft, granular texture that would make it ideal for granita and ice cream making? If the answer was yes to all these questions, they set to work with special, wide-toothed saws to cut it into blocks, then they used wooden spades to extract them.

Each slippery block weighed 60 kilos, and it had to be wrapped in a clean sack made from waxed cloth and stuffed with straw, then tied up with rope like a gigantic parcel. One of the illustrations in Houël's book shows *nevaioli* bent double beneath the weight of blocks as they made their way through the Grotta dei Ladroni and up its precipitous steps. It is a vivid image of brutally hard work. Of course, there were no roads on the upper reaches of Etna, only paths too narrow and uneven for a cart. Mules were the only viable form of transport, and they would have been waiting outside the *neviera* with their *bordonari*. I've seen photos of those animals taken at the beginning of the twentieth century, while bales of ice weighing a total of 120 kilos were being roped across their backs. Their ears are laid flat and their tails appear to be swishing in the way they only swish just before a well-aimed kick.

The mule train would set off from the *neviera* before dawn in a race against the sun, its load diminishing with every step. The *bordonari* timed their journeys to arrive when the heat was greatest and demand for snow at its peak in cities, towns and villages on Etna and the Catania Plain. They went to snow stores built into the city walls of towns and cities, made deliveries to the shops lining the Via Neve, to middlemen and traders. Sometimes they even sold snow on street corners themselves, shouting *neve, neve!* ever louder as the temperature rose. As the day progressed and snow became scarcer, they were able to increase their prices with every hour that passed.

To find out why such enormous quantities of snow were deemed essential to daily life on Etna, we must go back to the sixteenth century, and into the company of an extraordinary scientist and mathematician from Naples called Giambattista Della Porta. He was only fifteen years old in 1559 when he published his first book, *Magia naturalis*. Thirty years later he brought out a second, greatly expanded, edition, including this time his instructions for artificial freezing. By now he was one of the most famous natural scientists in Europe, and the new edition was a compendium of all the knowledge he had gained over three decades by reading ancient manuscripts, carrying out experiments of his own, and talking to, or corresponding with, the most knowledgeable people in Europe. It was the sort of book you might consult for advice about preserving fruit, only to find yourself, as I did an hour later, learning how to train a dog to do tricks (leave it in the company of an ape), or how to make a silent bullet (mix fat with the gunpowder). It reads like an enormous how-to of everything from optics to alchemy, from breeding animals to cookery. And it was here, in the cookery section, that Della Porta explained how salt could be used to lower the freezing point of snow. Just like Seneca, he deplored the fashion for 'wine cold as ice' himself, and yet because it was 'the chief thing desired at feasts . . . especially in summer', he made wine the focus for his first experiment. The result, he said, sounding almost vindictive, was a drink so cold 'that you cannot drink it but by sucking, and drawing in of your breath'. This was the first time anyone had achieved artificial freezing. It was a true marvel, and a gateway to new chapters in the history of both food and medicine.

Like a magician concocting a spell, Della Porta achieved his end by diluting wine with water, pouring it into a glass carafe, and sinking it in a wooden container filled with snow and strewn with saltpetre. By mixing it with saltpetre, he lowered the snow's freezing point, thereby boosting its power to induce freezing in other substances. All he had to do now was turn the carafe continuously on its snowy bed and watch the wine 'congeal by degrees'. Of course, its alcohol content prevented it from freezing solid, but nevertheless it was considered a great wonder. It was only a matter of time before it became common knowledge that you could put a mixture of fruit juice, sugar and water into a metal canister, or *pozzetto*, and turn it continuously in snow mixed with saltpetre, or even sea or rock salt, until the contents froze into the soft, creamy mix we call granita.

With Della Porta's discovery, iced wine, ice cream, granita, and even ice sculptures became essential elements of any decent banquet. You can glean a lot of detail about these events from handbooks written by the fashionable stewards who organized every aspect of banqueting in great houses. In *Lo scalco alla moderna*, 'The Modern Steward', for example, Antonio Latini describes the late seventeenth-century celebrations he organized for numerous noblemen and women, cardinals and princes. The pinnacle of his career came in the household of Don Stefano Carrillo y Salcedo, First Minister of the Spanish government. Whatever happened at his banquets set the tone for hospitality among the elite all over the kingdom, and in a chapter entitled 'Triumphs', Latini describes the ice sculptures used to decorate tables on special occasions. Among them were pyramids, obelisks, vases, bowls and statues, enormous frozen ornaments arranged like an icy spine down the middle of the table, and then left to deliquesce in the flickering light of the candles. Latini's instructions for making them are so clear that filling a mould with spring water and sinking it carefully into a bed of snow mixed with salt in exactly the right proportion sounds like the simplest thing in the world. That done, he suggests filling those icy bowls and vases with fresh fruit, or even suspending bright berries in the ice as it froze. At the end of each course the ornaments would be whisked away and replaced with a fresh set of entertainments. A platter of figs, melon slices, plums or peaches, perhaps, nestling on a bed of snow, or baskets full of frosted fruit and flowers.

Latini dedicates a whole chapter to *sorbetti*, a word used interchangeably at this time for granita and milk-based ice cream. He gives the exact proportions of snow to salt needed for freezing them, but his recipes are otherwise rather vague because, as he put it, 'It seems that in Naples everyone is born with the instinct and talent to make *sorbetti*.' And if they weren't, he had no intention of spoiling the trade by passing on its secrets. Better to look to Vincenzo Corrado for them, and the *Credenziere del buon gusto*, 'Steward of Good Taste', which he published in 1773. He prefaces recipes for granita and ice cream with a warning that 'you need a lot of practice in the seriously hard work of ice cream making'. That said, he proffers thirty-six recipes, including an ice cream made from violets.

You might think these treats and treatments the preserve of the rich, but in the late eighteenth century Patrick Brydone remarked that, 'even peasants ... regale themselves with ices during the summer heats'. At the beginning of the nineteenth century, William Irvine, a Scottish army doctor stationed in Sicily, described 'wretches whose rags have scarce adhesion enough to hang on their bodies, yet find a baioc [an almost worthless coin] to spend in the ice shop'. Sorbets and granitas were also sold on the street, and even those 'wretches' would be given a silver spoon to eat them with. All in all, according to Brydone, 'a famine of snow', or so he was told, would be considered 'more grievous than a famine of corn or wine'.

The shops on Via Neve in Catania used to stay open day and

night like twenty-four-hour chemists, selling snow to treat bruising, diarrhoea, smallpox, and many other common conditions, including high fevers and terrifying haemorrhages during childbirth. In 1775 a Neapolitan doctor called Filippo Baldini published the first book devoted to the medicinal uses of *sorbetti*. He described acidic, fruit-based recipes as the cure for diarrhoea and any other condition improved by increasing the fluidity of the humours. Aromatic *sorbetti* made with cinnamon, chocolate or coffee were best for boosting fertility and curing melancholy. This was all urgent business, and William Irvine was genuinely shocked by the scramble for fresh deliveries of snow. 'The noise and tumult at the houses where the snow is sold, as fast as it arrives from Etna is even alarming to a stranger;' he said, 'and I thought, the first time, that nothing less than murder could have occurred within, seeing the doors besieged by so clamorous a mob.'

People would indeed resort to desperate measures if there was no snow to be had. For example, when the snow stores in Siracusa were empty in 1777, Jean-Pierre Houël saw panic set in among the locals. Pity the crew of the snow ship that happened to be sailing along the coast when 'without a moment's deliberation everyone ran down and demanded that the ship be unloaded, and when the crew refused, the ship was attacked . . .'

Despite its precarious nature, the snow trade continued to flourish throughout the nineteenth century, and in 1904 an entrepreneur called Giuseppe Leotta (although everyone called him Don Puddu) set up a whole new snow business in Fornazzo. The place was no more than a few huts and houses then, lived in by woodcutters, charcoal burners, and others scratching a meagre living from the woods. But Don Puddu had seen its potential as the centre for an ambitious new business dealing in all the gifts Etna had to offer – snow and ice, as well as timber, charcoal and firewood. Before long everyone in Fornazzo was involved in this new enterprise in some way, whether as *nevaioli* supplying the snow trade, as foresters felling trees and chopping firewood, as charcoal makers or sawyers in the timber mill. Donkeys and mules were also key to the business, and Don Puddu brought muleteers to Fornazzo from as far away as Adrano and Paternò on the opposite side of the mountain, some with a dozen or more animals apiece.

Before long Don Puddu was having to provide accommodation for all the people flocking to the village to work for him, so that in no time at all both the lives of Fornazzo's inhabitants and the place itself had been transformed. He also built two *neviere*. You can still see the remains of one of them on the edge of the road running through the centre of the village. The other is in the forest high above Fornazzo, where it emerges from the undergrowth like a monumental shrine to the snow trade, its walls nearly 20 metres long and 10 metres high, the space between them 10 metres wide. The broad, sloping entrance would have been easy to access by mule, and a rough track still links it to the road.

I am lucky enough to have been inside the handsome house Don Puddu built for himself in Fornazzo, where the visitors' book was once filled with the names of actors, artists and other well-known figures from Taormina and Catania. How extraordinary, for example, that Filippo Tommaso Marinetti himself, founder of the Futurist movement, should be among its signatories. Futurists were generally much more interested in machinery than the natural world, but Marinetti was a great fan of volcanos, and described Etna as a *macchina naturale*, 'a natural machine'.

Baron Wilhelm Von Gloeden, still notorious for his homoerotic photographs of young men and boys in Taormina, was another famous figure in Fornazzo at the beginning of the twentieth century. And when his international circle of gay friends in Taormina was scattered by the First World War, he returned to Etna and settled in Milo. Local people were galvanized by his arrival, and there were rumours that the rooms of his house in Via Bellini were filled with caged birds and papered with worthless German bank notes.

Don Puddu's snow trade went on being so successful that in 1921 he and his son Salvatore decided to build the first cable railway on Etna. Four kilometres long, it was designed to carry snow and ice, charcoal, timber and firewood off the mountain in the fastest and most efficient way possible. No wonder Marinetti wanted to see it, for this was just the kind of technical innovation he loved. However, building on that steep, unstable ground was an enormous challenge, and unfortunately for Don Puddu the work was not complete by the time he died in 1923. Perhaps that was just as well, because in 1928, just three years after they finished the job, Etna staged its cataclysmic eruption. Over the course of only three days lava destroyed almost the entire railway, forcing Salvatore to return to the old system of transporting everything by mule – excellent news for local muleteers. However, a poster from this period advertising Leotta's Etna snow suggests that business continued to thrive. 'Everybody prefers Etna snow!' it said, under a lovely line drawing of the volcano. 'It is the best snow in Sicily, compact, as white as can be, and completely clean, unlike snow from other sources, which many local councils forbid their vendors to use as it often turns out to be harmful.' The poster summoned snow traders to the station yard at Giarre from 31 December, where they would be able to buy 100 kilos of this excellent product for only four lire.

In 1926, Don Puddu's son invested in a machine that compressed snow into regular sheets of ice. These were thought to be more hygienic than old-fashioned bales of *neve ghiacciata*, and were certainly much easier to transport. However, the first artificial ice machine had already arrived in Catania fifty years earlier, and by the outbreak of the First World War there were over a hundred artificial ice shops in the city and the end of the snow trade was in sight. It did not come to a definitive end, however, until the 1950s, by which time most families in Sicily owned a fridge, making one of Etna's greatest and most abundant gifts properly redundant once and for all. That said, granita is the true legacy of Etna's snow trade, and the sound of the granita van roaring, hooting and whistling its way up the hill marked the start of every summer day for me on Etna. It always stopped in the lane just below my window, where each morning I heard a version of the same shouted conversation between the granita man and my neighbour Lucia, who may or may not have had a granita-filled brioche for her breakfast that day. Me too, if I could get down the steps before he roared off again.

The recipe for genuine granita has never changed, and in a shiny kitchen behind the Bar Pasticceria Santo Musumeci in Randazzo, Giovanna Musumeci still spins it from nothing more than sugar, water and fruit juice. She is *maestra gelatiera*, ice cream professor, in the bar her late father set up in 1967, and like him she has won some of the highest international awards for her work.

'Who invented granita?' Giovanna demanded, eyes flashing behind huge glasses. The granita enthusiasts gathered in the kitchen sensed the weight of the question. It made the honeymoon couple from Canada look hard at their own feet, had the chef from the luxurious San Domenico Hotel in Taormina smiling, and his colleagues exchanging knowing glances. Barely pausing, Giovanna answered her own question with all the energy and panache of a stand-up comedian. The Tuscans say they invented it in Florence, the inhabitants of Val di Zoldo in Friuli say they did it, and of course the Sicilians know it was them.

'These are the three schools of thought,' she said pragmatically, 'and each has its own story to tell. However . . .' and here she paused for laughs and dramatic effect, 'Sicily had certain advantages when it came to making granita . . .'

We know all about that now, but as well as Etna's abundant snows, Giovanna harked back to those Arabic settlers in the ninth century. Many of them were farmers from the desert fringes of North Africa, and although the plants and trees they brought with them were commonplace in the Caliphate, they were entirely new to Sicily. Citrus fruit and sugar cane were among those new crops, and without them *granita al limone* – that quintessentially Sicilian summer treat – might never have been invented.

Giovanna had already prepared 600ml of *acqua profumata*, by grating the rind of a lemon into it, right down to the pith. 'It's a terrible thing to take only the juice from a lemon', she said; 'the pith is the best bit, it's the sourness you feel in your saliva glands.' She warmed the perfumed water to just below boiling point, whisked 200g of lemon juice and 200g of cane sugar into it, and popped the mixture into one of a team of industrial ice-cream makers standing against the wall. But as she explained, she could just as well have put the same mixture into a metal container, sunk it into a saucepan packed with ice and salt, and stirred the contents with a spatula until it froze.

What passes for granita in other places can be an uneasy, brightly coloured, granular mix, an act of aggression in the form of ice and fruit juice, but when Giovanna's granita emerged it was the colour of damp snow, and still soft enough to drop from the spoon.

'It's magic,' she said simply, 'and when you put it into your mouth the heat of your body should melt it immediately.' Which is exactly what happened to a mixture so smooth that it seemed to turn to cream in my mouth, delivering a huge, fresh-lemon punch as it did so.

On a board outside the bar there was a list of all the *granite* Giovanna produces in her small kitchen. It changes from week to week and season to season, but each and every one showcases the flavours of the fruit from which it is made. At the gentler end of the summer spectrum come the creamy flavours of toasted almond, flat peach or apricot, while at the opposite end are variations on raspberry, and the fabulous *assoluto di mandarino*, made entirely without water so that it does indeed capture an absolute definition of mandarin's flavour. Whatever the fruit, the time of year or time of day, each mouthful of granita will always encapsulate the memory of the strangest trade ever practised on the slopes of Etna.

10.

Into the Woods

A swathe of forests encircles Etna's middle like an undulating green girdle, and until the beginning of the twentieth century, every aspect of daily life on the volcano was enabled by their timber. People found all they needed there for making the beams, rafters, doors and window frames of their houses and barns, not to mention the firewood to keep them warm and fuel their ovens. They also used wood for making wine and water barrels, boats, carts, ploughs, household utensils, shop signs, furniture and tools. In fact, timber was such a valuable resource that people sometimes compare its past role in the lives of Etna's people to that of oil today. Meanwhile, shepherds sent their flocks to graze among the trees in summer, while others came to collect the fallen acorns to feed their pigs, pick mushrooms, or climb trees to perilously gather honey and wax from wild bees' nests. Over the summer, charcoal burners produced the fuel for firing furnaces, and *resinatori* milked the pines for resin to make pitch. The Boscosa was also a hunting ground for animals such as deer, rabbits, hares, wild boar and wild goats, many of them hunted to extinction.

Trees grew much closer to Etna's summit crater than anyone dared to live. Ever quixotic, Etna would nurture them with shelter, rich volcanic soil and an abundance of water for centuries before sending lava to plough through them, toppling and igniting great tracts of the forest as it came rolling through. Sometimes, among the tumbled lava of a petrified flow, you may find the ghost of a tree preserved as what they call a *pietra cannone*, or cannon stone. A large tree is most likely to be preserved in this way because it is full of sap that slows combustion, giving the lava time to solidify slowly around its trunk, just as volcanic ash once enfolded and preserved casts of the bodies of Vesuvius' victims in Pompeii. Over time, whatever remains of the trunk will rot away, leaving nothing but a lava cylinder, a hollow effigy of the tree with the unique imprint of its bark inside. Although not easy to spot in the chaotic jumble of a lava landscape, a *pietra cannone*, named for its resemblance to the barrel of a cannon, is a rich source of information for volcanologists. Under expert scrutiny it will divulge secrets about the direction the lava flowed, its thickness, and even the original layout of the landscape before the eruption.

Despite the pressures of human exploitation, eruption, disease and climate change, Etna's forests endure, reminding us of a time when ours was a civilization built around wood. Take the holm oaks that have always grown at the intersection between the Coltivata and the Boscosa on the east flank of the volcano. Their unusually dense and heavy wood was perfect for making things that needed to be particularly strong, such as handles for tools, clamps, vices and presses of all kinds, including the gigantic, wooden screws used in machinery for crushing sugar cane. I found the ancient holm oak called Ilice di Carrinu, 'little Charles's holm oak', growing in the forest high above Milo. I had been to visit it in spring, when the path took me through woods swaying with the seedheads of long grasses, asphodel's pale flowers emerging from metallic buds as scaly as insects' backs, yellow leopard's bane, and bright blue clumps of lungwort. The tree's very existence struck me as a monument to the ancient multispecies relationship between Etna's people and her forest, and its position next to a ruined farmhouse as an enduring statement about the age-old entanglement of plant and human life on the mountain.

What struck me first about the Ilice di Carrinu were its strange proportions, as if it had spent its 700 years reinventing the meaning of 'tree'. Its twisted trunk, for example, was really remarkably short, and the muscled, horizontal branches it threw out to either side quite exceptionally long. The branches themselves were twisted too, like dough before it is plaited into a loaf, or pastry turned for decorating the top of a tart. Its bark was as scaly as the skin of some imaginary reptile, and where its stabilizing roots thrust into the ground, they looked like elephant's feet marking the spot where it had germinated on the surface of a lava flow from 1285. Those long branches helped it to balance on the steeply sloping ground, but over time the shade beneath them must also have convinced the people living in the farmhouse to spare it the axe. This decision passed from one generation to the next until it seems almost as if the tree had taken agency over the duration of its own life by growing in that peculiar way. It has survived longer than all the people whose existence played out beneath its branches, and now it lives in gentle symbiosis with insects, birds and fungi, providing them with a habitat, and thus helping to maintain the forest's rich biodiversity and resilience.

Ilice di Carrinu is among thirty ancient specimens on Etna that have been included in the European Register of Monumental Trees. The enormous, gnarled and nobbled Castagno dei Cento Cavalli, 'hundred-horse sweet chestnut', in Sant' Alfio on the east flank, is another. Legends are entangled in the branches of all these ancient trees, and the name of Castagno dei Cento Cavalli comes from the story of Giovanna d'Angiò, the fourteenth-century queen of Naples, who happened to be riding past it when a terrible storm broke out. The tree was already so big that the queen and her entire retinue of a hundred knights on horseback are all supposed to have found shelter beneath its enormous canopy. Handed down from generation to generation, legends like this perpetuate the intimate relationship between trees and human life on the volcano. Some, and Castagno dei Cento Cavalli is certainly one of them, have become an important part of the local community's identity.

Sweet chestnuts have always grown especially well on the volcano's east flank, where rainfall is higher than anywhere else, and Etna's great bulk protects them from the coldest winds. Unlike the Ilice di Carrinu, always left to its own devices, the Castagno dei Cento Cavalli bears testament to a long tradition of coppicing. This ancient technique involves cutting the tree back to its base to form what is known as a 'stool'. Treated in this way, fresh, straight growth springs up from the outermost edge of the stool so rapidly that the 'poles', as they are called, can be metres high in as little as five years.

In the past, people found uses for chestnut poles of every diameter on Etna. The thinnest were woven into baskets, the medium sized used as posts for supporting vines, and the largest of all were turned into beams or planked to make floorboards. Until twenty or thirty years ago, sweet chestnut was the only wood used locally for making roof and window frames and doors for barns and houses. These have always been its principal uses, but there is a long list of other objects traditionally made from chestnut wood, objects revealing that chestnut trees were once essential to the fabric of everyday life on Etna. They include the stakes still used to this day for supporting vines, staves for wine barrels, musical instruments, boats, parts for ploughs, collars for cows, flagons, spoons, ladles, furniture, milk vats, milk buckets and spinning wheels, so that it goes almost without saying that chestnut also made a substantial contribution to the economies of all villages engaged in forestry on the volcano. The variety of chestnut tree grown on Etna was selected for the high quality of its timber rather than its nuts, which are actually quite small. Nevertheless, driving out of Milo after a windy autumn night, I have often had to dodge people wrapped up warm against the cold, bottoms up, collecting fallen chestnuts before they got squashed by drivers like me.

It is a long time since anyone has dared wield an axe around the Castagno dei Cento Cavalli, but centuries of coppicing have left it with three separate trunks. It had many more in the eighteenth century, judging by Jean-Pierre Houël's painting of a horse grazing in the shade of the trunks' branches, and a small house nestling in the circular space between them. Despite the myth surrounding it, sceptics have always suspected that the tree is, as Patrick Brydone wrote, no more than 'a bush of five large trees growing together'. However, in 2021 a team of scientists took leaves from the branches of each of the three trunks in order to analyse their DNA, and the results confirmed that all three originated from the same seed. After scraping away the leaf litter and soil at their base, they were able to measure the gargantuan stool produced by hundreds of years of coppicing. Its radius was an astonishing nine metres, and by multiplying this figure with the average growth rate of sweet chestnuts, they reached the conclusion that the Castagno dei Cento Cavalli was 2,200 years old. This made it both the oldest and the largest sweet chestnut in Europe. Older than Christ, it was throwing out its tap root at the same time as Sicily was being annexed as the first province of the Roman Empire. It has shrugged off diseases like the canker that massacred millions of chestnuts all over Europe at the beginning of the twentieth century, and seems unaffected by the sweet-chestnut blight running amok on the mountain today. No wonder people engaged in forest conservation are so keen to capture its genetic ID, because this will be key to understanding and preserving its capacity for adaptation in the face of rapid climate change, human pressure and disease.

Historians often refer to the age of our dependence on forests as the Civilization of Wood. It began to crumble in Sicily, as it did everywhere, in the second half of the twentieth century, when more convenient, modern alternatives to timber became available. Why bother with painting window frames and doors when you could install aluminium ones? And why make wooden tools when you could buy almost the same things made from plastic? As in so many cases, however, Etna is an exception, being one of very few places in Sicily that still has a thriving timber trade. There are sawmills in Biancavilla, Nicolosi and Trecastagni on the south face, Zafferana Etnea on the east and Linguaglossa on the north. And of course, Fornazzo has been at the heart of the timber trade ever since Don Puddu set up his multifaceted business there in 1904, for as well as dealing in snow he was a timber, charcoal and firewood merchant.

The eco-museum in Fornazzo was built in 2017 to celebrate the people of Fornazzo – past and present – who dedicated their lives to working with local timber. Its director is Lavinia Lo Faro, one of those rare people who recognize the value of the ordinary things in the everyday life of a community, things that can so often seem eternal but can quite suddenly disappear. This compels her to champion the work of the five, family-owned sawmills in the village, and the quality of the chestnut timber they produce. One morning she led me down narrow lanes and bumpy tracks to the tin barn where the Patanè family have been running a sawmill since 1946. Its roof was supported on chestnut rafters, there was a chestnut ladder leading to the loft, and vertical piles of chestnut at every stage of processing leaning against the walls. It took me a moment to adapt to a place where for once the ground's deep, soft covering was not black lava but a huge build-up of golden sawdust. It coated everything, the floor, the walls, the cobwebs, and the hair, skin and clothes of people working there.

Alfio Patanè, the mill's current owner, was one of many people I met on Etna with a trade that had been in his family for generations. And like so many others in their fifties, he could remember how things were done in the old days, before mechanization made it all so much easier. However, nothing could change the high winds and heavy snows high on Etna's slopes, where he and his team were often obliged to abandon their winter work of felling trees and chestnut poles. Nevertheless, ever since the 1960s, the chainsaws used for felling, the forklifts for moving timber, and the motorized planes and saws for processing it have put an end to all the heaviest labour.

There were two men working with Alfio in veiled, golden light that day, men with huge forearms and steady hands. They were feeding a length of timber through a bandsaw, slowly, seriously, and with utter concentration. Until thirty years ago, four people would have been needed to saw up the same length of wood, arduously tugging away in turn with a huge saw. Now one of the men simply processed slowly forwards, guiding the timber to a blade that cut through it like butter. Meanwhile, the other man backed slowly away as he received it, so that it looked as if both were engaged in a graceful, slow-motion dance. Things were certainly easier now, but like so many people I had met on the mountain, Alfio had huge respect for the wisdom of his ancestors, and for the heavy, hands-on practices he learned from them as a young man. He believed his training in the old traditions of the wood trade had given him an understanding of timber that people often lack today. 'It's the wood that tells you what to do with it,' he said, 'and if you don't know it, you won't understand what it is telling you.'

Versed in the language of trees, Alfio was one of several people I met whose work still seemed to knit the present to the long traditions of the past. Meanwhile, Lavinia Lo Faro, director of the Ecomuseo in Fornazzo, made sure that the village never forgot its original identity as the crown jewel of Etna's timber trade.

On the hottest days of summer, when towns on Etna's slopes blazed like ovens, and even the beaches were too hot, I sometimes took refuge in the shade of Ragabo, the Calabrian pine forest that is part of the Boscosa on Etna's north face. Sunlight was tempered by flickering shadows among the trees, the warm air full of green scents and resinous smells, and birds, struck dumb by the heat at lower altitudes, were busily vocal. It was the epitome of peace, and yet, if any more proof were needed of how hard trees in the Boscosa used to work, this was the place to find it.

Ragabo has belonged to the town of Linguaglossa since 1634, and this link is incised in the landscape in the form of a shockingly steep track called the *trainara*. It was used for hundreds of years to haul (for that is what the verb *trainare* means) enormous pine trunks straight from the forest to huge woodyards in the town. The timber naturally followed the easiest slopes downhill, taking the same route century after century, so that the *trainara*'s impression appears to be worn almost subcutaneously into the land. In places, you can still find the marks of cartwheels cut deep into the rock. The oxen must have done as much restraining as they did hauling, or those vast tree trunks would have careered off under their own steam, bouncing between the drystone walls built for just this eventuality to either side of their route. A safe haul to the woodyard would see valuable pine trunks graded, sorted, and sent off again to be sold in bigger towns like Acireale, or in the shipyards of Catania and Messina.

The august pines in Ragabo, with their towering trunks and

classical ancestry, are covered in bark that seems to veer from flush-pink to grey, depending on the light. Many of them have been inscribed with long, narrow, slightly pointed marks that look like the beautiful symbol of some arcane cult, but are really the signature left by resin collectors. They came to Ragabo in the Middle Ages from Lombardy and Liguria, places in northern Italy that already knew the value of pine resin. According to Antonio Filotei degli Omodei, a local man whose book about Etna and her eruptions was published posthumously in 1591, they were the first to introduce the idea of using resin from pines to make pitch. The northern Italian dialect, or *lingua*, they still spoke sounded coarse, or *grossa*, to local people on Etna, and this is why the town they eventually founded was known as 'Linguagrossa'. This eventually evolved into Linguaglossa, a name just as tautological as Etna's Mongibello, the 'mountain mountain', for both *lingua* in Latin and *glossa* in Greek mean the same thing – 'language'.

Omodei says those *resinatori* sought out the oldest pines to tap, the ones that had become fat on their own viscous juices. Their resin would have flowed so freely it oozed, perfumed, golden and unbidden, out of knots and broken limbs, and some people even used their roots and branches as torches, easily lit and 'feeding off their own fat'. Consequently, pines were still known in dialect as *ddeda* on Etna until the nineteenth century, a word derived from *taeda*, Latin for 'torch'. There were many more uses for the resin than that though, and the *resinatori* started to milk the trees each year as soon as the last snow thawed in June. They began by stripping back the bark at about waist height to reveal a lozenge of tender sapwood. Each week they carved two V-shaped incisions that would bleed resin, so that by the end of the season each lozenge-shaped mark looked like the delicate spine and bones of a fish. Despite the abundance of resin, the trees bled slowly, and the *resinatori* only expected to empty the tins you still find nailed to their trunks about once a month. The season ended in October, and by then they could hope to have harvested a couple of kilos of resin from each trunk. This took its toll on those hard-working trees, disrupting the flow of sap that carried nutrients and water from their roots to the tips of their branches, and shortening their lives so much that they had generally been felled for timber by the time they were sixty years old.

As well as being processed to make pitch, resin was used over the centuries for treating wounds in animals and repelling stinging insects. It was also an ingredient in turpentine, varnishes, paints and thinners, and this made it so important to life on the mountain that the unbroken tradition of milking Ragabo's pines continued until the invention of plastics and synthetic resins finally put the tree tappers out of business in the 1960s.

Altitude determines the species that grow in the Boscosa, so that one kind of forest gives way to another as you climb. Above the pines come swathes of enormous beech trees with smooth trunks that look ice blue in certain lights. You would not expect to find beech growing at such a low latitude, but like the silver-birch trees that also grow on the volcano, beeches were driven south from northern Europe by plummeting temperatures during the last Ice Age. They took refuge at high altitude on Etna and remained after the ice retreated. The trees growing there today are relics of much bigger forests that thrived in the colder, wetter weather after the Ice Age. On the north and north-east flanks of the mountain they grow like shrubs with horizontal branches right up to an altitude of 2,300 metres, the highest ever recorded for their species. Like every other kind of wood in the Boscosa, beech had multiple uses. In his *Trattato dei Boschi dell'Etna* of 1828, Salvatore Scuderi says it was sometimes painted and varnished to look like walnut, and then used to make floorboards, tables and trays. He lists shovels, pack saddles, yokes for oxen, cannon wagons, slippers and oars among its other uses, a list that serves to reveal something of the lives being lived on Etna in the nineteenth century, and to reiterate yet again the idea of timber being essential in ways we can scarcely imagine today.

Silver birch, that other migrant, still grows on Etna's east flank, and like beech it scrambles right up to the tree line. Adapting to conditions on the volcano has compelled it to develop so many unique characteristics that it has become a variety in its own right – *Betula aetnensis*. One of its most striking characteristics is its pure white trunk, and scientists at the University of Catania think this helps it reflect the unwelcome heat of the sun. In the past, people used its roots for making pipes, tobacco boxes, cups and spoons.

Those high-altitude beech and birch forests have never been a place to live, although if you are lucky you might find one of the *pagghiari*, or huts, that have been preserved in memory of a time when the Boscosa was still enfolded into everyday life on Etna. Those little buildings have been made to the same design ever since the Sicani, the volcano's earliest inhabitants, settled on her slopes during the Bronze Age. Their circular walls have always been made of lava, and their roofs thatched with branches cut from broom that grows to the size of a tree on Etna. They are the places where shepherds bringing their flocks up to graze on high ground took shelter, and the charcoal burners who knew the fuel value of every kind of timber decamped with their wives, children and often a few hens every summer. As late as 1955, when the journalist, doctor and political activist Carlo Levi spent a few days on Etna, he saw *pagghiari*, 'Or rather, the little cone-shaped structures made of straw – with small, low doors in which the peasants of the mountains live, all higgledy-piggledy.'

At lower altitudes the Boscosa is still inscribed with the marks of hundreds of years of human use and habitation, relics of a time when what it had to give was essential to every aspect of life. Walking in the middle of nowhere, I often glimpsed the overblown flowers of a cultivated rose climbing high into a tree, a blazing declaration that this isolated spot was once dear to someone. There was usually a ruined cottage nearby, the remains of a circular sheep pen perhaps, or a *neviera*, the narrow steps cut into its side leading to nothing but a chaos of brambles on the forest floor.

The people who lived among the trees, or commuted to the Boscosa for seasonal work, were its guardians. They kept the ground clear of the leaf litter and fallen branches that act like tinder for forest fires. Now there are so many wildfires that you get used to seeing fire-service planes buzzing overhead like bees, their pollen sacs bulging with water. You also get used to the shocking rumours about arson. Sicily's firefighters only get paid when they are called out, so it's no wonder people suspect, or even know, that some can only make ends meet by starting fires themselves, and then rushing off to fight them. This desperate situation has triggered research about a return to sustainable practices in the Boscosa. For example, Lavinia Lo Faro has brought academics and silviculture experts from all over the country to Fornazzo to discuss how Etna's chestnut forests can be better managed and protected. One of the ideas that emerged was that of grafting a nut-bearing variety of chestnut onto the rootstock of the existing trees. This would be an incredibly labour-intensive project, but cultivating trees for their nuts would bring people back to work in the Boscosa throughout the year, safeguarding it and simultaneously making it more sustainable. In the meantime, the only people working there are timber merchants like Alfio Patanè, beekeepers who put their hives among the chestnut trees when they are in flower, and shepherds who drive their flocks up through the forest to summer pasture, grazing as they go.

Those beekeepers and shepherds were my neighbours in Milo and Zafferana Etnea, and they would turn out to be key to helping me to understand the Boscosa's ongoing role in the lives of Etna's twenty-first-century inhabitants.

II.

Shepherds and Cheesemakers

Shepherds have been driving their nibbling flocks through the Boscosa ever since the ancient Greeks first settled on Etna, and making cheese ever since the cyclops Polyphemus milked his sheep and made a creamery of that vast cave overlooking the sea. To this day, his life rings true in a place where grocers' shops are still stacked high with huge wheels of *pecorino* made from local sheep's milk, oozing baskets of fresh ricotta, pear-shaped *provola*, and enormous *provoloni* tethered with string like fat puppies. Nothing could be simpler than asking for *pane imbottita* in one of those places, a golden sourdough roll *imbottita* – stuffed – with slices of cheese and tomato, dressed with olive oil and a sprinkling of the oregano that grows wild on Etna's slopes. The only complication comes with choosing the kind of cheese you want. Will it be *pecorino stagionato*, tawny, seasoned *pecorino*, studded with peppercorns, or *pecorino fresco*, milk pale, mild and fresh, or something in between? It is so good to be spoilt for choice.

Walking through the Boscosa in summer, I sometimes heard the distant sound of sheep bells and barking dogs, or met with the trademark stink of goats hovering above a hot path. This could only mean one thing, and before long I would be crossing paths with one of the shepherds who still wander the mountain with their flocks. Their dogs were true professionals. Fierce to the core, mangy, flea-bitten, fly-ridden, they wore their filthy working clothes full time, for there's nothing so time-wasting as washing a goat dog. Nevertheless, when they drove long-eared, long-haired Pinzirita sheep along invisible paths across a lava flow, that procession of animals looked like a beautiful string of pale beads.

Nomadic shepherding has been part of life on Etna for thousands of years, and Pinzirita, the indigenous breed of sheep, is one of the oldest in the world. Until the 1970s, shepherds with no land to call their own were an essential part of the volcano's agricultural community. They would overwinter their flocks on the same farms in the Coltivata each year, where they were welcome to graze their animals among vines and fruit trees in return for supplying the household with ricotta, *pecorino* or goat's cheese. They left again long before the vineyards and orchards put on their tender spring growth, and began their annual transhumance up through the Coltivata and Boscosa to high-altitude summer pastures. I know someone on Etna in her forties who grew up on a farm where these ancient understandings were still ingrained in the cycle of the seasons. However, by the time she was born, many other farms on the volcano would already have been abandoned by families who had emigrated, or moved to the city. And today, even working farms like hers no longer embrace the same extended communities they once did.

With no grazing to call their own, nomadic shepherds have often been driven to live on the edge of a society that has made vagrants of them and their flocks. Now they take their animals wherever they can to graze, and there is constant, low-level conflict between them and winemakers, farmers and other landowners. They refer to them as *abusivi*, 'illegals', and blame them for turning a blind eye when their animals wander onto private land, doing unforgivable damage to other people's vines and crops. Some are suspected of poisoning the farm dogs that would otherwise see them off, and some of laying claim to common land with ramshackle fencing. They are also accused of ignoring rules about vaccinating their flocks for brucellosis and TB, and insisting on making ricotta in the age-old way by heating the milk in a copper pan over an open fire. I will never be in a position to comment on any of these local tensions. All I know is that Etna's last wandering shepherds are some of the few remaining pastoralists in Europe. I also know that there will always be people

Shepherds and Cheesemakers

happy to take the risk of eating the delicious ricotta made by *pecorai abusivi*, because I am one of them.

There is a second kind of *pecoraio* on Etna, one who gets their sheep vaccinated but still prefers to look after them in a traditional way, milking them by hand and driving them up to high-altitude pastures in summer. When I say pastures, don't imagine lush, Alpine grazing. The fodder Etna offers is for animals happy with a mixed diet of grass, wild herbs and leaves pilfered from the low-growing branches of trees and shrubs. Again and again friends and neighbours in Milo told me to contact Zio Pino, old uncle Pino, if I wanted to meet a shepherd straddling old and new traditions in this way. I already bought his rich sheep's milk ricotta from the village shop each week, but nobody seemed to have a clue about where to find him at any given time. People knew I was looking for him though, so when he rolled into the village in his old Fiat Panda one afternoon, Silvia from the *pasticceria* rang to let me know. 'He's just delivered our ricotta,' she said, 'but he can't stay. How soon can you get here?' I pelted down to the piazza like someone responding to an emergency call, and there was Pino, waiting peacefully for me in a car that looked as if its working life had been almost as long and demanding as his own. He was seventy-eight, he told me, his weathered face appearing above a dashing pink T-shirt in the car window, and he had been a shepherd and cheesemaker ever since he was nine years old.

After a lifetime in the job, Pino was beset by demands from people everywhere, not to mention the sheep, but he seemed happy for me to visit him at milking time, or while he was making ricotta; it was up to me. He interrupted our conversation regularly to say, 'I think you understand me already,' although in truth I understood only about 40 per cent of what he said, for despite his best efforts he kept slipping back into dialect. Somehow we made a date, a milking date, for 5.30 that very afternoon. It all seemed so easy, and I got to our meeting place by the side of the Mareneve road above Fornazzo a little early. Five thirty came and went, but I stayed on, secure in the knowledge that sheep must be milked. At about 5.45 I tried to ring him, only to realize I was in one of many places on the mountain without a signal. I gave up after an hour or so, convinced I had stupidly misunderstood our arrangement, but my phone rang as soon as I got home, and it was Pino, of course. He had run out of petrol, and now he suggested we try again for eleven o'clock milking the next morning. And there I was, patient and trusting on the side of the road while, I learned as soon as I got home, he was at his grandson's first communion, having forgotten all about our arrangement.

The following day, Silvia rang from the *pasticceria* to say that Pino's son had dropped off some ricotta for me by way of an apology. The invitation was still open, but my luck had already changed by then because I had met Alfio, who had invited me to join him while he milked his sheep in a *dagala*, one of those spits of trees surrounded by lava in the Boscosa. Sheepdogs lay panting in the shade on the scorching day I chose to visit him, their eyes and noses buzzing with flies that swarmed between them and old, gnawed bones they had abandoned among the trees. The chestnuts were in flower, filling the still air with their suggestive perfume, and with the bees come to milk them of their nectar. The ewes and their grown lambs were in two rough pens on an area of levelled ground. Like cows waiting to be let into the dairy, the sheep seemed glad to be brought into the pen where Alfio had set up his three-legged stool. His wife, Angelina, drove them gently towards a small gap in the fence just beyond the shelter. Alfio stood next to it, letting lambs and dry sheep through until he saw a ewe in milk. Then he closed the gap, grabbed her from behind and settled on his milking stool. Soon the clatter of sheep's bells and arbitrary bleating was set against the rhythmic sound of milk spurting into the bucket he gripped between his legs. Every so often a lamb, hefty and half grown, butted its way under a ewe as she was being milked, claiming whichever teat was not in use as its own. They were orphaned, Alfio told me, when he sent their mothers to the slaughterhouse, and because of that he tolerated their outrageous assaults again and again.

Soon after visiting Alfio, I went to see another, thoroughly modern kind of shepherd on Etna, the kind who observes all the health-and-safety regulations, keeps flocks on permanent pasture, uses milking machines, and makes cheese in the pristine surroundings of a modern creamery or *caseificio*. Ignazio Coco is one of these, and like so many others on Etna, his skills are rooted deep in childhood. I wonder if working so hard at one trade from a very early age would shape your body to meet its specific demands. If so, cheesemakers like him must build muscle peculiar to lifting the dead weight of curds and stirring vast quantities of milk. And in Ignazio's case, perhaps cheesemaking explains the expression of infinite patience in his pale green eyes – as if some skills might mould your character as well as your body. Just like Alfio Patanè in his sawmill, Ignazio inherited a trade that had been in his family for generations. He learned to make cheese from his grandfather over forty years ago, and they worked *all'antica*, in the old-fashioned way, heating the milk in copper pans over an open fire, and driving their animals up from the family farm outside Lentini on the Catania Plain, to graze high above Fornazzo each summer. However, just over twenty years ago Ignazio moved the creamery and shop up from Lentini to Via del Gattopardo in Zafferana, and now, instead of being driven up the mountain each summer, the sheep, goats and cows stay put on permanent pastures all year. This means that Ignazio must jump out of bed in Zafferana Etnea at four o'clock each morning, or to be more precise, because precision matters when the hours are so small, at 3.50, to make the winding, 500-metre descent of almost 60 kilometres to Lentini and the farm. After doing the milking, he and his brother see the milk tankers filled and send them off up the mountain to Zafferana. Soon after that, Ignazio will get to work in the gleaming room they call the *laboratorio*. It looks a little like an operating theatre in there, with its tiled floor, walls and ceiling, its stainless-steel surfaces, thermometers and gauges.

'Ricotta is for winter,' Ignazio said firmly when I dropped in to the *caseificio* one summer morning. 'It's what you feel like eating on a rainy Sunday.' So why on earth was he making it on a day already skewed by late-July heat? Because he knew, I suppose, there would always be someone who wanted to eat fresh ricotta sweetened with honey for breakfast, and someone who fancied a snack made from ricotta with olive oil and a squirt of lemon juice, whatever the time of year. And of course, there is a perpetual market for ricotta to stir through hot pasta with spinach, blob onto pizzas, or mix with eggs and parmesan as a filling for all kinds of creamy, savoury tarts. When thoroughly drained of whey, ricotta can also be sieved to make a dense cream. Sweetened with sugar, chocolate or candied fruit, this becomes the filling for numerous pastries, or the basis for *cassata*, made from a voluptuous mix of that creamed and sweetened ricotta with green pistachio paste, layers of liqueur-soaked sponge and crystallized fruit.

Ignazio makes ricotta as it has been made on Etna for thousands of years, by stirring fresh milk into the greenish, watery whey left over from starting to make *pecorino*. Soon the room was echoing with the cappuccino-making clamour of steam issuing at high pressure from pipes in the walls of the stainless-steel vat. In the old days down on the farm, Ignazio's grandfather might have stirred salt into the warm milk and broken up the curds as they formed with a twiggy stick. These days Ignazio uses its modern equivalent – a wooden baton fitted with teeth like a gigantic, two-sided comb. Wearing the cheesemaker's pale uniform of white trousers, gumboots, T-shirt and hat, with sunlight turning the steam around him to gold, he could have been a milk magician casting a spell. What happened next reminded me of being in a photographer's darkroom, watching an image float to the surface of a blank sheet of paper immersed in chemicals, as if something had been made from nothing. Ignazio's blank paper was milk, and there really was something magical about the sudden appearance of a soft, white layer of ricotta floating to its surface. He scraped the foam off it, putting it aside as a treat for the sheep back on the farm. Then he picked up his stirrer again and cut the sign of the cross into its surface. I've seen this done by shepherds making cheese in Tuscany, too. 'We do it to thank God for the chance to make this good food,' Ignazio told me, 'and for helping the ricotta to turn out alright yet again.' Then he gave me a spoonful of ricotta that had just floated to the surface of the whey, so fresh that it had not yet firmed up.

When spooned warm from the vat, ricotta is known in Sicily as *zabbina*. It is a rare privilege to eat *zabbina* warm from the pot these days, but when the modernist writer Elio Vittorini wrote *La città del mondo* in the 1950s it would still have been a familiar experience. Nomadic shepherds in the novel make ricotta over a fire beside the sheep pen, and for them the taste of *zabbina* seems to encapsulate all that is fresh, good and natural in the world. Sloppy, warm and smelling intimately of sheep, I found it evocative only of dark, enclosed spaces and the fug of the lambing shed.

Ignazio and his cousin Salvo spooned dripping, wobbling curds into the plastic baskets that would be both sieves and moulds as the ricotta drained and solidified. If you have ever bought fresh ricotta in Italy, you will know the lines and stripes that always pattern its sloping sides. Originally these were made by indentations left by baskets woven on Etna from broom twigs, but now plastic baskets are designed to create the same effect, 'for anyone who remembers what ricotta used to look like'.

Ignazio and Salvo worked with a delicate touch, taking care not to break the soft curds as they moved them into the baskets. When they were all full, Ignazio's sister, Alfina, wheeled them away to drain on a sloping surface in the cool room. Pausing for breath, Ignazio told me that even after four decades, making ricotta is different every time, every day. The qualities of the milk change throughout the year, with each season bringing its own peculiarities. Its fat content alters according to the animals' diet, and the speed at which the ricotta can be made is also affected by the time of year. The soaring temperature on that day ensured that everything happened very fast.

Each region in Sicily makes its own particular version of ricotta. In Messina and Palermo, for example, they make it with a slightly more solid texture, while on Etna and in Catania it is always meltingly soft. Over time, people have also invented many ingenious methods for preserving it. Alfina always baked part of each batch until its base and edges were slightly blackened and its interior gloriously golden and bouncy. This is *ricotta al forno*, and it comes out of the oven looking like an inflated, golden cushion, almost too big to manage. Chop it into squares though, and enjoy its mild, smoky flavour with an *aperitivo*, or eat it in slices with a summer salad and it soon disappears. It will keep for a few days longer than the fresh cheese, but the very best way of preserving ricotta is to salt it and leave it to age for at least three months. The result is *ricotta salata*, a semi-hard cheese with a pungent, farmyard flavour that is the making of many summer pasta dishes on Etna. Catania's *Pasta alla Norma* is one of them, a sumptuous mix of tomatoes and fried aubergines named in honour of the opera by local boy Vincenzo Bellini. My next-door neighbour always promised to make it for me, proposing to devote the whole of Sunday to the task. Sundays came and went without an invitation, but as I couldn't live through a Sicilian summer without eating it, I often made *Pasta alla Norma* myself. Perhaps the scent of fried aubergine relieved him of his obligation by drifting over the fence. My first step before embarking on any traditional recipe was always to ask advice from those formal ladies at the village shop. That's where I learned to reproduce the depth of genuine *Pasta alla Norma*'s flavour, which comes from tossing *ricotta salata* into the tomato and aubergine sauce before mixing it with the pasta. That and the quintessentially rich flavours of tomatoes and aubergines from the sun-baked soils of the Coltivata.

Sheep and goats have always been more common than cows on Sicily's parched ground, but in this, as in so many other ways, Etna has been an exception. Her rich soils and relatively high rainfall make cattle farming viable, and in the eighteenth century Sir William Hamilton said the volcano was renowned for 'the finest horned cattle in Sicily'. They were no bigger than ordinary cows, he said, but their horns were 'nearly twice the size' of any cows he had ever seen. Ignazio's own cows produced the milk he used to make *mozzarella* and *provola*. Like *caciocavallo*, *scamorza* and *provolone*, these were both *pasta filata* cheeses, made from curds that have been cooked and stretched. For these cheeses the milk's freshness is especially important, and as Ignazio was able to start making his *mozzarella* within only a few hours of milking, its flavour was guaranteed to be excellent.

We all pitched in, Ignazio, Salvo, Alfina and her daughter, to shred the curds that lay like pale lungs on the steel counter. Then Ignazio poured boiling water over them and began stirring, lifting and stretching them with a stick until thin, threadlike strands, as glossy and white as elastic, began to form. Mozzarella's name comes from the verb *mozzare*, 'to cut off', and he plunged his hand into the scalding water, selected a thread and cut it free from the rest of the curds by squeezing it between his index finger and the base of his thumb. Each ball of *mozzarella* emerged from this stricture as bulbous and shiny as a balloon in the process of being modelled. He added no salt to the curds themselves, but dropped each new-minted *mozzarella* into a bucket of brine to soak up some seasoning.

Mozzarella is not one of Etna's traditional cheeses, and Ignazio had spent years learning how to make it. However, he insisted his *fior di latte* (the name for *mozzarella* made from cow as opposed to buffalo milk) would never be as good as that produced in its places of origin, Puglia and Campania. He gave me some to take home anyway, telling me to leave it soaking in the brine for twenty-four hours or so before eating it. After slicing it with tomatoes and sprinkling it with oil, oregano and fresh basil to make an *insalata caprese*, I found myself struggling to agree with this harsh judgement.

When it came to making *provola*, it was suddenly my turn to shape a slice of smooth pasta into the classic *provola* pear shape. I tried to follow Ignazio's example of turning the pasta constantly in one hand, while simultaneously squeezing a neck for it and folding the top in on itself with the other. Mine emerged like a toddler's attempt at pottery, but examining it as if he were the tutor at an abstract sculpture class, Ignazio tried to encourage me by saying, 'It's only your first attempt, and yet the concept is already there.'

Salvo and Ignazio had already produced *tuma* that day. It is the first stage in the long process of producing *pecorino*, hard cheese made from the milk of ewes (*pecore*) and rennet. *Tuma* is at the melting heart of *arancini*, and it is layered into warm slices of *scacciata*, the quintessential street food for winter all over Sicily. Each part of the island has its own recipe for *scacciata*, and on Etna it is nearly always made from *tuma* with some combination of highly seasoned winter vegetables like cauliflower, spinach or broccoli, all crushed between very thin slices of pizza dough that turn golden when baked in a wood-fired oven. *Tuma* is also the essential ingredient of a *pizza siciliana* – made from pizza dough wrapped around a stark combination of *tuma* with salted anchovies, and then deep fried until it is crisp, golden and surprisingly light and tasty.

After a little salting, *tuma* changes its name to *primosale*, and sharpens its flavour to become a filling fit for any panino. Salted again and aged until its rind hardens and darkens, it evolves into *pecorino* shot through with crushed peppercorns that Ignazio's sister, Alfina, sells fresh, semi-mature and mature in their shop overlooking Via del Gattopardo in Zafferana Etnea. Ignazio also makes a special *pecorino ubriaco* in winter, 'drunk' *pecorino*, its rind red from an eighteen-month soak in Etna rosso wine. In summer Alfina adds an especially delicious, fresh *pecorino* to the cheese counter, with bright green strands of Etna's wild fennel running through it.

The shop at the front of the creamery felt a long way from those old-fashioned shepherds trailing through the Boscosa like outlaws. Nevertheless, all three kinds of shepherd at work on Etna sprang from the same ancient tradition, and each served their own markets and observed the law to their own degree. Thinking about them now, they strike me as a perfect example of the layering of past and present practices common to so many of the trades on Etna, as if nothing in that landscape could ever be truly forgotten.

12.

City of Honey

In a country with a beekeeping tradition reaching back to the Iron Age, it is brave of Zafferana to call itself *Città del Miele*, but that is what's emblazoned on its road signs. And with good reason. There are honey shops on the main street; a honey 'boutique'; honey sold from vans, doorsteps, garages and roadside stalls; honey-tasting outlets and a beekeeping supplies store. Of just over 9,000 people living in this unusual place, 700 are beekeepers, and they produce 25 per cent of Italy's total honey output, all of it processed in sticky local workshops. What makes these facts extraordinary is that Zafferana's history as a honey town goes back only to 1954, when Michele and Maria Di Prima set up as the first professional beekeepers and honey producers in town.

Michele was already ninety-four years old when we met on a hot day in high summer, and his face told me that beekeeping had given him plenty to laugh about. The business he founded with his wife is called Dolce Parco. These days it's run by their son Alfio, assisted by Marica, his daughter. However, Di Prima honey is still spun, bottled and sold from Michele and Maria's house on a sharp corner between Zafferana and Milo.

Michele and Maria remember a time just after the Second World War when most of Zafferana's men still worked as shepherds or winemakers. There was only one serious beekeeper in town, and that was Maria's father, Alfio Lizzio. Maria told me he began to keep bees almost by chance, after coming across a swarm in the vineyard where he was working. The hive he used for them was made from the strong, feather-light stems of fennel's gigantic relation, *Ferula communis*, which grows wild all over Etna. Every Sicilian beekeeper

I've ever met seems to have one or two of these old-fashioned *villici*, as they are called, still tucked away on a high shelf. They are oblong boxes made by boring holes into the ends of lengths of *ferula* stem and pushing olive twigs through to bind them together. One end of the box has an entrance in it for the bees, and the other can be removed to harvest their honey. The whole thing used to be sealed with a skim of cow dung. Light as air and regular as bricks, *villici* could be strapped to either side of a mule when bees needed moving to fresh territory, or neatly stacked under a shelter to keep them warm and dry in bad weather.

After a few years of keeping bees in this old-fashioned way, Alfio happened on an article about the box hives we use today. Inspired by this modern vision of beekeeping, he commissioned a local carpenter to make two wooden hives, and then tracked down two more swarms of wild bees to live in them. When they lived in *villici*, his bees had been expected to construct their own honeycombs, but now Lizzio inserted removable frames of ready-made wax combs into the upper layers of the new hives, which made the honey very much easier to harvest.

Although highly skilled, Lizzio was always an amateur beekeeper, and the history of Zafferana as *Città del Miele* didn't really begin until Maria and Michele got engaged. Maria must have told the story of their engagement hundreds of times, and yet she seemed to relish the retelling, which was a vivid reminder of how much life has changed since the 1950s for young women living in rural parts of Italy, and on Mount Etna in particular.

Michele and Maria both grew up in the country outside Zafferana. Although their fathers were friends, Sicilian girls still lived such secluded lives in the 1950s that they had never met. Or almost never. 'He had met me,' Maria said, 'but I hadn't met him.' Now Michele chipped in to explain that his mother had taken him to visit Maria when he was eight years old and she was a new-born baby.

'But I never saw him again,' she said, 'because my parents didn't let me go out unless we were going to Mass together. I had to stay indoors, and I didn't have any friends apart from my sister.'

'Until I stole her!' Michele interrupted, eyes gleaming.

'One day,' Maria continued, 'Pappa said "there is a young man coming round this evening who wants to marry you. Sit down with us if you like the look of him, otherwise you can just leave the room and I will know what you mean." Well, he was *bello*, so I sat down, and here I am sixty-eight years later, still sitting next to him.'

They married in 1955. By then Lizzio had passed on his hives to Michele and Maria, who were now working side by side in their own business. Michele still had much to learn in those early days. He subscribed to a monthly magazine that put him in touch with the latest developments in beekeeping, and connected him to the national beekeeping community. For him, the lessons were never over.

'I've always compared beekeeping to learning music,' he told me. 'Once you start studying, you have to carry on for the rest of your life, because there is always something new to learn. You can't change Nature, but you can always make little improvements.'

At first, they kept *Api nere siculi*. I've asked a few people about these native black bees and words that recur in relation to them are 'furious', 'stinging', 'agitated' and 'wild'. Despite over 2,000 years of domestication, it's said they dislike hives, always preferring to escape back into the wild. It wasn't until the mid-sixties that Maria and Michele invested in their first *Apis mellifera* (European honeybee) queen, a blond bee renowned for being very productive and much more docile than the Sicilian bees they had always worked with. By then, Michele and Maria knew exactly how to produce honey – or provide optimum conditions for bees to do their job – but they struggled to find a market for it on the island. Like so many of the conundrums here, this one had ancient origins. Sicilian beekeepers had once had a monopoly over sweetness, and Sortino, Forla and Pantallica near Siracusa had been centres for honey production ever since the Greeks settled there. However, their status soon changed when Arab farmers arrived on the island and began to cultivate sugar cane for the first time. Between the ninth and eleventh centuries, when Sicily was part of the Caliphate, cane sugar became so fashionable that the rich gave up eating honey altogether. Bad news for beekeepers was perpetual, and by 1839, Sicily was spending twenty-five times more money on sugar than coal. The next disaster came with the introduction of sugar beet to Sicily in the 1950s, because now the island could produce its own sugar again, which made it even cheaper. All in all, this should have been a terrible moment for Michele and Maria to make honey their business, and yet Michele was clever enough to forge a contract with a dealer who could export their honey to the mainland and abroad, and with this reliable outlet the Di Prima business thrived.

Meanwhile, Michele and Maria were bringing up Alfio and Sebastiano, their two sons, to be beekeepers. When I met Alfio Di Prima for the first time, he told me he had been working in his parents' business ever since he was six:

> We thought of nothing but *la famiglia* in those days – and by that I mean the real family, not the Mafia. We didn't just go to school as children do today. We worked during the school holidays and we worked on Sundays, as children always had on Sicilian farms. The jobs were important, and we had a real obligation to come home from school and get to work.

So, Alfio learned beekeeping from a very young age, just as his mother had done, and just as his daughter Marica did. However, he made a point of saying that Sicilian children don't grow up in the same way anymore, and although Marica works alongside him now, 'she went out to play as a child, and we didn't expect her to work at all'.

As the family business became more and more successful, another narrative began to unfold in Zafferana Etnea. Keeping sheep and making cheese was still one of the main occupations for people living there, but shepherds' lives had always been hard. As Michele put it, 'It's a terrible job. You have to wake up before dawn to milk the sheep. There's no Sunday, no *festa*, no rest, no shifts, because sheep need looking after every day.'

The shepherds spent winters down on the Catania plain, where there was enough grass for their sheep all year. 'They had no transport other than a horse or mule,' Michele told me, 'so they had to stay down on the plain for months at a time without coming home. And at night they just slept on top of a sheepskin on the ground.'

It's hardly surprising that shepherds began to see beekeeping as an easy alternative. Or as Michele put it, 'They thought they could just stay at home and leave the bees to get on with it.'

How wrong they were. Beekeeping is as hard as any other form of farming. Alfio Di Prima spelt this out for me when I met him first. Like most Sicilian beekeepers, he moved his hives around so that the bees would gather nectar from a single species of flower or blossom at a time. Managed in this way, they produce mono-floral honeys with distinctive colours, flavours and scents. Some people root this style of beekeeping in the ninth century, when Arab farmers started to grow citrus trees on Sicilian soil for the first time. And as soon as Sicilian bees discovered that pungent *zagara*, as citrus blossom was known to the Arabs, they made it their chief source of nectar.

Zafferana beekeepers have always been obliged to practise transhumance, for it is only in May, when the sweet chestnuts in the Boscosa are in flower, that bees can gather nectar close to home. During the rest of the summer beekeepers must take their bees all over the island to find flowering plants and trees at their peak. They must also seek out suitable spots for the hives. Sheltered, hidden from roads and footpaths, away from the cattle or other large animals, the hives must also be in sight of the landowner, who can generally be trusted to keep an eye on them in return for a steady supply of honey. When I met Alfio for the first time, he was just back from a 450-kilometre round trip to harvest honey from hives he was keeping on a friend's farm near Trapani. He had left home at dusk the previous day and worked through the night, while the bees were at their quietest. When he got back early that morning, the truck was full of honeycomb. A few dazed bees had inadvertently hitched a lift; sleepy and disconsolate, they blundered around the windows of the honey shop, hundreds of kilometres from the queen that was their focus for existence.

One conversation with Alfio made it clear to me that beekeeping is no soft option, and yet hundreds of people in Zafferana began to turn to it in the late 1950s and early 1960s as an alternative to more traditional work. Some were former shepherds, and others were people who didn't want to go back to the hardship of old jobs after a stint working abroad. 'People who didn't even know what a bee was were buying bees,' Michele said. And because they knew nothing, they made all kinds of mistakes. Some let their bees die of cold, and some produced such poor honey that Michele compared it to molasses. He was humble about his role in those early days of beekeeping in Zafferana, but he did admit to advising a few people, and to having become what he described as a sort of *carabiniere* for bees', policing both their welfare and the quality of the honey on sale in town. He also set up an association for local beekeepers and served as its president for many years. I noticed that if ever his name cropped up in conversation with younger beekeepers, they spoke of him with the utmost respect.

When it came to producing honey, Michele was very clear. 'There are two kinds of beekeepers,' he said, 'the ones who put their paws into the honey and the ones who don't. The secret of good honey is to do nothing to it. It has no need of anything.'

Although he despised flavoured honeys himself, he conceded that the problem stemmed from customers, who often expected honey made from the nectar of fruit-tree blossom to taste of the fruit itself. The opportunity this offers is just too tempting for some producers. 'And if honey tastes of fruit,' Michele said, 'you can be sure they have added flavouring to it.'

All the Dolce Parco honey is extracted and bottled in a room on the ground floor of Michele and Maria's house. It was Marica who took me there, dreadlocks tied up in a bun, and one of those regulation, food-production white caps on her head. Initially the workshop was spotless, but then Alfio delivered a pile of honeycomb, and things began to get very, very sticky. At first glance, the comb in its wooden frame seemed to contain nothing but an opaque sheet of white wax.

'This is the operculum,' Marica explained, holding the frame under my nose. 'It's the wax the bees use to close each cell in the comb as they fill it with honey.'

I had already backed away before I noticed that nothing was dripping from the frame she held horizontally between her hands. 'Don't worry' she said, 'the operculum seals the honey inside the comb. In fact, it's so strong that if I put this comb into the centrifuge we use for extraction, the wooden frame would simply break without releasing the honey.'

Balancing one end of the frame on the table, she started to run the edge of a flat blade under the wax to reveal the glistening honey beneath. She had honey on her fingers now, honey on her wrists, and the air was steeped in the scent of it. She handed me a large flake of operculum on the blade of her knife. 'Take it! Taste it! All of it!' she said, with an intensity I had grown used to among food producers on Etna. She watched carefully as I enjoyed its honey covering, and then set about chewing a hard ball of wax that remained in my mouth until I plucked up the courage to swallow it.

'We collect the wax that rises off the honey as it settles, cut it into slices like a tart and sell it to people with digestive problems,' she told me.

Apparently, taking a spoonful of *opercolo* with your breakfast each day can resolve all kinds of intestinal troubles. 'There's nothing bees make that isn't good for us,' Marica said.

The Di Prima family were the last beekeepers in Zafferana to *disopercolare* their honey by hand, but last year they bought the machine that Marica showed me now. It was basic. It simply fed the frame containing the honeycomb between two vertical blades. The blades did only a rough job of removing the wax, so the process often had to be completed by hand.

You might think the honey would pour from the comb as soon as it was free of wax, but again, not a drop escaped, despite Marica shaking the frame as hard as she could. Why? Because the honey had been left to ripen in the hive, a process that allows the water to evaporate naturally, encouraged, extraordinary as this may sound, by bees fanning it with their wings at night to speed the process.

'If we harvested the honey before it was ripe it would ferment after a few months, but ripe honey is eternal,' Marica said. 'They found some in Etruscan tombs, and some in the pyramids.'

Marica put the wax-free combs into the extractor, and soon honey began to spatter against its glass sides as it was flung out of the unsealed combs by centrifugal force. Honey ran out of the machine through a filter designed to remove any wax that remained. Now it had to be decanted.

'Decanting honey is the opposite of decanting wine,' said Marica, 'because everything moves from the bottom to the top, so that all the impurities float on its surface.'

And what were these impurities? Well, they were not really impurities at all, just tiny bits of wax, pollen and propolis, apparently, and all the air that had entered the honey during the extraction process. Next the honey flowed into a big container where, as Michele put it, 'honey from thousands and thousands of different bees, with all its infinitesimal variations, is homogenized'. Before it could be bottled it had to be decanted once more into barrels, where it would settle one last time before being poured into the jars.

When I first visited their shop, the Di Prima family were selling four kinds of honey: *sulla* (made from *Hedysarum coronarium*), orange blossom, eucalyptus and chestnut. Marica advised me to start tasting them at the light end of the spectrum, where the clear, delicately flavoured, pale-gold *sulla* honey sits, made from the nectar of a little leguminous plant that had stopped me in my tracks in spring, and had me gazing at hillsides carpeted with its magenta-pink flowers. Next came very slightly darker orange-blossom honey, still the most popular Sicilian honey, both locally and abroad. However, it's much more difficult to produce these days because – as Michele explained – oranges have been cross-bred to be more productive, and they blossom for a much shorter period, and all at the same time, so that 'By the time the bees realize they are blossoming, it's over already.' Then I jumped to the dark end of the spectrum and rich, almost caramelized flavours. First came eucalyptus, and then my absolute favourite, the less sweet, powerful, smoky honey made from the Boscosa's sweet chestnut flowers. As I worked my way through these different flavours, I heard Michele murmur, 'Honey is the finest liquor that the sky distils on earth.'

They use honey for everything in the Di Prima family, and always have. 'Eucalyptus honey mixed with lemon juice will cure a cough,' Maria said, and Alfio told me that a hundred grams of honey dissolved in a litre of water would cleanse my system and solve all manner of ills.

Before beekeeping changed its fortunes, Zafferana Etnea was little known beyond the mountain. Thanks to its powers of reinvention, however, I saw coaches rumbling into town almost every day, bringing visitors to taste the extraordinary range of seasonal honeys produced by its industrious bees throughout the spring and summer.

13.

Donkey-Milk Dairy

Of all the trades and other occupations I sought out on Etna, milking donkeys struck me as the most curious. But then I come from Britain, where we milk cows a lot, goats a little, and sheep hardly at all. Here in Sicily it was well known, and then forgotten, that babies tolerated donkey milk better than any other substitute for breast milk. These were not babies from wealthy backgrounds, because their parents could afford a wet nurse if they needed one. Donkey milk was for poor babies, ones who had lost their mothers or had mothers who couldn't feed them, and then it might make the difference between life and death.

In the past, nobody knew why babies thrived on donkey milk, but today's analyses have shown that it resembles breastmilk more closely than any other substitute. More importantly for all those babies and young children with cow's-milk allergies, it contains fewer of the proteins that so many of them are allergic to. It is also rich in the antibodies and antioxidants that foals and babies all need to build up their immune systems. Among them is lysozyme, a powerfully antiviral and anti-bacterial enzyme completely absent from cow's milk. Added to all these built-in benefits is the sweetness that comes from high levels of lactose in donkey milk, because this makes it delicious to babies of every species.

Hot climate, scarce water and rough terrain have always conspired to create conditions in Sicily best suited to goats and sheep, so that cow's milk has never been part of the traditional diet. As a result, more babies and children suffer cow's-milk allergies here than anywhere else in Europe. And as if to prove it, I met two such people, each born about thirty years ago to parents living in what

Donkey-Milk Dairy

I came to think of as the land of donkey milk and honey. This was a steep stretch of ground between Zafferana Etnea and a donkey-milk dairy not far from my home in Milo.

Marica Di Prima was the first. Alfio, her father, explained that his wife hadn't been able to feed her when she was born, and they soon discovered that she had a violent allergy to all the alternative kinds of milk, because even formula specially made for babies contained cows'-milk proteins in those days. While paediatricians and dieticians argued about the best way forward, Marica lost weight at an alarming rate. In desperation, her parents turned away from the hospital experts and returned to what they knew: honey. They began to feed her with that simple mix of honey and boiled water, and within a week she had stopped being sick and begun to gain weight. The next step, Alfio told me, was to dissolve the finely ground crumbs of homemade bread and biscuits in the honey and water, and later still they began to add protein to her diet. You only have to look at Marica today to know she thrived, and it's little wonder she chose beekeeping as her future.

The other baby born with the same allergy was Guglielmo Grasso from Milo. His mother, Ketty Torrisi, was an equine vet, and unlike most other people on Etna, she still knew all about donkey milk's unique properties. The Di Prima family had drawn on their own knowledge to solve their daughter's problems, and Ketty did the same by setting off at once to look for a donkey. Fifty years earlier she would have been spoilt for choice, for as Guglielmo told me, there were still donkeys all over Sicily then, carrying loads, powering oil and flour mills, and pulling ploughs. However, her informal review of the island's donkey stock in 1997 revealed that it was shockingly diseased and diminished. Shockingly because, barely sixty years before, the island's donkeys were so famous that the Fascist government had chosen Sicily as the ideal place for a breeding programme. This aimed at improving the standard of mules used by the Italian army. A mule is a cross between a donkey stallion and a horse mare, and at the end of the 1920s government experts sought out the finest animals on the island to enrol in their programme. They went to the Nebrodi Mountains to find San Fratellano mares, and to Ragusa in the south of the island for the donkeys. Having made their choice of breeding stock, they ordered the animals' owners to bring them to *stazioni di monta* (literally 'mating stations' or studs) that they had set up in local towns. Horse owners were also required to sign an undertaking to bring foals back to the stud for inspection every year. Mules mature slowly, so they might have had to return three or four times before those government officials decided whether their foal was good enough to join the army. Luckily for their owners, the state paid for their keep every year.

What made a foal fit for military service? One consideration was the colour of its coat. The darker the better, for this would make it easier to camouflage. It needed to have stamina too, and the muscle to carry heavy loads of ammunition and other military supplies across ground too rough or remote for wheeled vehicles. Guglielmo had seen the names of foals eventually chosen by the state because they had all been entered into stud books that survive to this day. The people in charge certainly lacked imagination, for he told me that many had names like *costa poco* ('very cheap'), *vale molto* ('worth a lot'), and even more literally, *giùdilì* ('from down there').

The breeding programme also focused on improving the available stock of donkey stallions, and so as well as bringing stallions, or jacks, to stud with horses, local farmers around Ragusa were also called on to bring their donkey mares, or jennies, to breed with another cadre of carefully selected jacks. The countryside around Ragusa had always been known for the quality of its donkeys, but through this other breeding programme the Ragusano donkey was officially recognized as a pedigree breed. Enormous numbers of mules were needed as pack animals in the Alps and in Greece and North Africa throughout the Second World War, and this meant both horse and donkey breeding also had to continue apace.

The fall of Mussolini in 1943 had put an end to the breeding programme, and by the time Ketty set out to look for a donkey in 1997, Sicily's three main breeds, the Ferrante or Sicilian grey donkey, the

Pantesco and even the Ragusano, were represented only by ancient specimens harbouring every imaginable disease. Through persistence and determination, she eventually came home with an old jenny called Santina. When I say old, remember that donkeys can live for up to forty-five years. Perhaps that's why they take a leisurely twelve months to produce their foals, something any heavily pregnant woman on Etna is likely to know, because there is always someone to say, 'What, not born yet? Are you doing it like the donkeys?'

News of Santina's arrival spread fast on the volcano and elsewhere, and soon other families with babies and children suffering similar allergies began to get in touch. By 2000, so many people wanted a share of Santina's milk that Ketty set herself the difficult task of amassing a whole herd of milking donkeys in order to set up her own dairy that year. Once again it was a tremendous struggle to find decent animals, but she eventually managed to gather twenty donkeys.

Cut to the present, and Asilandia, the donkey farm that Ketty set up in a shady valley below the village, is home to over 450 animals, and Guglielmo and his sister, Maria Costanza, help her to run it. Preserving local biodiversity is at the heart of all they do, and although Ragusano donkeys are the most common breed both on the farm and in Sicily as a whole, they also have substantial numbers of much rarer Pantesco and Ferrante donkeys in the herd. They keep other rare and endangered local breeds on the farm as well. Those ringleted Pinzirita sheep, for example, and a collection of peculiar, heritage breeds of chicken. Like those beekeepers from Zafferana Etnea, Ketty Torrisi was a pioneer, and she made the volcano one of the first places in Sicily to have a donkey dairy. Since then the efficacy of donkey milk has been widely recognized, and dairies have popped up in almost every province on the island.

Ketty calls the milk they pasteurize and sell in glass bottles Asilat. It is chalk white, coats the palate like animal milk, and yet tastes as light as any plant milk. And no wonder, because Guglielmo told me it contains only 1 per cent fat, so that in Sicily people often add a drop of olive oil to the mix in a baby's bottle. There was another visitor tasting milk when I was there. He was a toddler, and his mother seemed quite astonished to see him guzzling a mug of the stuff and asking for more. Apparently he had refused milk of any kind ever since he was weaned. Ketty, who must have seen similar performances again and again, was not remotely surprised because, as she explained, all small children who have been breastfed love donkey milk simply because it reminds them of breastmilk.

Asilandia, Asilat: both names derive from *asino*, the Italian for ass or donkey. In Sicily, however, you are more likely to hear a donkey referred to as *sceccu*, the dialect word for sheikh. Ask why, you'll always be told a version of the legend reaching back to the ninth century, when the Arabs completed their slow conquest of the island. The emir forbade Sicilians to ride horses, or so the story goes, and they responded furiously by poisoning every single horse on the island. Now nobody had any transport, and the emir had to send to North Africa for an urgent delivery of new steeds. This really is a story about animal suffering, because all but one of the ships sank during a terrible storm at sea. When the surviving ship docked it turned out to contain nothing but donkeys, so now they were the only form of transport for Sicily's proud 'sheikhs'. Like a fly caught in amber, the comic image of a proud sheikh on a donkey is revived every time a *sceccu* ambles past.

Of course there was a *sceccu* everywhere you looked at Asilandia, some of them feeding foals with coats like thick brown velvet, and outsized ears and eyes. They were given sole use of their mother's milk while they built up their immune systems during the first three weeks of their lives. Then they had to share. The older ones seemed indifferent to separation, casting themselves down to sleep in furry piles, but the younger foals were restless when separated from their mothers at milking time, and most rushed over to be stroked. Guglielmo absent-mindedly held their little heads between his hands, pulling their ears and playing with their muzzles as he told me their names. Next to them were yearling jacks that appeared, like any other decent adolescent, to have dyed their hair bright red. They would lose their red coats as they grew older, Guglielmo said, but for now everything else about their futures was uncertain. They might keep an especially fine jack on the farm for breeding, but otherwise they would all be sold. Once you start to notice the quantity of donkey meat for sale in Sicily, it's no mystery what would happen next. However, Ketty sends only six donkeys to the slaughterhouse each year. She won't touch the meat herself, and so she sells it on.

Asilandia was the first donkey dairy in Sicily to be given permission to sell pasteurized milk, and it is still one of the few farms on the island where donkeys are milked every day, as opposed to being milked only on demand. Milking time there was much like milking on any other dairy farm. The jennies waited quietly to be allowed through the gate into the parlour. Then they trotted onto the raised concrete platform of their own accord, and stood obediently still as Guglielmo attached the milking clusters to their teats. On average they produced only about a litre of milk each day (as opposed to dairy cows, which average about twenty-two litres) and the whole process took less than ten minutes. Then they were off, suddenly in a rush to be reunited with their foals. A small proportion of their milk goes into making Asilat's milk soaps and cleansing creams. I took a bar of soap home with me to Milo, and it was as pure and white as the milk that made it. Who knew there could be so many roles for donkey milk in our modern world?

14.
Soil and Society

Of all the wonderful resources she gifts to her inhabitants, Etna's fertile soil has always been the most famous. People often refer to volcanic soil as if it were obvious how the sterile, black landscape of a lava flow could be transformed into something so valuable, but for a long time this seemed as opaque as alchemy to me. Eventually, however, finding out about the processes surrounding the slow breakdown of lava would prove to be a natural precursor to also discovering how Etna's rich soils have shaped social history on the volcano.

Lava is like a vacuum. Nature abhors it and almost as soon as it has cooled after an eruption the elements join forces to break it down, as if that outpouring of the Earth's insides were a mishap that must be erased. Wind, snow, frost, rain and sun are first to weather its surface. After only a decade or so they begin to work in harness with the snow lichens that colonize the flow wherever they can find a few tiny drops of moisture, a microscopic accumulation of dust or volcanic ash. And before very long the chaotic lava landscape begins to look as if a pale-grey veil has been thrown over the embarrassment of its nakedness. Lichens respond to fluctuations in moisture by expanding and contracting on the flow, and this pulls fragments from its surface. Their tiny, root-like structures then penetrate the lava and loosen the flow beneath its surface. More astonishing still, to me at least, they also secrete organic acids capable of dissolving it. The lichens are joined by mosses, and together they flourish, then die and decompose. This forms the tiny traces of organic matter that will eventually enable more complex plants to take root. Among these pioneer plants will be the fiercely thorny Sicilian milkvetch (*Astragalus siculus*), which grows in clumps like plump cushions on volcanic sand and lapilli, thriving in those desolate conditions at anything up to 2,500 metres. Etna soapwort (*Saponaria sicula*) is another, and it also grows high above the treeline, on even the steepest lava-covered slopes. Working alongside other endemic species, these plants improve the growing conditions by stabilizing sand and lapilli with their roots, stopping moisture from simply draining through the porous lava, and laying down the organic matter from which soil is formed.

Then come trees, another set of brave pioneers. Take the Etna broom (*Genista aetnensis*). In other places it would be a modest shrub, but on the volcano it can grow into a substantial tree five metres high. As well as managing to thrive in the first sparse soils covering a lava flow, it enriches them with nitrogen, paving the way for yet more plant species. And when it flowers in June and July, it sets the slopes ablaze, turning some high-altitude roads into glorious, golden tunnels, and sending its perfume wafting across the landscape like the spirit of the place.

Calabrian pines and Etna birch trees are among the first to colonize new lava flows. In fact, a touchingly tender, pale-green, bonsai version of the forest of Ragabo is already beginning to grow on the lava that ploughed through it in 2002. There is no soil to be seen among the charred and broken relics of trees, so that at first glance the survival of those fragile saplings is a mystery. However, as usual on Etna, what goes on underground is as important as what can be seen on the surface, because each of those infant trees is in a symbiotic relationship with the mycorrhizal fungi among its roots. Under normal conditions the trees would scavenge all the nutrients they needed from the soil, but of course that is impossible in the extreme conditions of a young lava flow. Fortunately for them, however, mycorrhizal fungi are capable of burrowing into solid lava and mining all the minerals the tree needs as nutrients. And when it comes to water, a terribly sparse resource at that altitude, the fungi's questing hyphae are a hundred times longer than the tree's roots, and they can seek out moisture anywhere. All this the fungi give to the tree in return for a share in the sugars, lipids and carbon it extracts during photosynthesis, an exchange that makes the impossible possible in this high-wire act of survival.

First-time visitors to Etna often ask, as I did, how long it takes for a fresh lava flow to weather and break down into soil. Unfortunately, there is no simple answer, because it might be only a few decades before the first lichens begin the process by settling on the surface of a new flow or, as is equally likely, the lava could resist change for hundreds of years. So the proper response to the question 'how long?' all depends on the type and texture of the lava, and the minerals and other compounds it contains. Altitude, microclimate and exposure also play their part, so that lava flows high on Etna and fully exposed to the elements are likely to break down faster than those in sheltered spots at lower altitude. Meanwhile, those pioneer trees and plants make me think of philanthropists, or members of some penitentiary order, laying down their lives for others. And seeing them slowly colonizing a flow is like watching life on Earth evolve over and over again.

Lava flows have criss-crossed almost the entire surface of Etna. At any one time, some may be only a few weeks old, and some will have been produced by Etna's ancestors, tens of thousands of years ago. Overlapping and overlaying each other, the flows break down in myriad ways, and this makes soils in the Coltivata very diverse. I have seen soils that span the whole gamut of textures within metres of each other on the same farm. At one extreme were feather-light, ash soils that are the legacy of Ellittico, Etna's ancient forbear, and at the other was lava apparently so unredeemed that the soils appeared to be little more than a jumble of lava boulders.

Almost all Etna's soils are rich in valuable nutrients such as phosphorous, potassium and magnesium that enable plants to thrive. They also contain good supplies of iron and copper, the micronutrients essential to processes like photosynthesis. Lava soils are continually weathering and breaking down, releasing more nutrients to feed the soil, so that its quality is never exhausted. This has always made it possible to farm intensively and grow superb cash crops on Etna. However, it is not just the abundance of the harvest that makes those crops exceptional. That cocktail of minerals also imbues fruit and vegetables grown on the volcano with such rich flavours that they seem to become the perfect version of themselves. Pistachios grown there are the most valuable in the world, and wines made from Etna's grapes are a true expression not just of the volcano, but of the intimate patch of soil where they were grown.

Etna's soils have always been a wonderful resource, and yet her people have not always had equal freedom to benefit from them. These disparities are engraved on the landscape today, so that when I circumnavigated the volcano by train, I had noticed a huge contrast between styles of land management on her east and west flanks. On the east side of the volcano were little farms and farmhouses packed together on heavily cultivated slopes, while on the west, the windows of the carriage framed a much wilder view of wide, empty, sparsely populated spaces. Since making that journey, I had learned about extraordinary events in the town of Bronte that might be held responsible, at least in part, for this contrast. For unlike the east flank, where land was owned and farmed by multiple families for almost 200 years, most of the territory surrounding Bronte had belonged to one of the biggest private landowners in the whole of Sicily. Vast estates like this were so common elsewhere that even in 1952, gazing across the Simeto River on Etna's western boundary, Carlo Levi saw nothing but 'desolate, bare feudal estates, corn country, but destitute, yellow, treeless, uninhabited, sun-smitten, mysterious in its nakedness'. These vast, feudal fiefdoms were the legacy of the Romans, who carved much of Sicily's interior up into enormous monocrop arable estates. They were known as *latifundia*, and they tended to be owned by rich landlords from the mainland, who valued them purely as business opportunities to be managed at a distance and worked by badly treated peasants and slaves. This miserable arrangement laid the foundation for a feudal system that would suffocate Sicily's economy, and exploit the majority of its population for the best part of 2,000 years. In fact, feudalism lasted so long in Sicily that at the beginning of the nineteenth century *latifondi*, as they are now known, still accounted for about 80 per cent of the island's agricultural land.

Etna's climate and steep gradients had always made it unsuitable for growing wheat on the grand scale of the *latifondi*. But nevertheless, from 1799 to 1981 Bronte and its surroundings were part of a huge, private estate. Imagine my surprise when I first learned that, instead of being the feudal fief to some ancient, local family, the Duchy of Bronte had belonged to none other than that great British hero Admiral Horatio Nelson, and then to his descendants. This unhappy history began when King Ferdinand III made Nelson the first ever Duke of Bronte. He gave him the estate as a reward for whisking him and his family to safety on the eve of the Jacobin invasion of Naples, and then brutally suppressing supporters of the Parthenopian Republic set up there in his absence. The king invented the dukedom and its duchy for this purpose, although much of the land he parcelled together for Nelson had been part of a feudal estate since the fifteenth century. Nevertheless, *contadini* living there had never really accepted the authority of their previous landlords, nor had they given up their claim to timber and water on the estate, or their rights to the common land they believed was theirs. By the time it was given to Nelson, therefore, the estate was entangled in lawsuits stretching back hundreds of years. And, to cap it all, the king chose an old monastery in Maniace that had been derelict for years as the seat for this dubious duchy. Nelson never managed to see all this for himself before he died at the Battle of Trafalgar in 1805, but he was delighted by his new title, albeit that it was attached to a place nobody in England had ever heard of.

Some say the king's gift was a joke, for Nelson had already lost an eye, and Bronte takes its name from Brontes, the cyclops. Some say the relationship between Nelson and the duchy's inhabitants was poisoned from the start by his treachery in Naples, where he violated the terms of the anti-royalists' surrender by putting them to death. Some say, or to be more specific, the *Corriere della Sera* newspaper said in 2010, that Nelson's 'money-grubbing family' and estate managers treated Bronte as if it were a colonial possession, and ran the estate 'just as they would have run a banana farm in Rhodesia'.

It is true that, in the letters that successive generations of the duchy's British estate managers wrote to their employer, they sound like old-fashioned colonialists living somewhere very far from Europe. The misjudgements and misfortunes of generations of Britons in Bronte make for extraordinary reading. For all their bias, and their authors' shocking insistence on their own superiority, however, the letters give a vivid impression of the brutal realities of life on Etna's west flank in the first half of the nineteenth century. In general terms they considered Bronte 'a bitter wilderness', where they were surrounded by 'vagabonds', 'ruffians', 'scoundrels' and even 'savages'. At first they were obliged to live just as everyone else in Bronte did, and in 1817 a new manager complained of finding 'no butter, no cheese, nor even milk enough for my children . . . [and] no habitable house to shelter my family in all seasons'. British employees and their families lived in constant fear of cholera. They also suffered terribly from coughs, digestive problems, boils, and other disgusting, pus-filled infections and chronic conditions that made their lives a misery. All in all, as one estate manager said, 'The privations and inconveniences of Bronte are to us even who have seen various foreign places almost beyond sufferance.'

Among those 'inconveniences' must surely have been Etna's eruptions, which were unusually frequent between the mid-eighteenth and mid-nineteenth centuries. Their lava flows destroyed arable land and crops, as did numerous rivers on the estate. The Simeto was the biggest and most dangerous, but they were all prone to flooding, and regularly sent cascades of thick mud to uproot crops and sweep them from the fields. Worse still, after the floods receded, water remained in the ditches until it became stagnant and malarial. Two of the duchy's estate managers died of malaria, which was endemic on Etna until the 1950s. Crops and animals on the volcano's west flank were also prone to disease. Sheep and cattle caught foot and mouth, vines were eradicated by phylloxera, and locusts decimated the grain. Weather on the landward side of the mountain was harsh because it enjoyed none of the east flank's sea breezes or damp winds. Summers were scorching, and winters sometimes began in September with the first snowfall. Local *contadini* and their families had withstood all these hardships for centuries, and yet one British estate manager found them so overwhelming that he shot himself.

You only have to look at the layout of Bronte to understand just how much those *contadini* had to endure. Corso Umberto is its main street. Spanning a stretch of level ground, it is lined with handsome, eighteenth-century palaces built by doctors, lawyers, and other professional people who lived there in great comfort, often sending their sons to be educated at the famous Real Collegio Capizzi, alongside the offspring of other wealthy families from Sicily and the mainland. Meanwhile, *contadini* and *braccianti* lived in chaotic conglomerations of hovels and shacks above and below the *corso*. Many of the tiny buildings clinging to the slope are derelict today, and yet there were still people living in them as best they could when Carlo Levi arrived in 1952 to research the conditions of rural life in the Mezzogiorno. Although Levi had done more than anyone to open the eyes of the Italian north to extreme poverty in the south, even he was surprised by what he found on leaving the main street. In *Le parole sono pietre* he describes scenes that would have been shocking in any century, let alone the mid-twentieth:

> For lack of drainage streams of foul water flow along the ground, through the streets and the sloping courtyards, and the smell catches you in the throat. The houses – if they can be so called – are mere hovels with roofs of reeds through which the rain comes; they are smoky and bare and windowless, and eight, or ten, or twelve people live huddled together in a few square yards.

He saw children 'with faces lovely as angels' whose stomachs were swollen by malaria, and a man who could only enter his house on all fours.

Physical hardship was not the only challenge on Etna's west flank, however, and anyone living there in the nineteenth century knew that violence was always just beneath the surface. Brigands roamed the slopes, and armed robbery and cattle rustling were both commonplace. Bronte was also renowned as a litigious place, and the *Brontesi* were insistent on what they held as their ancient privileges. As a result, successive British managers found it impossible to prevent them felling valuable trees, drawing water, and grazing animals all over the place, without asking permission or offering payment of any kind. These frictions had always made the town unusually prone to political upheavals, revolts, and other crises cooked up in steep, narrow streets that could have been made for plotting that would result in tragedy soon enough.

As well as exposing the everyday hardships of nineteenth-century life on Etna's west flank, letters from those hapless estate managers reveal the elaborate economic arrangements that were common to large estates all over Sicily. Absentee landlords traditionally handed the management of their estates to local farmers, who agreed to oversee them and ensure the *contadini* paid their rent in return for a share of the profits. This created a new rural class known as *gabellotti*. The word translates as 'rent collector', but in nineteenth-century Sicily it signified much more than that. The *gabellotto* came between the landowner and his tenants by renting the land himself, and then subletting it at an exaggerated price to the *contadini*. He increased his income still further by supplying seeds or renting out farm equipment at great cost, and extorting protection money from *contadini* working in Etna's dangerous countryside.

Bronte and the duchy were the *gabellotto*'s little kingdom, where he could fix the price of anything he liked, and intimidate the *contadini* until they paid up. In theory he passed any rental income on to the estate, but in practice he invented arcane taxes that enabled him to cream off an ever-expanding quota for himself. By applying the same methods to the sale of all estate produce he became richer still. Extortion, intimidation and protection rackets were all routes to riches, and they made the *gabellotto* the most powerful figure in the local community. For the first British estate managers arriving in Bronte, however, those *proto-mafiosi* were all to be discovered.

Back then, Etna was linked to the outside world by only the roughest roads and most treacherous mule tracks. This might have preserved it as a world apart, but, to the contrary, Bronte serves as a lens through which we can view nineteenth-century politics all over Sicily. When revolution convulsed Palermo in 1820, one faction supported the king while the other campaigned fervently for independence and a truly Sicilian monarch. Already much given to fighting and factions, Bronte was soon split along the same lines. In 1848, the year of revolutions all over Europe, the king's refusal to undertake any constitutional reforms provoked another uprising in Palermo. Rebellion was bred in the bone in Bronte, and when they heard about this new rebellion, *Brontesi* of every social category used it as the chance to settle old scores, and the *contadini* welcomed it as an opportunity to lay claim to land they believed to be rightfully theirs. The fervour of their beliefs compelled the duchy's estate manager to run for his life.

Dramatic as they were, events in 1848 resolved nothing in the town, which remained riven by resentment between different social and political groups. Matters there had been exacerbated by a ruling of the supreme court in 1841 declaring that the *contadini* did indeed have inalienable rights to the timber of mature chestnut, beech and oak trees on duchy land. This was the outcome of a court case that had lasted for centuries, and in compensation for the rights denied them for so long, the court ordered that a third of the duchy's lava fields and 25 per cent of its arable and grazing land should at last be divided between *contadini* living there. Guess what? Instead of redistributing these riches, Bronte's town council simply passed them over to Bronte's elite, so that by 1848 the *contadini* were in the grip of unprecedented rage and resentment.

That was the situation on Etna's west flank when Garibaldi and his army of 1,000 volunteers landed on Sicily in May 1860. They came announcing their intention of overthrowing the Bourbons and making an independent Sicily part of the new Kingdom of Italy. According to a royal dispatch, their arrival incited 'a delirium of revolution' all over the island. Like *contadini* everywhere, those living in the duchy were convinced Garibaldi had come to fight alongside them for freedom, and to deliver justice by redistributing the land at last. In reality, this was wishful thinking, and when their aspirations for land and freedom were shattered again, Bronte exploded into a full-scale peasant revolt on 1 August 1860.

Exasperated by generations of grinding poverty, oppression and hunger, deprived of education or any prospect of improving their lot, *contadini*, *braccianti* and 'communists' (supporters of the redistribution of common land) embarked on a violent war of attrition. This was pure class warfare, and it's said that revolutionaries armed with scythes, sickles and axes poured through the streets like a torrent of incandescent lava. No one who owned land, a business, a shop or property of any other kind was safe. Policemen, lawyers, landowners, local aristocrats, businessmen, notaries and priests were all at risk, and there were no limits to the fury of the mob. Victims were forced from their houses, stabbed, shot and then hacked to pieces, as if one mortal blow could never avenge so many centuries of deep wrongs. There were many eyewitness accounts the events that followed and these became the source for a barely fictionalized story by the nineteenth-century novelist Giovanni Verga, who gave his tale the bitterly ironic title of 'Libertà'. It was, as Verga put it, as if a starving wolf had entered a sheep pen: 'it doesn't think of filling its belly, but just slaughters everything in sight from pure rage.' The mob burned down forty-six houses, the theatre and the government archive. They burst into the richest houses and helped themselves to the contents. Anything they did not want, they smashed up and threw out of the windows.

What happened next is spoken of much more in Bronte now than the macabre events preceding it. On 6 August a battalion of voluntary soldiers rode into town under the command of Nino Bixio, Garibaldi's fiercest commander. Their public mission was to restore public order, punish the perpetrators of the uprising and make an example of them. In Bronte, however, they dwell on the fact that Bixio was also sent to protect the duchy, following a special request from the British ambassador to defend 'Mrs Nelson's' property – another nail in the coffin of Britain's reputation.

Even a patient person with unlimited time would have struggled to cut through the ancient rivalries and antagonisms of that traumatized community, and find the true perpetrators of the uprising. Bixio was not that person. In fact, he was renowned for his impatience and sudden outbursts of rage. He did everything in a rush, a rush that saw five men chosen almost at random and hauled up as culprits. They were lined up against a wall at the top of the town and shot. The firing squad was formed from Garibaldi's soldiers, and as the victims fell to the ground, his promises of freedom and justice died with them. That act of violence, by the very people who came to liberate Sicily from oppression, has been seen for evermore as a turning point in history, for it spelt out to the *contadini* of Bronte that they would continue to suffer exactly the same injustices as they had for centuries. Less than eighty years earlier, Goethe had described Sicily as 'the clue to everything', but now it was Etna shining a spotlight on a truth that rang true for the entire Mezzogiorno.

Say the word 'Bronte' to the British and it means only one thing – the Brontë sisters. (How often must we be reminded that their father's real surname was 'Brunty' before he changed it in homage to his hero?) Say it to an Italian, and as likely as not they will recall the *Fatti di Bronte* – the Bronte business – for those terrible events have been inscribed in Italian consciousness. They are seen now as a counter-narrative to Italy's Unification, revealing the stark truth behind all its promises, bluster and glory. There is a memorial on the site of the executions, and if you walk through town with anyone truly local, they are bound to take you there.

All this happened during the first sixty years of the duchy's history. You might have expected the Nelson Hood family to sell up and leave after all their troubles, but instead successive generations forged an ever closer and more affectionate link with the estate. Immediately after Unification, General Alexander Nelson Hood, fourth Duke of Bronte, was the first to take on the management of it himself. He made improvements by bringing steam-powered machinery from England, digging wells, building and repairing bridges, and introducing new crops. He also built the first proper road between Castello Maniace and Bronte, so that it was possible to reach the castle by carriage for the very first time.

People used to compare Castello Maniace to a British public school: spartan, cold, and occupied only by men. But now the family seemed bent on turning it into an English country house transported to Etna's wild, western flanks. Frances Elliot was one of a succession of British visitors, and in her 1881 *Diary of an Idle Woman in Sicily* she described the drawing room as:

> half hall, half parlour, filled with the scent of flowers. Great logs are blazing on the hearth, a piano, pictures over consoles, vases of spring daffodils and wood hyacinths, hats and gloves ranged on a table against a wall, a letter-box, sofas with dogs asleep on them, dogs also wandering about inclined to bite, a long vista of convent corridors, lighted by ranges of lamps, leading to bedrooms.

That huge room and the bedrooms beyond it had often lain empty over the years, but when Alexander Nelson Hood appointed his nineteen-year-old son Alec as estate manager, it was lived in almost full time. Nevertheless, Elliot's account also suggests that the family had come no closer to integrating with the local population. They flew the British flag perpetually over the castle, and couldn't stray far from it without armed guards, for Sicily, as she put it, 'is a land of brigands'.

Elliot's arrival coincided with a visit to the castle by the rest of the Nelson Hoods. Her description reveals their determination to translate all the pleasures of upper-class life in Victorian England to the slopes of a Sicilian volcano. Huge and almost uncontrollable horses were brought round to the house for them to ride. They ventured down impossibly steep and rutted tracks in flimsy carriages. They staged an elaborate picnic on the edge of a lava flow, and surrounded themselves with dogs, indoors and out.

And what of Bronte's *contadini*? What had their rebellion achieved? Between 1862 and 1868 the duke at last parted with most of the common land on the estate, and signed nearly 2,000 long, low-rent tenancy agreements. It seems almost inevitable, however, that the realization of a goal pursued for almost 400 years should be a disappointment. And so it was, for the *contadini* felt the rents were too high, the boundaries uncertain, the ground too poor, too remote, too difficult to farm. So many people abandoned the plots they had been allocated, or lost them during boundary disputes, that a progress report thirty years later could identify only 700 of the original tenants.

The fortunes of some people on the estate did improve when Alec Nelson Hood succeeded his father in 1904. He was the first in his family to be fluent in the local dialect, and the first to do his share of manual labour on the estate. He also introduced a new kind of tenancy agreement to Etna. *Mezzadria* contracts, as they were called, were a partnership that committed him and his tenant to providing half – *mezzo* – of the working capital that needed to be invested into the land each year. This perfectly equitable arrangement meant that his tenants also received half the produce. As the citrus trade was booming at the beginning of the twentieth century, they installed irrigation on the lowest slopes of the volcano and planted tens of thousands of citrus trees, as well as almonds, olives and more pistachios. Suddenly everybody was making good money, and because *mezzadrie* contracts left no room for middlemen, the *gabellotti* were excluded at last. Alec also planted vines on duchy land for the first time. He set up winepresses, cellars and a distillery for making brandy, and engaged a French winemaker to produce Duchy of Bronte fine wines and brandies, and export them to London. In 1911 he built La Falconara, a large villa overlooking the sea in Taormina. He entertained the British King and Queen there in 1925, and over the years his presence and that of his inner circle helped launch Taormina as Europe's most fashionable gay resort.

Alec Nelson Hood renovated Castello Maniace, making it more comfortable than ever before. He entertained a succession of well-known people, and it also became something of a second home for various writers, poets and musicians. This was Maniace's heyday, and I happened upon a surprising link to it while visiting a chemist in Catania to buy treatment for a late-summer cold. I suggested Vitamin C, but this led to a long discussion, for surely vitamins were not enough to fend it off. I would need other things it seemed, and many of them. Even the pharmacist got involved, and realizing I was English he swapped his pharmacist face for something far friendlier, and came out from his dispensary. He had grown up in

Bronte, he told me, where his mother developed the extraordinary habit of drinking tea at five o'clock every afternoon. She also made good, solid fruitcake using a recipe given to her by the tea-drinking English people at Castello Maniace. 'And now I have inherited the fruitcake recipe,' he said, 'and if I haven't had my cup of tea, no sugar, by 5.30, my children know there will be trouble.'

Among Alec's guests at the castle was D. H. Lawrence, who, chippy as ever, disliked his host so much he remarked, 'money maketh the man, even if he was a monkey to start with.' The Scottish poet and novelist William Sharp was a frequent visitor. He was a mysterious figure, whose greatest success came under the pseudonym of the Celtic Revival writer Fiona Macleod. Few knew Macleod's true identity, and this left Sharp free to promote her writing shamelessly, apparently acting as her agent, turning down interviews on her behalf, and even pretending to whisk her off to secret locations if he ever came close to being rumbled. He told some people they were cousins, implied to others they were lovers, and went on adding more depth to her character until his premature death at Castello Maniace in 1905. He was buried there, in the beautiful English cemetery where his grave now emerges from long grass and wildflowers. Alec Nelson Hood died in 1937, and was initially laid to rest in the garden of La Falconara. When the villa was sold, however, his body was exhumed and re-buried close to Sharp in Maniace.

When Italy declared war on Britain in 1940, both the duchy and La Falconara were seized by the Fascist government, not as enemy property, as you might expect, but because it said the duchy had failed to comply with new laws about building accommodation for *contadini* on its land. The government began building these houses itself as soon as it took possession. Some were farmhouses and some were part of a new village right in front of the castle. This new development was almost complete by the time the Allies reached Maniace in 1943, and several families had already moved in.

Peter Nelson Hood, the new Duke of Bronte, moved back to Castello Maniace in 1946, but it took over a decade for his rights to the duchy to be accepted. Having bulldozed the new development beneath the castle walls, he continued the long process of selling and redistributing land. Nevertheless, when Carlo Levi visited Bronte in 1952, he described all the *contadini* he met there as inhabitants of 'Nelson's feudal estate':

> That is how the labouring class lives in Bronte ... thousands of landless peasants ... who for a century and a half have been fighting a daily peasant war against a persisting feudal system for the lands of the Duchy ... who are turned out and then go back patiently, tenaciously, and who remain in spite of everything, full of human vitality, and still manage, in their fetid courtyards, to have hope in the future.

And there was hope, because after the war the duke tried to improve the lives of those on the estate by building a school, employing a doctor and midwife at his own cost, and extending and repairing the local infrastructure of roads and bridges. By the time of his death in 1969, he had redistributed so much of the original 50,000-acre estate that only 3,000 acres remained.

Then came Peter Nelson Hood's son, another Alec Nelson Hood. He was the only prospective duke to have grown up at the castle, or rather that is where he lived when he wasn't at boarding school in England. However, he had no interest in farming, and soon after inheriting the estate he sold the remaining land to local farmers. The town council bought Castello Maniace on condition he left all the Nelson memorabilia behind. I visited it once its interminable restoration was over. However, all that remained of the interior created by generation after generation of the family was a terrible, frozen formality. The drawing room Frances Elliot described so vividly is scattered with arbitrary furniture in strange configurations. There are bookshelves too, jammed with a random collection of English country-house classics, interspersed with veterinary textbooks and agricultural manuals. Dusty parterres and roses cling on to life in the parched garden, and the swimming pool lies empty beside the derelict pool house. There was little about the place or its history to make you glad to be British.

15.
Sicilian Emeralds

You can buy pistachio nuts anywhere, but it is only by coming to Etna that you can properly understand their true potential. For example, there is a restaurant in Bronte's Corso Umberto called Pepe Rosa, where they feature in every course on the menu. You might begin your meal there with *bruschetta* spread with pistachio paste, and then choose a *primo piatto* of potato gnocchi with slightly granular pistachio pesto, as full of subtle flavours as the freshly picked nuts. That was enough for me on a hot, hot afternoon. Had I been willing, however, I could have gone on to eat a fillet of veal with savoury pistachio cream, and then walked further up Corso Umberto to buy a soft, creamy pistachio ice cream in Pasticceria Gelateria Conti. That ice cream would have been the colour of an avocado bathroom suite, and come with an emerald sprinkle of chopped nuts on top. Sometimes I went there and made a meal of it by having an *arancino* as my first course. The Conti had its own take on that familiar recipe, and beneath the usual crisp exterior of fried breadcrumbs and rice was a savoury heart of melting pistachio pesto and *mozzarella*.

Pistachios are central to the offering of every bar, restaurant and *pasticceria* in Bronte, and no wonder, because although pistachios grow in other countries all over the world, nowhere else can produce nuts of the same vivid, emerald green as the *Pistacchio Verde di Bronte*. Their nickname on Etna is *Smeraldi di Sicilia* – Sicilian emeralds – and their intense colour, combined with an exceptional flavour, makes Bronte pistachios twice as expensive as those grown anywhere else. Such a valuable crop would be bound to attract the wrong kind of attention wherever it grew, and in September 2009 thieves made off with 300 kilos of ripe nuts. Police have patrolled the fields at harvest time ever since, sometimes even hovering overhead in a helicopter.

Nino Papero is one of the largest pistachio producers in Bronte, and he had invited me to meet him one morning in early September at Caffetteria Luca, a bar on the edge of town. Morning light glanced off glass cabinets crammed with a glistening army of cakes and pastries. When I asked the barman their names he began with *bignè al pistacchio* (choux pastry puffs filled with sweet green pistachio cream), went on to *cannoli al pistacchio* (Sicily's deep-fried alternative to the brandy snap, filled with a mixture of ricotta and pistachio cream), and then *canestrelli al pistacchio* (biscuits with pistachio icing). And so it went on, food from a fairytale, a poem written in pastry and dedicated to pistachios. Despite being entirely different from each other in size and shape, every cake in the case wore the same vivid green uniform of belonging to Bronte. It was breakfast time and my order was simple – *un cappuccino ed un cornetto*. '*Crema, marmellata o pistacchio?*' the barman asked, as barmen must and always do. Of course I chose one filled with emerald cream, its sweetness tempered by the almost savoury nuttiness of Bronte pistachios, and its abundance soon apparent all over my hands.

I had spoken to Signor Papero only twice on the phone, but I passed the time as I waited by trying to match the memory of his voice with people coming into the bar. The game eventually played out perfectly when a small, solid man in his early eighties strode in, wearing a striped T-shirt and gripping the stub of a cigar between his teeth. He cast a gaze around the room, greeted a few people, and then walked confidently over to my table. Looking approvingly at the remains of my *cornetto* he told me it would be much cheaper for Caffetteria Luca to make all their pastries with nuts from abroad. 'But I was mayor of Bronte once,' he said, 'and I told them I'd shut them down if they didn't use Bronte pistachios.' I believed him. My offer of coffee was met with a gentle hiss of disapproval. Could I at least pay for my own? 'Hospitality is sacred in Sicily,' he said firmly, settling up and setting off for the door.

Most farmers around here drive battered Fiat Pandas, and Papero was no exception. I followed him out of town and turned off the main road before stopping abruptly in front of his gates. Pistachio trees lined the drive, flinging out their narrow, trailing branches as if to embrace us as we left our cars. We could only reach his house on the terrace at the end of the drive by treading on the nuts that had been shelled and spread out to dry all over the ground. Papero led the way, making it clear that crunching over the most precious pistachios on Earth was nothing to worry about.

Papero told me that people come from all over the world to see trees growing from the ancient lava flow that is his farm. He seemed to take particular delight in telling me about a group of agricultural experts from France. 'They said that when it came to farming, all of us pistachio farmers in Bronte were just idiots compared to them. And they were right, but as they put it, "you are so lucky God gave you this wonderful land".' Papero couldn't agree more, but when I stepped down from the terrace into the *pistacchietti* – or *lochi* as they are known in local dialect – they didn't look God-given at all. There was nothing nice about the arrangement of the trees, nothing ordered or regular. They jostled for space on that troubled terrain, growing at wild angles on black crags and knolls of lava, and crowding each other out of dark hollows and across sooty slopes. They were small trees with sun-stricken leaves. You might have called them squat if they hadn't been so insubstantial, and with their ashen trunks and tentacle branches, they bobbed like pale octopuses in a lava sea.

Everything about those trees looked casual, almost impermanent, and yet pistachios have a history of cultivation reaching right back to the Book of Genesis. Jacob considered them one of the greatest luxuries of the land, and told his sons to pack them in their saddlebags to take as gifts to Egypt. They crop up again in *Naturalis historia*, a vast encyclopaedia of natural science written by Pliny the Elder in AD 77. He paired them with hazelnuts as a treatment for coughs and catarrh, and with pine nuts as an effective antidote for snake bite. He also explained their arrival in Italy. Apparently, it was Lucius Vitellius, a Roman governor in Syria, who brought the first trees home with him to Liguria in AD 35. Before long they were recorded growing in Sicily as well as Liguria, Puglia and Campania. However, as far as we know, none of them deigned to produce nuts until the ninth century, when Arab farmers began to cultivate them in Sicily.

It is impossible to know exactly what those farmers did to persuade Sicilian trees to start cropping. However, in Ibn-al-Awam's great 'Book of Agriculture' (*Kitab al-Felahah*), he instructed twelfth-century farmers to encourage their pistachio trees by placing gold at cardinal points around the base of their trunks. Not a lot – just the equivalent of seven or eight grains of barley. More importantly, the Arabs were much better farmers than any of their predecessors on the island. They knew more about soil and its fertility than the Romans, and they had better techniques for storing and capturing the water they needed to grow the exotic plants they had imported from all over the Caliphate. The Romans had grafted fruit and nut trees, but Arabic farmers are thought to have had the idea of grafting the only nut-bearing member of the *Pistacia* genus, *Pistacia vera*, onto the terebinth or turpentine tree (*Pistacia terebinthus*) – a wild relation that already thrived on the island.

Despite being a member of the same extensive pistachio clan, the terebinth is an altogether tougher tree. It is drought tolerant, and has such a deep and powerful root system that it can drill right down into volcanic soil and even bore through lava. Terebinths are slow growers, and it takes ten years for the grafted trees to bear nuts for the first time. But they are also long lived, and once established they can be productive for 300 years. This is much longer than most fruit or nut trees, and longer than the emirs would rule Sicily before being ousted by Normans. Nevertheless, the Arabs were the first to cultivate pistachios successfully on a grand scale, and the first to notice how well they grew in places like Bronte. The breakthrough made by those Arabic farmers was written indelibly into local dialect, where the pistachio tree is a *festuca*, a word derived directly from the Arabic *fastuq*. In the dialect peculiar to Bronte, they used to describe anything green as *frastuchino*, and a pudding made from pistachios was a *frastucata*.

From the sixteenth century onwards, pistachios appear again and again among the ingredients for recipes made in wealthy Italian households. Bartolomeo Scappi, the most famous cook in Renaissance Italy, published his *Opera* in 1570. It is a wonderful mix of recipes, descriptions of dinners cooked for his grand employers, and household tips. It is full of good sense – throw away pistachios after a year because they will be rancid – and straightforward instructions: candy them and put them in small bowls among a wonderful array of other delicacies on the sideboard during formal meals. Scatter a handful into a roasted quince tart; steep them, chop them and slip them into fish pies during Lent, or into cherry and plum pies in summer. It also encompasses the impossibly labour-intensive processes I associate with sixteenth-century life in general, and sixteenth-century cooking in particular. How do you extract oil from pistachios, for example? By heating them over a fire, grinding them lightly with a wooden pestle, putting them into a hot cloth and then squeezing for all you're worth. Pistachios make their final appearance in Scappi's book in a soup for convalescents. There they are soaked for six hours and then ground up with sugar and a few melon seeds and heated gently with water over the fire.

The curative properties of pistachios were called on again over a century later, when Bartolomeo Stefani published *L'arte di ben cucinare* – 'The Art of Good Cooking'. Here they appear alongside a recipe for cooking oysters. Stefani acknowledges that some people eat oysters raw, 'but they are very difficult to digest, and people who consume them in great numbers must counteract the effect by eating pistachios in proportion to the quantity of oysters'. And when he says 'great numbers' he really means it: 'For fifty small oysters you need to eat four ounces of pistachios, and if the oysters are bigger, you must increase the weight of the pistachios in proportion.'

In Bronte, pistachios were the happy ending to its troubled social history, for instead of being defeated by the great expanses of lava handed over to them in the mid-nineteenth century, some of the duchy's tenants revived the ancient tradition of cultivating pistachios. When the trees began to crop, the quality of nuts grown on Etna was so high that they found themselves with a secure income at last. The success of this enterprise grew year on year, as more and more lava fields outside Bronte were reclaimed as *lochi*. At summer's end the town's narrow streets were spread so thickly with drying pistachios that there was scarcely space to walk along them. The success of Bronte's farmers was soon well known in Sicily, and when Mussolini made a speech demanding that every clod of Italian earth should be made fertile, an obsequious Sicilian agronomist remarked that the pistachio could do even better than that, for it exploited rocks as well as soil, thus 'taking us beyond even the goal set by our great leader'.

These days most farmers in Bronte have plots of about 1.5 hectares, but Nino and his nephew Alfio have amassed 22 hectares of land, all of it planted with pistachios. Alfio has always been so serious about Bronte's pistachio industry that he even chose it as the topic for his university thesis. He and his uncle do the job of growing and harvesting pistachios today in much the same way as it was done when Stefani was writing in the seventeenth century. The techniques have been handed down from generation to generation of the same families in Bronte.

Nino and Alfio keep a constant lookout for the wild terebinths that seed themselves wherever they can find a spoonful or two of soil. The seedlings then develop roots to drill through the lava until they can dip them into one of the hidden streams flowing beneath it. This ability has earned them the nickname of *spaccasassi*, or 'stone breaker'. In dialect they are *scornabecco*, so that lovers so close they seem grafted together are sometimes compared to the *festuca* and the *scornabecco*. The men wait until each little incomer is properly established before grafting onto it. Grafting is generally done at the beginning of June, and some say it's more successful with a waxing moon. However, as one of the other men on the farm chipped in to tell me, 'They're like babies – incredibly delicate – and it doesn't matter when you graft, they won't do well if the weather is too hot or too cold.' Whenever it's done, the process is the same. The men lift a plump bud and a sliver of bark from a pistachio, slip it beneath the bark of its sturdy relation, bind them tightly together and settle down for a long wait. Using self-seeded terebinths as rootstock may give Bronte's *lochi* a haphazard appearance, but it also conjures the wonderful thought that every tree has chosen to grow exactly where it is. For some this means underneath a larger tree, for others it entails growing almost horizontally from the side of a lump of lava. Whatever the spot, it's their choice and they thrive in it.

When it comes to pollination, however, things are not so straightforward. The female pistachio must be pollinated by one of a scattering of self-seeded male terebinths if it is to bear fruit. Unfortunately, terebinths flower a little earlier than pistachios, and anyway, there is only about one male tree to every twenty females in Bronte's orchards, making this process so hit and miss that it reminds me of pandas breeding in captivity. Another of the pistachio's eccentricities is its alternate cropping. 'I'm eighty-three,' Nino Papero told me, 'and I still don't really understand why, but on years with even numbers we just remove the flower buds, so that trees only crop on the alternate, odd years.' He told me that some people had experimented with letting trees fruit every year, but the results had been very disappointing. 'It's the tree that decides,' he concluded. Alfio pointed out that alternate cropping was an organic form of pest control because it disrupted the insects' life cycle. Over the years a few farmers in Bronte have tried to resist this age-old tradition by making their trees fruit on even years. 'And then all the birds and insects flocked to their farms,' said Alfio, with some satisfaction I thought. 'And they were forced to use pesticides, which we never have to do with the old-fashioned system.'

During the harvest it was Alfio's job to ferry sacks full of pistachios back to the farm from the *lochi* where the pickers were working. He was about to set off again and so I jumped into the car beside him for the treacherous journey across lava fields on an almost vertical route. We pulled up at last in front of one of the little houses built on the edge of *lochi* everywhere. There is employment for anyone who wants it during harvest, and by camping out in those small buildings, families were able to turn a stint of very hard work into a sort of holiday in the country. Alfio led me along the whisper of a path beside the building, over a great bolus of lava and down into the *loco*. Suddenly we were among another tight-knit community of trees, growing from the lava wherever it had fallen in lumps and mounds, or as a loose, sharp scree. Pistachio farmers in Iran and California plant their trees in rows on even ground, and pick the nuts with a machine. A machine capable of coping with Bronte's awkward, tree-packed landscape has never been invented. So picking, and other jobs, like weeding between the trees and pruning, must all be done by hand, just as they have always been done, ever since Arab farmers worked these slopes. Alfio told me that some people rebelled against these conditions by purchasing ready-grafted trees from a local nursery. This gave them the advantage of being able to plant the trees wherever they liked, but unlike trees grafted on to wild rootstock, nursery-grown trees were delicate and had to be watered.

When we first arrived the *loco* looked deserted, but then I began to spot the pickers, like birds hidden among the trees. Some were young, some old, some Sicilian and some Romanian. Some talked and others were silent, but they were all working hard under the eye of Sebastiano. Tightly upholstered in a sporty white shirt and clean jeans, Sebastiano headed up that disparate team, pointing out nuts that had been missed or dropped and tying the tops of full sacks. He also selected a few people to sling those 50-kilo bundles over their shoulders before staggering off across the uneven terrain to Alfio's car. Meanwhile, every tree made slightly different demands on the pickers. Some were able to stand comfortably beside the tree while pulling pale pink clusters of nuts from its branches. Others were tackling trees that demanded deference, and could only be picked while they squatted or even knelt on the sharp lava beside or below them. And then there were trees that had their pickers clambering up among their all-too-bendy branches. Everyone wore the kind of heavy boots you use to climb Etna, which is, in effect what they were doing as they scrambled across that lava field from first light each day. The other essential equipment was a bulky plastic basket worn with a strap across one shoulder. By positioning themselves beneath a branch, the pickers could pull the nuts directly into the basket. With each new handful it grew heavier, and the job of staying upright on the uneven ground got ever more difficult.

One of the pickers was a boy dressed in bright jeans and a flowery shirt, with a baseball cap perched backwards on his head. 'You're looking smart,' I said. 'Me? These are just my old clothes. I'll be throwing them away after harvest because of the *colla*.' All the members of the *Pistacia* family are full of this sappy resin, or 'glue' as he called it, and pickers must wear gloves to protect their hands. Smart nevertheless in his orange jeans, he told me he usually worked on his father's cattle farm, but in common with 60 per cent of Bronte's population, he had taken time off for the harvest. The streets were virtually empty, in fact, from the end of August to the middle of September, when everyone was out in the country picking nuts. Like everybody else he was keen to chat while he worked. 'Pistachios are hot,' he said, 'and if you eat too many you'll get a temperature.' For a moment lava wasn't the only thing that had ground to a halt on the hillside, and we were two ancient Greeks well-versed in Galen's doctrine of humours. If either of us had been naturally choleric, we would have been fools to feed our anger with 'hot' pistachios. Now his friend chipped in with, 'Pistachios are supposed to be an aphrodisiac, but I've never eaten enough of them to know.' Another time warp, and we were returning to beliefs that might have echoed across those slopes in the ninth or tenth centuries, when Arab farmers might have hoped to increase their virility by eating pistachios. Chatter ricocheted easily from tree to tree, and every so often a joke or a question echoed across the mountainside. By now it was midday, the heat was striking up from the lava underfoot, and beating down from the sky above. The men passed round a plastic barrel of water like a wine sack, throwing back their heads to glug it down without allowing their lips ever to touch the spout.

Sebastiano told me they would be back in the *lochi* in January to prune out dead or crowded branches. It would be a very different place then, the air cold and crisp, and the vast, snow-covered summit of Etna always in the background, like a full moon in the sky. The trees would be bare, the tips of their branches straining groundwards, as if they were gymnasts reaching out for balance during some complex move. The team would return again in May for the 'green pruning' peculiar to pistachios. This only happened during a rest year for the trees, and involved the meticulous removal of all the *occhi*, or 'eyes', as the flower buds are known. Sebastiano was well versed in the logic for cropping only on alternate years. 'This terrain is full of minerals,' he said, 'but it isn't easy for the trees to access them, and if they produced nuts every year they would become exhausted.' He said *l'anno di riposo* – the rest year – allowed them to accumulate the water and nutrients they needed to bear a good crop.

Despite late spring cold and ferocious summer heat that year, the trees were laden with nuts. 'Eat, eat!' Sebastiano insisted, stripping a spray from the end of a branch and handing me a plush yellow nut flushed with pink. We all know how to open the split shell of a pistachio and slip the nut from its bitter, outer skin, but Sebastiano also taught me the technique for prising open those annoying shells that are sealed tight like a clam. Holding the tiny nut delicately between his huge fingers, he pointed out the little yellow button on the end of the shell where it had been attached to the stem. Then he put the opposite end between the very tips of his big white teeth, pressing down gently until it popped apart like a tiny spring. And there it was. Damp like a thing newborn from the parched landscape, a dazzling gem with a bright purple outer skin, emerald-green flesh, and a flavour so sappy and fresh it was like eating the very essence of tree; a little sweet, a little caramelized, even a little savoury, and utterly unique.

By now the last sacks were being loaded into Alfio's car and, for lack of an alternative space, I lay indecorously down on top of them for the bumpy journey back to the farm. There the nuts went into the queue for *smallatura*, the shelling done by a machine that needed constant feeding to keep it rattling and chugging away all day. Stripped of their shells, they were tipped onto the ground and raked over again and again until they were dry. With the late-summer sun still blazing, it would have been only two or three days before they were ready to leave the farm, to be either eaten whole or processed into grains, bright green flours, pesto or sweet cream.

Walking through Bronte later that day, I noticed a cacophony of strange and urgent sounds coming from behind the pink front door of a house as I passed. The door was ajar and inside, not that I should have been looking, was a huge bin full of pistachios. It stood in what should have been the small front room, but instead of chairs and sofas it was furnished with big, busy, elderly machines. The one closest to the door appeared ready to shoulder its way out onto the street. But instead it was trapped in a perpetual dance in that small space. It was grading nuts by sending them through sieves of different sizes, shunting the biggest into the bin I had seen by the door, and shooting smaller ones of various sizes into different sacks. Although the nuts had been shelled immediately after picking, they were all tightly enclosed in a second layer of woody protection. Removing this husk was the job of the other machine in the room. Imagine the cacophony of shaking metal and shaking nuts, then add the sound of the nuts rolling round and round a metal drum until they fall through holes that will strip them of their husks.

In the tiny room next door were two more machines expressly designed to process this most demanding nut. They were big machines in a small space, and the two men bent over them were like a vision from the early years of the industrial revolution, a cottage industry of the kind that involved ruining your eyesight while bending double. One man sat in front of a pyramid of nuts on a small table. It was his job to sort them one by one, spotting any rogues still wearing their husks. The other was peering at a bucket of nuts beside the machine that should have blown any dust or shredded husks away. He was the equivalent of the proofreader in that long process, the one entrusted with spotting any final errors that might undermine the quality of the entire product.

Of course, nuts are also processed in Bronte by modern machinery in conventional, industrial units. But here's the thing about the town's pistachio business: it is open to anyone, so that even people with a single tree in their gardens are part of an international trade that has made emerald-green pistachios grown in Bronte's lava fields famous all over the world.

16.
A Winemaking Revolution

Of all the stories embedded in Etna's landscape, there is none so dramatic as that of winemaking, with its rollercoaster succession of triumphs and disasters, and two periods of quite extraordinary success. The first of these high points straddled the eighteenth and nineteenth centuries, and the other is still unfolding as I write. This miraculous vinous renaissance has attracted attention all over the wine-drinking world and fuelled the creation of a new, dynamic and international community of winemakers.

When the Greeks arrived on Etna 3,000 years ago, they began to cultivate and train the wild vines they found scrambling over the flanks of the volcano. They were quick to understand the benefits of growing vines there, for as the Greek geographer and historian Strabo wrote at the end of the first century BC:

> although the ash is an affliction at the time, it fertilizes the country for future seasons . . . making the soil well-suited to the vine, and beneficial to other crops.

Winemaking was established on Etna by the time the Romans arrived, and they delivered a wealth of new knowledge and techniques from all over the empire, embedding practices that endure to this day. Etna wines were soon so popular that local traders exported them to the mainland, and even to Rome itself. During the Middle Ages, there were thousands of hectares of vineyards on Etna, many planted on land that belonged to monasteries or the Church. Some of these institutions would donate young vines to new tenants, in a bid to get them off to a good start.

Jump to the sixteenth century, and the prospects of tenant farmers on Etna improved still further when a local bishop was made Count of Mascali, the small town that would eventually be eradicated during the eruption of 1928. He revolutionized land tenure by granting local *contadini* long, or even perpetual, leases on stretches of Etna's precious soil under the *emfiteusi*, or emphyteusis, system. In return they were obliged to pay a modest rent and invest in improving the land. The clue as to what these improvements might be was in the name, for *emfiteusi* derives from a Greek word meaning 'to plant' or 'graft'. *Contadini* in Mascali now had all the security they needed to make the long-term investment of clearing the ground of lava, building terraces and retaining walls, and planting vineyards in the rich soil. And the yield of those vineyards improved year on year, because now the *contadini* had time to maximize productivity by repeatedly selecting and propagating the best vines. Over time, their efforts created such healthy biodiversity that by the mid-nineteenth century there would be over forty different varieties of vines growing on Etna, not to mention all the fruit and olive trees they planted to grow among them.

Land on Etna's maritime flank had been managed in the same way for over 200 years by the time a young Florentine called Domenico Sestini arrived in 1774 to study winemaking in Mascali. He was so startled by the contrast between its landscape and that of the bleak, feudal estates he had seen elsewhere, that he described it in almost biblical terms. It had been transformed, he said, from a 'horrid place, and uncultivated land . . . into a delightful garden . . .' The slopes surrounding the town were carpeted in beautiful vineyards and, instead of being abandoned by their absentee landlords, they were looked after by local farmers who lived in 'fine and comfortable homes', so as to 'better attend to the economy of their lands'. A few years later the French political scientist, politician and historian Alexis de Tocqueville was so impressed that he went so far as to describe Etna as:

> a kind of enchanted country which anywhere would be striking; but in Sicily is ravishing. Orchard succeeds orchard, surrounding

cottages and pretty villages; no spot is lost; everywhere there is an appearance of prosperity and plenty.

He also named it 'the only part of Sicily where the peasant is a proprietor'. A good thing, he thought, in a country where 'the higher classes are sunk into hereditary sloth and vice'.

The little houses in that intensely worked landscape often formed one side of a small farmyard enclosed by a stable, a bread oven and a pigsty. Almost every house also had a *palmento* beside it, where eighteenth-, nineteenth-, and even late-twentieth-century farmers continued to make wine in much the same way as the Romans. The international wine merchants who now began to arrive on Etna were drawn by the promise of wines stable enough to be shipped without deteriorating, or worse still, turning to vinegar. Wines made from grapes grown on that volcanic soil were naturally stable because of the acidity imbued in them by the mineral content of the soil, and the response of the grapes themselves to the dramatic drop in night-time temperatures typical of the volcano. Long hours of sunshine also contributed to the wines' stability by developing the grape sugars that ensured all Etna wines were high in alcohol. Alongside these natural characteristics were the skills of the winemakers in those little *palmenti*, of course, and according to one commentator, their wines were not only 'suitable for navigation', but might even be expected to improve in transit, so they would reliably be of 'good quality, grateful to taste, and much appreciated at the table'.

At first there was no port for sending off the wine the merchants bought, and it was shipped in boats from a small jetty on the coast below Mascali. As demand grew, however, that obscure little place was transformed, and by the end of the 1770s it was a thriving port full of shipwrights, sailors, dockers, coopers, shopkeepers, lawyers, and above all, wine merchants. They called this new place 'Riposto' because of all the warehouses where barrels of wine were *riposti*, 'stored'. And never mind who made it or where it came from, the whole lot was mixed together and named *Vino di Riposto*, just as Marsala was named for the port from which it was exported.

The volcano may have been an isolated place, cut off by poor roads from both its own interior and the rest of Sicily, but this new port put it at the heart of the international wine trade. And no ship carrying wine ever left Riposto without a wonderful mix of other products from the mountain. Farmers all along Etna's coastline now began exporting fresh and dried fruit, pistachios, almonds, olive oil, rice, honey, spices, cured meat, salted anchovies and raw silk. There were also plenty of false pepper trees (*Schincus molle*) growing in parched ravines around Etna. Local bandits sold their bright pink fruits as pink peppercorns and exported them all over Europe, although truth be told, they were completely unrelated to true pepper. Meanwhile, more honest farmers were tapping into the American citrus trade with oranges, lemons and mandarins grown in the warm coastal climate.

Vino di Riposto was soon so renowned that the British Royal Navy began to stock up on it. To grasp what this might have meant for the income of Etna winemakers and merchants, you only have to consider the 40,000 gallons of table wine that Nelson and his fleet picked up in Sicily in 1798, on their way to the Battle of the Nile. This is not a comment on how much sailors drank, for there were thousands of men in the fleet. However, it is some indication of what the demand for wine might have been during the Napoleonic Wars, when the Royal Navy made Riposto its centre of operations for a blockade to stop the French taking control of the Mediterranean. Its presence created an additional opportunity for winemakers, because behind the Royal Navy blockade cargo ships were able to make regular crossings to Malta, which soon became one of the most important markets for Etna wine, as well as brandy and grappa, not to mention snow.

It seems almost inevitable now that Etna's honest, traditional winemakers should eventually have been corrupted by merchants struggling to satisfy an ever-increasing demand for *Vino di Riposto*. The grapes produced on Etna's almost magical soils were as good as ever, but by 1814 wine was already being so poorly made that it had to be 'polluted' with great quantities of sulphur to stop it turning to vinegar. Or so said William H. Smyth, sent to Sicily to survey its coastline for the Admiralty in London. Things had gone from bad to worse by 1839, when Diego Costarelli, an interesting local figure, who was both a priest and an expert in education, urban planning and viticulture, wrote an essay on the subject, tellingly entitling it *Considerazioni sullo stato economico e morale delle popolazioni abitanti sulla costa orientale dell'Etna* ('Thoughts Regarding the Economic and Moral Condition of the Inhabitants of Etna's East Flank'). He was the first person to blame the sharp decline in the quality of local wines on the merchants in Riposto, whom he accused of dragging everyone on the mountain down to their own disgraceful level. This was easily done by rewarding producers to make wine of such poor quality that they could buy it from them at rock-bottom prices, and then sell it on at an enormous profit. If a determined producer insisted on making better and therefore more expensive wine, he could find no one to buy it. And in this unscrupulous way Riposto's wine merchants broke the spirits of even the best winemakers on the volcano.

Despite its poor quality, the demand for *Vino di Riposto* was still relentless by the time tiny, aphid-like phylloxera hitched into France on the roots of vines imported from America. As they worked their way through the country, destroying vineyards everywhere, French wine merchants began to seek supplies in Riposto. Until now *Vino di Riposto* had always been a table wine, but the French were after the much coarser cutting wine known as *vino da taglio*, for blending with any northern European wines they could still get their hands on. There were even whispers that they sometimes bottled those blended wines and passed them off as their own under false labels. Etna winemakers rose to the occasion, business boomed, and farmers all over the volcano grubbed up the last remaining orchards and olive and nut groves and replaced them with yet more vineyards. The demand seemed almost insatiable, and some winemakers sought to meet it by installing the first pneumatic or electric presses. In the town of Viagrande on Etna's south flank, they added another strand to their success by making an anise liqueur that could be sold to the French as a substitute for their absinthe.

Of course, the inevitable happened and in 1880 phylloxera arrived on Etna, putting an end to the business that shapes the landscape of Etna's east flank to this day, spelling bankruptcy for wine merchants, and the many people in Riposto who depended on trades and businesses associated with wine. And things were no better in the countryside. There winemakers had lost their customers, vineyard owners had lost the market for their grapes, and foremen, labourers and grape pickers had lost their jobs. Even timber merchants went out of business, because no one needed the sweet-chestnut stakes used for training and supporting vines anymore, or sweet-chestnut wood to make barrels. Thousands of people emigrated to Australia and America, taking with them skills and traditions learned over many generations on Etna's soil.

Etna lost yet more of her rural population during the First and Second World Wars, and in 1928 she added to the suffering of those who remained with the colossal eruption that engulfed Mascali and all the remaining vineyards around it. Winemaking had reached its nadir, and there were abandoned vineyards all over the volcano. Left to its own devices, the ground was infested by a shady tide of myrtle, gorse and bramble, and weed trees hogged the terraces, dismantling them with their roots. The volcano added to the dismal atmosphere of those desolate plots by gradually interring them in layers of ash so that, still enclosed by walls, they looked like forgotten rooms in some ruined mansion, dusty, drab and deserted.

There was nothing in this bleak scenario to presage what would happen next, and the story of how winemaking on Etna was not only revived at the beginning of this century, but raised to a whole new level, is told again and again, as if people were still struggling to believe the miracle unfolding before their eyes. Every version of that winemaking renaissance begins in 1988, when Giuseppe Benanti bought land on Etna's north and east flanks. Benanti was a local man and a scientist, and he was so appalled by the poor wines now produced on Etna that he set out to revive the tradition of

A Winemaking Revolution

high-quality wines made exclusively from native grapes. Working with a young oenologist called Salvo Foti, he released his first vintage in 1990, and it immediately won prizes at festivals both in Italy and abroad. This was wonderful news, but one successful *cantina* was never going to be enough to revive Etna's international profile as a wine region. Her true renaissance came only when three remarkable winemakers arrived on the volcano at the beginning of the twenty-first century, because all three already had an international following, and they drew attention to Etna simply by being there. But what brought them to Etna in the first place? Ask Marco De Grazia, now owner of the Tenuta delle Terre Nere estate between Solicchiata and the town of Randazzo on Etna's north face, and he will tell you that he first came to Etna on business, but then recognized its wonderful, untapped potential.

By the time he arrived in Sicily, De Grazia was already renowned as a maverick in the wine world and an exporter of fine Italian wines. During the 1980s he had been one of the so-called 'Barolo Boys', who revolutionized winemaking in Piemonte and made Barolo into one of the most famous red wines in the world. Andrea Franchetti was another new arrival on Etna. He already produced famous wines at Tenuta di Trinoro, his estate in a remote corner of Tuscany. On Etna, he chose a tumbledown farmhouse and *cantina* in Passopisciaro, and planted acres of vineyards climbing the slopes to almost 1,000 metres. Frank Cornellisen, a former wine trader from Belgium, and a key figure in the world of natural wines, was the third in this constellation of stars.

Once again, Etna's soil is at the heart of this success story. Almost as soon as they arrived, De Grazia and Franchetti were struck by the difference between it and the soils of other wine-producing regions in the world. Elsewhere, vines grow in soils formed by geological events many millions of years ago. On Etna the soil rests on, or directly derives from, the lava flows of eruptions that may have occurred only thousands – or perhaps even hundreds – of years ago. This creates a vast variety of soils on which grapes can be grown. What is more, the regulations for Etna DOC (*Denominazione di*

Origine Controllata) wines defined an area of production extending from 400 to 1,000 metres above sea level. This created an extraordinary contrast between vineyards at the highest altitudes, where conditions were similar to those in northern Italy, and those on the lower slopes, where the climate was more Mediterranean. A change of only 50 metres can make a huge impact on the ripening of grapes and the concentration of sugars in them, so it is not hard to imagine the diversity of wines that came with the 600-metre difference between the highest and lowest vineyards on Etna. The DOC also encircled the volcano like a crescent moon from the north to the southwest, with all the variation in rainfall and wind exposure this implied. Notwithstanding all these variations, ever since those DOC regulations were ratified in 1968, the wines had been defined simply as Etna Rosso, Etna Rosato (rosé), Etna Bianco and Etna Bianco Superiore. This was only a small step up from selling them all in the eighteenth and nineteenth centuries under the generic title of *Vino di Riposto*.

Like Franchetti, Marco De Grazia considered the ancient parcels of agricultural land on Etna known as *contrade* to be an equivalent of the French *crus*. The boundaries of Etna's *contrade* have always been defined by a combination of social history, geography, geology, tradition and growing conditions. Their names often give away something of their pasts. For example, De Grazia grows some of his grapes in a *contrada* called Feudo di Mezzo, 'half a fief', and others in one called Guardiola, the 'guard house'. Shortly after arriving on the mountain, he began campaigning for the change in DOC regulations that would allow producers to label their wines with the name of the *contrada* where the grapes in them had grown.

While De Grazia was fighting his battle over labelling, Franchetti was founding a very local wine festival that he called *Contrade dell'Etna*. He invited every single winemaker on the volcano to come to the inaugural event in 2008, bringing wine from their latest vintage with them. This was an opportunity for producers great and small to meet, and to taste each other's wines. By also sending invitations to journalists from Italy and abroad, Franchetti ensured that word of these exciting new wines began to spread. Despite his death in 2021, the festival continues to showcase, publicize and celebrate the infinite variety of the mountain's different *contrade* every year.

De Grazia finally won the campaign for diverse labelling in 2013. This has made for fascinating drinking ever since, for now as well as knowing the geographical zone of production, we can compare the nuanced flavours and aromas imbued by unique soils, microclimates, and aspects of individual *contrade* all over the volcano. Of all the wines I have tasted on Etna, the ones that spell out these differences most clearly come from De Grazia's own vineyards, where vines grow at various altitudes on lava flows from multiple different epochs.

I visited Tenuta delle Terre Nere one afternoon not long before my season in Sicily came to an end. Bleached grass grew to either side of the narrow road running towards the estate from Randazzo, so that driving down it felt like following a parting on the scalp of the landscape. The Alcantara valley in all its reliable gentleness lay to the left, and Etna's perpetual promise of uncertainty to the right.

It was a hot day, and so instead of walking out to the vineyards we chugged up there in a car slick with dust. Tenuta delle Terre Nere's forty-five hectares are divided into twenty-nine vineyards and seven *contrade*. Their names read like a poem: Calderara Sottana, San Lorenzo, Bocca d'Orzo, Guardiola, Santo Spirito, Moganazzi and Feudo di Mezzo. All are between 600 and 1,000 metres above sea level, and even within the same *contrada* there can still be enormous variations in conditions.

Everything seemed silenced by heat that afternoon, and the leaves of the vines in Santo Spirito were sunstruck and drooping. 'Watch this,' Marco said, as he slammed on the brakes. The car was immediately enveloped in feather-light ash soils so thick we could see nothing through the windows. Then came Calderara Sottana, one of only a handful of places on the north and east flanks of Etna where the product of eruptions between 15,000 and 60,000 years ago from the Ellittico, Etna's ancient ancestor, has survived. This may be almost absurdly young in geological terms, but it is the oldest soil available to winegrowers on Etna, and by happy chance it has never been overrun or submerged by more recent lava flows. We drove on, and within only a few metres we had left that ash landscape for soil mixed with visible pieces of lava. Then came different tones of grey volcanic sand, and eventually a particularly beautiful vineyard surrounded by lush woodland, where the young vines appeared to be growing almost like pistachio trees from the cracks between huge lumps of basalt and lava.

Most of the wines made on Etna's north face are red. Etna Rosso is pale, cherry coloured, and lean in the mouth. It is a fine wine, and instead of the sunny, overripe flavours usually associated with Italy's deep south, its mineral edge combines with aromas of red fruit and spices. These are no more than generalizations though. For the differences between the wines we tasted gave me the deepest and most visceral experience I have ever had of the range of nuanced flavours and styles that can be coaxed, metre by metre, from this terrain. The first wine Marco gave me was an Etna Rosso made from grapes grown in the ash of Santo Spirito. It was slightly dry, as all Etna Rosso is, and yet it encompassed a wonderful array of spicy, sensual, even voluptuous flavours that lingered on in the mouth. Remember that, as I tried so hard to do when we moved on to tasting the next wine. It was from Guardiola, another vineyard, another *contrada*, separated from Santo Spirito by no more than a few metres and a low stone wall. Across that short distance the soil changed, and the ground began to climb steeply uphill. Grapes growing in those colder temperatures are always the last on the estate to be harvested. This means they will also be among the last in Sicily, and perhaps even in Europe too. Instead of being curvaceous and sensual like the wine I had just tried, this was steely and blade like, and yet it also revealed a sweetness I found in none of the other red wines I tasted.

Next came a wonderfully fresh Nerello Mascalese Rosato (Etna rosé), and a princely Etna Rosso made from the grapes of forty- to fifty-year-old vines. Elsewhere, farmers grub up vines when their yields begin to drop at about thirty years old. Not at Tenuta delle Terre Nere, for like a few other lucky estates on Etna's north flank, it has two parcels of land where there are vines that survived the scourge of phylloxera. There is no official definition of what defines a vine as 'old', but those ungrafted vines have lived for at least 140 years, which makes wines created from their grapes uniquely precious.

The success of winemakers like Marco De Grazia has been the inspiration behind a comprehensive renaissance that sees anyone on Etna with a scrap of ground turning their hand to winemaking. And those not lucky enough to own land seek out a vineyard to rent. Roby Abbate is one of them. Like so many small-scale winemakers on Etna, he has another job, one that makes his living. Nevertheless he produces a couple of thousand bottles of Etna Rosso and Rosato each year from grapes in a vineyard in Passopisciaro, the traditional heart of winemaking on Etna's north flank. Profit really isn't his motive, and this makes him a *vignaiolo per passione*, 'a winemaker for the love of it', as he states so clearly on his wine label.

It was mid-October when Roby invited me to join him on the last day of their *vendemmia*, and not long before I was due to make the journey home. There had been a smell of grape must and wood smoke hanging in the air for days, and the lanes always seemed to be blocked by trailers overflowing with grapes. Autumn had come suddenly, bringing cold, damp nights and precious, golden days unless, as was equally likely, it was pouring with rain. There were mushroom baskets for sale on the side of the road in Randazzo, and the woods were full of furtive pickers who would never show me what they had found. Golden crocuses and tiny pink cyclamen flowered on the verges, and in vineyards all over the mountain the *vendemmia* was in full swing.

I got to Roby's place about ten minutes early. There was time enough to take in the old vines, stems as thick as my arm and leaves just turning from green to autumn gold. And after that, still time left over to worry, as I always will, about finding my place in a close-knit team of strangers who have probably been working together for decades. Then the pickers arrived and came tumbling out the back of an old army lorry. A man called Sergio, his black hair severely parted in the middle, went straight to a little tree beside the barn and picked an apple. 'Have some,' he said firmly, offering a sliver on the blade of his penknife, 'it will be good for you because it's organic, *genuino*.' If you hang about with people producing food of any kind in Sicily, you get used to these forceful invitations. I was still chomping obediently through apple slices when another man strolled over, this time proffering a bag bulging with warm *cornetti*. They had all been working since first light, and this was breakfast. 'Will you do me the honour of accepting one?' Of course I would, I must, and now with apple in my mouth, a sticky *cornetto* in one hand, a camera, a pen and a notebook to manage, I was disabled by kindness.

Soon the air was full of the heavy thud of fruit dropping into plastic buckets. I wouldn't have dreamed of asking if I could help. Grape picking is part of a profession, and who was I to blow in and pretend anyone could do it? There was a constant stream of banter, but when the men reverted back to dialect, I understood only one word in every ten, making me a true foreigner to those who couldn't – or wouldn't – speak anything else. Still, they satisfied their curiosity by asking others all about me, the only novel thing to have appeared in that field for years. One man – and they were all men – was always smoking a cigar, so that a sweet, blue haze hung constantly above our heads.

Roby was a busy man that day, forever on call to answer questions or supervise the loading of the grapes onto the lorry, and yet he welcomed me into that field as if it were his own sitting room. When the pickers ran out of boxes I made a valiant attempt to help by running off to get them, calling back over my shoulder, 'I'll go, I'm doing nothing.' And so it was they allowed me to carry three plastic boxes down the row for a few metres before someone rushed to take them from me. Idle again, I watched a cat with no tail picking its way through the long grass, saw cloud pouring off Etna's summit, concealing and revealing it, casting us in cool shade one moment, and then back into baking sun. A lizard basked on a lump of lava, soaking up the energy radiating from its dark surface, the frantic beat of a minuscule heart quivering in its side.

Roby explained that most of the grapes they picked were Nerello Mascalese. This has always been one of the most common indigenous varieties on Etna. The literal translation of *nerello* is 'little black grape', a reference to the scarcity of pigment in their skins. And as for Mascalese, it refers to Mascali, of course, that great centre of eighteenth- and nineteenth-century wine production. Nerello is renowned for its sensitivity to place, and the only great wines ever made with it are from grapes grown on Etna's precious soils. Roby also pointed out a few of the Nerello Cappuccio vines so often thrown into the mix of an Etna vineyard. He told me they were named for leaves so big they look almost like a hood (*cappuccio*). Both vines have had thousands of years to adapt to conditions on the volcano, and they are well able to tolerate summer droughts on the north face, and the heavy autumn rains that often arrive just in time for the harvest. The *disciplinari* – regulations – defining Etna DOC wines stipulate that Etna Rosso and Rosato must contain at least 80 per cent Nerello Mascalese, and a maximum of 20 per cent Nerello Cappuccio. This gives winemakers the option of squeezing in a small percentage of the rare, local varieties that still survive in a few Etna vineyards.

Elsewhere, vines are usually trained horizontally along straight wires, but on Etna past and present conjoin, and they have been grown vertically up chestnut posts ever since the Romans first used a system now known as *alberello*, 'little tree'. In winter the vines really do look like miniature trees, with gnarled, contorted trunks, and three or four twisted branches emerging at knee height to form what are known as their 'shoulders'. Above that they fling their arms towards the sky, each one curving and curling on its own peculiar trajectory, as if they were dancing. The Romans also introduced the habit of planting those *alberello* vines in a quincunx, a group of five. This is still the tradition on Etna, as by spacing the vines at an equal distance from each other, it gives them all the same opportunity to benefit from sunlight, while allowing air to circulate freely between them. That said, the quincunx is also a means of fostering competition for, as Roby explained, this compels them to send their roots deeper into the ground, where they can take full advantage of the volcanic soil and all its minerals. Cultivating vines like this, in high-altitude, airy vineyards ensures they are healthy, and most producers on the mountain don't bother with pesticides or any other kind of treatment.

Like most other winemakers on the volcano's north flank, Roby focused his energies on producing Etna Rosso and Rosato. Etna's prized Bianco Superiore wines came from the high-altitude vineyards of my home in Milo on the east flank. It took only forty minutes to drive from Roby's vineyard in Passopisciaro to Milo, but for an Etna winemaker the journey ends amid such different conditions that they might almost belong to another country. Once again, the soil has a grand part to play in making the environment distinctive, because it is created from a unique melange of lava, mud and debris produced by the catastrophic collapse of Etna's east flank 8,000 years ago. Much more rain falls on Milo than anywhere else in Sicily, and this also plays its part. Then comes the length of the days. I knew all too well that they end sooner on the east flank than anywhere else because the sun must dip behind Etna's shoulder to set in the west. This leaves plenty of time for the air to cool at close of day, so that the drop in night-time temperatures can be as much as fifteen degrees. Taken together, all these conditions make Milo the ideal place for producing white wine, and indeed it is the only place where the DOC regulations permit Etna Bianco Superiore to be made. The DOC also stipulates that 80 per cent of the Bianco Superiore blend should consist of indigenous grapes. *Carico* means 'load', and the local Carricante vines were probably named for the sheer volume of grapes they produce. They seem to relish conditions in Milo's high-altitude vineyards, where they respond to the drop in night-time temperatures with high levels of acidity in grapes that give Bianco Superiore its characteristic freshness.

Marco Nicolosi describes Etna Bianco Superiore as the symbol of his family winery, Barone di Villagrande in Milo, and with good reason. Other winemakers have come and gone on Etna, but the Nicolosi have always been loyal to a patch of ground between the mountain and the sea. And their honest, decent, and now exceptional wines have run like a golden thread through the variable history of Etna winemaking for almost 300 years. Over the centuries the family has brought numerous innovations and improvements to winemaking on the volcano. For example, Marco's ancestor Paolo Nicolosi made the first ever Etna Bianco there in 1869. Carmelo Nicolosi Asmundo brought the first refrigerators to Etna in the 1950s, and it was Marco's father, Carlo Nicolosi Asmundo, who drew up the regulations defining Etna DOC wines.

When I tasted Barone di Villagrande's Bianco Superiore Contrada over lunch with Marco, I was struck first by minerality so sharp it reminded me of light glinting off the dazzling surface of the sea far below. The kitchen had whipped up a gloriously oily dish of fresh *mozzarella*, creamed aubergines and confit tomatoes for us, with warm focaccia to mop it all up. After a mouthful of that, I took the next sip of wine. It cut clean through the delicious oiliness of the confit, and as if that had employed all its acidity, it began to release sweeter, brown-sugar flavours, so that each sip thereafter had more to say. This complexity comes from age, for the Carricante grapes make Barone di Villagrande's Bianco Superiore one of those unusual white wines that can be guaranteed to go on improving in the bottle for up to a decade. Its acidity guarantees its long life, and yet given time, the wine develops nuanced flavours and perfumes so unusual in a white that many people now compare it to Riesling.

I never expected it to be so, but of all the conversations I had about Etna's famously fertile soils, the most illuminating were with winemakers. Other people talked to me about soil in general terms, but winemakers broke the surface of the volcano down, metre by metre, showing me what a cornucopia of opportunities it offered.

And by tasting elegant wines from Barone di Villagrande and Tenuta delle Terre Nere, I experienced those variations in the most visceral way possible, so that I came away with a sense of having glimpsed the volcano's very DNA. But Etna's restless landscape can never be stilled, and there is always something more to come, some new drama on the horizon. I drove away wondering what the next chapter would be in that sensational agricultural history.

17.
Eruption!

Although it felt irresponsible, and certainly un-neighbourly, I had spent much of my time on Etna hoping for a repeat of the eruption I had seen years before. Even at a distance it had cast its spell, sending me on a journey that would seem to have no destination without another show of that unbridled force at close quarters, and from a place of better understanding. It was this that sent me up to Etna's summit again, for even if she wouldn't erupt, at least I could look into the craters from which eruption might one day come. This time I joined a walk up to Bocca Nuova. The air was so thin up there that it made my legs heavy and my head light. I stood on the crater's edge and looked straight down onto the great slicks of colour – reds, whites, browns, yellows and acid greens – painting walls that enclosed a fuming, broiling bowl of unrest. Had I made that climb a couple of months earlier, there would have been only two modest vents at the bottom of the crater, each barely 10 metres wide. Since then, both of them had collapsed in on themselves, becoming vast pits with ragged edges, their dark depths unknowable. What's more, they were collapsing still and, despite the buffeting wind, I could hear the sound of rocks tumbling as their sides continued to give way. For now, the only thing emerging from them was a startling, stinking miasma of pale gas that billowed over me, hinting vividly at suffocation and setting my eyes and nose streaming. My hands were veined with the grey ash that had found its way into each tiny crack in my skin, as though the volcano were dressing me in her own clothing. The steep, sterile landscape surrounding me was made entirely from the Earth's insides, as if our planet had spent the past 15,000 years turning out its pockets. Nobody knew what might come next in that restless, impermanent, unpredictable place. Tracking the unfolding drama would be like trying to record a volatile political situation, the parameters changing from day to day.

Walking back home, across the top of Etna's west flank, I gazed right across the island in one direction to the north coast, and could even make out the Isole Eolie rising dark and mysterious from the dazzling blue water of the Tyrrhenian Sea. Looking in the other direction, I could just see the familiar, lava-strewn coast where Etna's lower slopes dipped into the Ionian. Those glorious, sweeping views placed me firmly in the Mediterranean. Yet I knew now that the volcano was also a world apart, an island within an island, with its own peculiar combination of climates and conditions that I had finally come to know and appreciate as if it were my own home.

I had learned so much more about all that Etna encompassed, and thanks to the people around me, I understood that, although she was a robber through and through, she was more likely to steal your livelihood than your life. And in return, as I had been told again and again, she would give back much more than she had ever taken away. I had a sense of what those gifts might be now. As well as heaping the table with what one friend described as 'the very best from land and sea', I had seen that Etna gave her inhabitants all they could ask for in the way of building materials, timber, water and the deep connections that form the fabric of any resilient and successful community. Nevertheless, the risks of living in a landscape as likely to explode into eruption as be riven by earthquake were undeniable, and I had observed people taking comfort from a unique cocktail of rigorous science emanating from the INGV, and church rituals that enlivened every season of the year. To outsiders, those saints' days and processions might have looked like religious events in Catholic countries all over southern Europe. But I had seen that they were peculiar to each small town and village, and had been finetuned to precisely meet the needs of people squaring up to the real and present dangers of living on Europe's most active volcano. I saw too how enacting those ceremonies could serve as an antidote to the absolute helplessness they might otherwise feel when confronted by Etna's unbridled power. Perhaps we should all be inspired by them to dig deep into the ancient rituals peculiar to our own local communities. Who knows what we might uncover there, but let's hope that it will be ceremonies from a time when we were more closely aligned with those untameable forces of the natural world.

Eruption hangs like a spell over Etna's landscape, impossible to imagine until it is cast. I knew something was happening at last when, one autumn evening, the sun set behind a tangle of thick, brown, ash-laden cloud pumping from the south-east crater. Lava is like fireworks, best appreciated in the dark, and so I went out again after supper to see what I could see. There were already a couple of other people down in the piazza in Milo. We stood side by side, gazing at a pinprick of light flickering like something alive in the darkness, and illuminating the first snow on slopes high above us. After so many months of talking and thinking about eruption, of reading books about it, looking at paintings, photographs and videos, this was how it started.

The following evening, the flow from the vent high on the crater was three times the size, and by the night after that a glorious, deep orange ribbon of lava was snouting a curving path downhill, the snow around it and the smoke billowing across it all doubly illuminated now by a full moon. And so it went on, night after night, until the mountain above us was a great mess of lava. The sight of it reminded me now of those long-exposure photographs of cars moving along a road in the dark, with the glowing lava standing in for the long red streaks of their rear lights on a multi-lane motorway. How many millions of people had stood as I was standing, and gazed up at this promise of destruction? How many poems, prayers and songs had been composed to capture exactly the emotions I was feeling? For a moment I had a sense of a great tide of human experience spanning thousands of years on the volcano, and like someone slipping into the waters of a gigantic river I felt myself become part of it, and be carried along.

During the day the crater belched dense, brown plumes of smoke that held their shapes, and set off across the sky like a parade of strange, stooped figures with bulbous noses and enormous ears. White smoke rose off lava as it tracked its way down the side of the crater. When the wind was right, it transformed Etna into a mystical, magic mountain, lost in a translucent white haze. However, the best special effects came at sunset, when the volcano was just an inky cut-out against the sky, and the setting sun backlit smoke and fumes pouring from her summit, turning them to gold.

The voice of the volcano was with me every waking moment of those final days, a deep bass sound like crashing waves on a cliff or distant thunder. In the morning her low grumbles were mixed with the sweet sound of birds calling in the woods, and the school bus toiling up the road below the house. But in the silence of my kitchen late at night, everything sounded louder and a little more threatening. Then it was as if someone were shifting heavy furniture in the attic I didn't have. Meanwhile, life in the village continued as normal; this was turning into what they call 'a tourist eruption', a pretty spectacle that does no one any harm. After a week or so, lava flowing from the vent in the side of the crater was tumbling into Valle del Leone, the steep valley immediately below it, and then flowing benignly into the Valle del Bove. Night after night I joined groups of onlookers in fields, gateways and laybys to watch the performance, a lovely decoration in the dark. The sky above was navy blue and studded with stars. Sometimes there were pinpricks of moving torchlight high on the slopes above, as people climbed to a viewpoint opposite the south-east crater, to watch the eruption at close quarters after dark.

The prospect of being right up there in the dark was irresistible. Eventually, a few of us, all drawn to the eruption, met up late one afternoon at Rifugio Citelli, where Biagio, the trusty guide from Etna Nord, was already pulling on his boots. We were headed for a high-altitude viewpoint that would give us a clear view of the eruption on the southeast crater. There was no easy way to get there, and so we set briskly off through the afternoon heat over rough, rocky paths overlaid with a purgatory of slippery ash. I was already familiar with the route leading up through the birch woods, and knew it to be precipitous from the start. At first the trees were dense, their clean limbs, as pale and smooth as human skin, giving us a solid, silken handhold as we hauled ourselves upwards. But they got smaller as we climbed, until they were no more than bushes crouching low to either side of the path. Now we needed to pick our way across smooth runnels through the rock still running with snowmelt from Etna's peak, even though it was already midsummer. Biagio paused to tell us that 70,000 years ago, snowmelt from the towering peak of Trifoglietto would have taken the same course down these rocky runnels, so that for a moment its ancient bones seemed to be breaking the surface of the ground.

The air thinned as we climbed, while the heat and the skiddy, ash-strewn surfaces underfoot made every stage of our walk feel arduous. However, after a few steep kilometres we reached one of the most spectacular lava caves on the mountain. We had to bend double to get inside Grotta di Serracozzo, but straightening up again we found ourselves under such a glorious pitched roof, it was as if we had stepped into the soaring architecture of a Gothic cathedral. Beyond it a rounded lava tube unscrolled like the smooth, sinuous belly of a gigantic snake. Light coming in through a small hole in the roof illuminated walls that had been striped and fluted with beautiful tide marks left by the lava that coursed through it during the eruption. Their varying colours and textures were the signature of each subtle change in its speed, and the cargoes of gases and minerals it carried with it. The place felt ancient, and yet it had only been created during the eruption of 1971.

A steep scramble took us away from the cave and on up the side of the valley until we tumbled over the crest onto Serra delle Concazze, one of the towering cliffs overlooking the Valle del Bove. Shadows were already falling across the valley hundreds of metres below, turning it into a dark scar, eerie and forbidding. On we went along the *serra*, light failing, wind rising over a vast wilderness of steep, loose lava that sunk and slid beneath out feet, filling our boots to the brim, and offering no respite or place to rest. We were in the *Deserta* again, and the only living things apart from us were a few sparse clumps of Sicilian milkvetch, concealing its vicious spines as usual beneath blameless leaves.

The sun was going down by the time we finally arrived at a magnificent viewpoint opposite the erupting vent in the side of the south-east crater. Biagio had ingeniously brought us to a spot almost level with it, and yet we were also at a perfectly safe distance. Dusk fell quietly over the slopes all around us, but the other side of the valley was a frenzy of activity. The sky was pale blue, and ash bursting from the vent turned pink in the last rays of the setting sun. Huge, white clouds came and went, concealing and then dramatically revealing the crater. Pink, white and pale blue, a pastel look for Etna I had never seen before. The darker it got, the brighter the exploding lava became, like a series of firework displays, firing black lapilli into the surrounding darkness. In the midst of all these swirling effects, one thing never changed, and that was the thump of small explosions that were as regular as Etna breathing. Watching this drama unfold in the gathering dusk, I knew where dragons came from, and all those flying sparks made the idea of Hephaestus' forge in the bowels of the volcano just as credible.

When darkness finally fell, the ash cloud turned black as diesel fumes, and the temperature dropped minute by minute. We had set off in hot, afternoon sunshine, but now it was barely four degrees in the icy wind. Eventually we had to turn our backs on the show and run away down soft, steep slopes made from the lava and ash of countless other eruptions, as if we were being chased out of the *Deserta* and back to the woods below, where trees and plants were filling the tepid air with the smell of life.

Four years have come and gone since I first arrived on Etna with few possessions and a bagful of questions. My season in Milo was over all too soon, but it is never long before I miss the crunch of lava beneath my feet, or the view of the moon rising from the dark sea far below, and so I return as often as possible. I used to ask myself if I could ever feel at home in a place defined by upheaval and impermanence, but running down from Etna's summit through that familiar landscape, I already knew the answer.

*The mind cannot carry away all that it has to give,
nor does it always believe possible what it has carried away.*

Nan Shepherd, *The Living Mountain*

Further Reading

Abate, T., and Branca S. (2016), *Il disegno delle eruzioni storiche dell'Etna: Percorsi iconografici dal XVI secolo ad oggi*. Palermo: Edizioni Caracol.

Antonelli, G. (1928), *Saggio di selvicoltura*. Torino: Paravia & Co.

Barbera, G. (2007), *Tutti frutti*. Milano: Oscar Mondadori.

Baron, A. (2011), *There's No Home*. London: Sort of Books.

Bjornerud, M. (2020), *Timefulness: How Thinking Like a Geologist Can Help Save The World*. Princeton, NJ: Princeton University Press.

Branca, S., Azzaro, R., De Beni, E., Chester, D., and Duncan, A. (2015), 'Impacts of the 1669 Eruption and the 1693 Earthquakes on the Etna Region, (Eastern Sicily): An Example of Recovery and Response of a Small Area to Extreme Events'. *Journal of Volcanology and Geothermal Research*, 303, pp. 24–40.

Bronte Insieme, 'A Short History of Bronte'. http://www.bronteinsieme.it.

Brydone, P. (1774), *A tour through Sicily and Malta. In a series of letters to William Beckford etc.* London: Forgotten Books.

Caffo, L. (2022), *La Montagna di fuoco, Etna: la Madre*. Milano: Adriano Salani Editore.

Calaresu, M. (2013), *Making and Eating Ice Cream in Naples: Rethinking Consumption and Sociability in the Eighteenth Century*. https://www.jstor.org/stable/24543621.

Cavallaro, F., Reitano, A. (2013), *Le Grotte dell'Etna, conoscerle e visitarle*. Palermo: Edizioni Danaus.

Chester, D. K., Duncan, A. M., Dibben, C., Guest, J. E., and Lister, P. H. (1999), 'Mascali, Mount Etna Region Sicily: An Example of Fascist Planning During the 1928 Eruption and its Continuing Legacy'. *Natural Hazards*, 19 (1), pp. 29–46. doi:https://doi.org/10.1023/a:1008001003888.

Conedera, M., Krebs, P., Tinner, W., Pradella, M., and Torriani, D. (2004), 'The Cultivation of Castanea sativa (Mill.) in Europe, from its Origin to its Diffusion on a Continental Scale'. *Vegetation History and Archaeobotany*, 13(3).

Crimi, V. (n.d.), *La resinazione del pino*. [online] Etnalcantara. http://www.etnalcantara.it/resinazione.htm.

D'Addezio, G. (2025), '25 Years of INGV's Education and Outreach: Bridging Science and Society'. *Journal of Geoethics and Social Geosciences*, (02, Special Issue). doi:https://doi.org/10.13127/jgsg-66.

David, E. (1995), *Harvest of the Cold Months*. London: Viking Adult.

De Amicis (1908), Edmondo. *Ricordi d'un viaggio in Sicilia*. Catania.

De Tocqueville, A. (1862), 'Extracts from the Tour in Sicily'. *Memoir, Letters and Remains of Alexis de Tocqueville. Translated by the Translator of Napoleon's Correspondence with King Joseph*. Boston: Ticknor and Fields.

Drago, E. (2022), *Quando il vino si fa storia: gli antichi palmenti rupestri siciliani*. [online] Le Vie dei Tesori. https://www.leviedeitesori.com/quando-il-vino-si-fa-storia-gli-antichi-palmenti-rupestri-siciliani/.

Duffy, C. (2013), *The Landscape of the Sublime 1700–1830: Classic Ground*. New York: Palgrave Macmillan.

Elliot, F. (1881), *Diary of an Idle Woman in Sicily*. London: Richard Bentley and Son.

Foti, S. (2020), *Etna: The Wines of the Volcano*. Catania: Maimone Editore.

Ganz, C. (2015), *Refrigeration: A History*. Jefferson, NC: McFarland & Co.

Giusti, M. (2022), *Il Castagno dei Cento Cavalli ha 2200 anni, e non solo*. [online] Agronomia. https://agronotizie.imagelinenetwork.com/agronomia/2022/09/20/il-castagno-dei-cento-cavalli-ha-2200-anni-e-non-solo/77071

Hamilton, W. (1771), 'An account of a journey to Mount Etna, in a letter from the Honourable William Hamilton, His Majesty's Envoy Extraordinary at Naples, to Mathew Maty, M. D. Sec. R.S.' *Philosophical Transactions of the Royal Society of London*, 60(60), pp. 1–19.

Latini, A. (2019), *The Modern Steward or the Art of Preparing Banquets Well*. Translated by T. Astarita. Arc Humanities Press.

Levi, C. (1959), *Words Are Stones*. Translated by A. Davidson. London: Victor Gollancz Ltd.

Mackay, J. (2021), *The Invention of Sicily*. London: Verso Books.

Mather, T. (2024), *Adventures in Volcanoland: What Volcanoes Tell Us About the World and Ourselves*. London: Abacus.

Further Reading

Mattioni, C. et al. (2020), 'Monuments Unveiled: Genetic Characterization of Large Old Chestnut (*Castanea sativa* Mill.) Trees, Using Comparative Nuclear and Chloroplast DNA Analysis'. *Forests*, 11(10), p. 1118.

Maxwell, G. (1959), *The Ten Pains of Death*. Stroud: Alan Sutton Publishing Ltd.

Mayor, A. (2001), *The First Fossil Hunters: Paleontology in Greek and Roman Times*. Princeton, NJ: Princeton University Press.

Mercatanti, L. (2013), 'Etna and the Perception of Volcanic Risk'. *Geographical Review*, [online] 103(4), pp. 486–97.

Mercatanti, L., and Sabato, G. (2019), 'Volcanic Risk and the Role of the Media: A Case Study in the Etna Area'. *AIMS Geosciences*, [online] 5(3), pp. 448–60.

Miller, M. A. (2009), 'Mountain, Become a Volcano: The Image of the Volcano in the Rhetoric of the French Revolution'. *French Historical Studies*, 32(4).

Nesto, B., and Frances Di Savino (2013), *The World of Sicilian Wine*. Berkeley, CA: University of California Press.

North Spencer, Benjamin (2020), *The New Wines of Mount Etna: An Insider's Guide to the History and Rebirth of a Wine Region*. Seattle, WA: Gemelli Press.

Nunziata, A. et al. (2020), 'Single Nucleotide Polymorphisms as Practical Molecular Tools to Support European Chestnut Agrobiodiversity Management'. *International Journal of Molecular Sciences*, 21(13), p. 4805.

Omodei, Antonio Filoteo degli (1992), *Aetnae Topographia*. Milano: Domenico Sanfilippo Editore.

Oppenheimer, C. (2020), *Eruptions That Shook the World*. Padstow: Cambridge University Press.

Oppenheimer, C. (2023), *Mountains of Fire: The Secret Lives of Volcanoes*. London: Hodder & Stoughton.

Poli Marchese, Emilia (2003), *Piante e Fiori dell'Etna*. Palermo: Sellerio.

Pollicino, D. (2020), *The Green Pistachio of Bronte*, Masters thesis. [online] https://parcoetna.it/?p=1295.

Riall, L. (2013), *Under the Volcano: Empire and Revolution in a Sicilian Town*. Oxford: Oxford University Press.

Riggio, G. (2013), *La Memoria del Vulcano*. Catania: Maimone Editore.

Further Reading

Rodwell, G. (1878), *Etna: A History of the Mountain and its Eruptions*. London: C. Kegan Paul & Co.

Rotoletti, A. (2015), *Vino e gente dell'Etna; Etna: Wine and People*. Milano: Adelphi Edizioni.

Russo, J. P. (1999), 'The Sicilian Latifundia'. *Italian Americana*, 17(1), pp. 40–57.

Scappi, B. (1988), *Opera, dell'arte del cucinare*. Arnaldo Forni Editore.

Sessa, P. (2005), *Milo, Viaggio nella storia di una comunità*. Caltanisetta: Edizioni Lussografica.

Sestini, D. (1991), *Memorie sui vini siciliani*. Palermo: Sellerio Editore.

Settaiolo, C. (1872), Degli alberi da bosco e dell'utile che apprestano. *Giornale Atti Regia Commissione Agricoltura Pastorizia Palermo*, 4, pp. 301–64.

Smyth, W. H. (1824), *Memoir Descriptive of the Resources, Inhabitants, and Hydrography of Sicily and Its Islands*. [online] London: John Murray.

Vittorini, E. (1969), *La città del mondo*. Torino: Einaudi.

Acknowledgements

My thanks go to all the inhabitants of Milo and Fornazzo who made me so welcome. I am especially grateful to Paolo Sessa for being such a wholehearted and generous source of information about all things Etna, to Lavinia Lo Faro and the Associazione Trucioli for introducing me to the owners of family-run timber mills in Fornazzo, to my kind neighbours Lucia and Affio, and to Alfiuccia Di Maio and her family for their unstinting kindness, support and friendship. I am also indebted to Roberta Bonsignore for her friendship and generous hospitality, and to Carlo Lombardo for his help, enthusiasm and good humour.

I am much indebted to Roby Abbate, Alice Bonaccorsi, Santo and Andrea Di Maio, Marco Nicolosi, Carlo Nicolosi Asmundo, Benjamin North Spencer and Chiara Vigo for all they taught me about Etna's wines, and to Valeria Lopis for kindly introducing me to so many of them. I am also very grateful to Marco De Grazia for a wonderful afternoon at Tenuta delle Terre Nere, and for generously sharing his rich knowledge of the history of Etna winemaking.

Many thanks to Maricò, Biagio and all their colleagues at Guide Etna Nord for being so supportive in every way – I cannot recommend them highly enough – and to Giuseppe Salerno and Boris Benkhe of the INGV for patiently answering so many of my questions in person and by email. Thank you to both Nino and Alfio Papero and to the staff of the Pro Loco and of the Consorzio di Tutela del Pistacchio in Bronte. Warm thanks to Raimondo and Salvo Lizzio for making me feel at home in the unlikely surroundings of their quarry, to Rossella Pezzino, the Di Prima family, and Guglielmo Grasso and Ketty Torrisi. Thanks too to Tommaso La Mantia, Francesco Pennisi and Roberto Lo Turco, and finally to

Acknowledgements

Ignazio and Donatella Coco for wonderful evenings together in Zafferana, and for being so hospitable in every way,

As always, heartfelt thanks go to my agent, Antony Topping at Greene & Heaton, and to all at Penguin, especially to Chloe Currens for her enthusiasm and understanding, to the inimitable Pen Vogler, and perhaps above all to Ana Fletcher of Unfolding Edits for inspiration and input.

Finally, love and thanks to Alex Ramsay, who has been obliged to live alongside this project for longer than I like to think.

Index

Abbate, Roby, 189–92
Aci Castello, 29–30, 31, 34, 86
Acireale, 95, 122
Agata, Sant', 54–6, 79, 80–91, 95
airports, 48
Alcantara, 187
Alfio, Sant', 78, 79
almonds, 164, 182
Andrea, Sant', 9, 78
architecture, 59–60, 94, 95
Asilandia, 149–51
Astragalus siculus, 12–13, 152–3, 199–200
Augusta, 9–10

Baedeker's guide, 44
Baldini, Filippo, 111
basalt, 57, 93; and Flavetta family, 95; international business in, 93, 95–101; and Lizzio brothers, 95–101; structures/buildings made of, 2, 9, 57, 93, 94–95; workforce in industry, 98–101
beekeeping, 126; *Api nere siculi*, 139; *Apis mellifera*, 139; Dolce Parco, 137, 140–45, 147; history of Sicilian honey production, 139–40; box hives, 138; operculum, 142–3; shepherds move to, 141, 142; use of *Ferula communis*, 137–8; *villici*, 137–8; Zafferana Etnea as *Città del Miele*, 137, 138, 140–45, *zagara*, 141
Bellini, Vincenzo, 134

Benanti, Giuseppe, 184–5
Biancavilla, 21, 120
Bixio, Nino, 161–2
brigands, 55, 158
Bronte: Castello Maniace, 156, 162–6; Corso Umberto, 158, 167; duchy/dukedom, 155–66, 171–2; *Fatti di Bronte*, 161–2; *gabellotti*, 159, 164; peasant revolts, 159–62, 163–4; *Pistacchio Verde di Bronte*, 22, 24, 167–9, 171–8; Real Collegio Capizzi, 158; social/political history of, 155–66, 171–2, 180
Brontë sisters, 162
Brydone, Patrick, 30, 40, 41–2, 49–50, 54, 66, 80, 110, 119
Burnet, Thomas, 39–40
Byron, Lord, 'Don Juan', 40–41

Caffo, Leonardo, 4, 5
Calabria, 1, 10, 26, 32
Carlo, Salvatore di (Saro Ruspa), 63–4
Carrillo y Salcedo, Don Stefano, 109–10
Catania: 1669 eruption, 20, 53, 54–7, 58, 93, 97–8; 1693 earthquake, 56, 93–4; artificial ice shops in, 113; basalt buildings/structures, 2, 93, 94–5; basalt elephant in, 94–5; Bishopric of, 54, 104, 105, 107; *candelore* in, 82–3, 86, 87–8, 89; Carthaginian march on (396 BC), 28–9, 41; Castello Ursino, 56, 57;

Catania – *cont*.
and the Circumetnea, 17–18, 19–20; *fercolo* of Sant' Agata, 78, 88–90; Agata as patron saint, 54–6, 79, 80–91, 95; horse-meat dishes, 83, 84; INGV in, 4, 66–7, 68–73, 74, 75–6, 196; Platania's painting of (1675), 55, 56; rebuilt after 1693 earthquake, 94–5; shipyards, 122; and snow trade, 104, 110–11, 113; version of ricotta, 133

Catania, University of, 32–3

caves, 62, 63, 64, 199; Grotta dei Ladroni, 105, 107; Grotta di Serracozzo, 199

cheese making: creameries, 131–6; from cow's milk, 134–5; *mozzarella*, 134–5; *provola*, 127, 134, 135; from sheep's milk, *pecorino*, *primosale*, 136; *tuma*, *zabbina* 9, 127, 132, 133, 135–6; ricotta, preserving, 133–4; regional versions, 133; shepherds making, 6, 9, 127, 128–9, 131–6.

Chiancone, 39

chocolate, 27

Christianity: and 1669 eruption, 54–5; and 1991 eruption, 64–5; adoption of on Etna, 77, 78–80, 81; Bishopric of Catania, 54, 104, 105, 107; Council of Trent, 79; debate about history of the Earth, 39–40, 41–2; Etna's saints' days, 78, 79–91, 95, 196–7; Festa di Sant' Agata, 80–91, 95; and Norman invasion, 104; processions to the lava front, 64–5, 79, 81; roadside shrines, 8–9; shaping of by Etna's people, 64–5, 79–80, 196–7

Circumetnea, 5, 16, 17, 19–27, 58, 155; construction of, 17–19, 23

Cirino, Sant', 79

citrus fruits, 2, 10, 18, 20, 26, 90, 114–15, 141, 144, 164, 182

Civil Protection, Department of, 69, 74

climate, local, 15, 22, 23, 25, 28, 43, 102

climate emergency, 3–4, 75, 106, 120

Coco, Ignazio, 131–5, 136

Coleridge, Samuel Taylor, 40

Cornellisen, Frank, 185

Corrado, Vincenzo, 110

Costanza, Maria, 149

Costarelli, Diego, 183

cow's-milk allergies, 146–7

cyclists, 8, 43

cyclopes, 31–2, 33, 127, 156,

Della Porta, Giambattista, 108–9

Diodorus Siculus, 29, 41

dogs, 37; Cirneco dell'Etna, 23–4; stray dogs, 10, 43, 73–4

donkeys, 73, 111–12, 150–51; Fascist breeding programme, 147–8; milking of, 146–7, 149–51; Sicily's three main breeds, 148–9

earthquakes, 16, 31, 32, 38, 53, 56, 69, 72, 76, 80, 93–5, 196

elephants, 32–3, 94–5

Eliodoro, 95

Elliot, Frances, *Diary of an Idle Woman in Sicily* (1881), 163, 166

Ellittico volcano, 38, 154, 187–8

Empedocles, 34

Enceladus, 30–31

eruptions, 1–14, 52, 157, 185, 187, 195–200; Bronte, 22; 1669 eruption, 20, 28, 29, 52, 53–7, 58, 76, 93; 1843 eruption, 22; 1928

Index

eruption, 52, 57–8, 59, 76, 113, 180; 1950 eruption, 11–12; 1971 eruption, 74–5; 1991 eruption, 52, 60, 61–5, 76; 396 BC eruption,; and *bottoniera*, 46; and changing attitudes to, 78–9; and disruption, 48; and poetry, 41; and prediction 66–77; and Sant'Agata, 81, 84; and Valle del Bove, 39; as metaphor for political ferment, 41

Etna, Mount: beaches, 24, 28, 29, 39; Boscosa region, 25, 106, 116, 117, 122–6, 127–31; Casa degli Inglesi, 44; climbing/ascent of, 3, 40, 44–51, 195, 198–200; *Coltivata* region, 12, 16, 17, 25, 49, 52, 117, 128, 134, 154; Deserta region, 25, 43, 44, 45–51, 199–200; eastern flank, 13, 16, 25–6, 38–9, 57–8, 61–2, 95, 117–18, 124–5, 155–66, 180–88, 192–3; first cable railway on, 112–13; funicular railway, 45; gendered names for, 4–5; impact on local climate, 15, 22, 23, 25, 28, 43, 102; landscape as 'cultural producer, 76–7; made a National Park (1987), 75, 96–7; monitoring of by experts, 66–7, 68–74, 75–6; north flank, 23, 24–5, 72–3, 122–4, 184–5, 187–92; Paternò's *salinelle*, 70–72; Piano del Lago, 48–9; Privitera surname, 57; restricted zone above 2,800 metres, 75; Rifugio Sapienza, 45, 64; Serra delle Concazze, 199; south flank, 45, 53–4, 183–4; south-west flank, 20–21, 70–72; Val Calanna, 60–61, 62–3; varying characters of each flank, 21–2; west flank, 22, 155–66, 180 *see also* geology of Etna; history of Sicily/Etna; people/inhabitants of Etna; summit craters; volcanology and entries for individual settlements and industries/activities

Fabrizio (guide), 45, 46–7, 48, 49, 50, 61
Faraglioni, 29–30, 31, 33, 34–5, 36–8
farming: and 1669 eruption, 53; abandoned farms, 24, 128; absentee landlords, 155–9, 180; and Arabic settlers, 114, 170–71, 174, 175; British estate managers in Bronte, 156–7, 158–9, 160, 163–4; of cattle, 61, 134, 157, 158; Circumetnea's impact, 17; *contadini*, 18, 59, 156, 157–8, 159, 160–62, 163–4, 165, 166, 180, 181; *contrade*, 186–7; donkey-milk, 146–7, 149–51; east-west flank differences, 26, 155–66, 180; *gabellotti*, 159, 164; and growth of Riposto, 182; *latifondi*, 155–66; *mezzadria* contracts, 164; and nomadic shepherds, 128; peasant revolt in Bronte (August 1860), 160–62, 163–4; pests and disease, 157, 183–4; and predicting of eruptions, 72–4; prickly pears (*fichi d'india*), 20–21; *scozzolatura* technique, 21; of sheep, 33, 73, 127–34, 140–41, 157; of strawberries, 23, 28; use of prickly pears, 20; in Val Calanna, 60, 62 *see also* beekeeping; pistachios; soil, volcanic

Fascism, 7, 19, 20–21, 52, 58–60, 147–8, 165, 172
Ferdinand II, King of the Two Sicilies, 38, 160
Ferdinand III, King of Sicily, 156
Ferdinandea island, 38

211

Index

feudal system, 18, 155–66
Filadelfo, Sant', 79
Finch, Heneage, 54
firefighters, 126
First World War, 184
fishing boats/fishermen, 2, 28, 29
Flavetta stone masons, 95
food: *arancini*, 30, 135–6; chilling/freezing technologies, 103, 108–10; donkey meat, 151; horse-meat dishes, 83, 84; *pane imbottita*, 127; *Pasta alla Norma*, 134; pistachio recipes/products, 167, 168, 171; *pizza secca*, 9; *pizza siciliana*, 136; *scacciata*, 136 *see also* cheese making; granita
forests, 25, 116, 126; Civilization of Wood, 120; beech and birch, 124–5; lava flows, 116–17, 153–4; *pagghiari*, 125; Ragabo, 10–11, 122–4, 153; *resinatori*, 116, 123–4; wildfires, 125–6
Fornazzo, 8, 10, 73, 131; and 1971 eruption, 74–5; and 1979 eruption, 13; as a centre for wood trade, 120–22; Don Puddu's business in, 111–13, 120; eco-museum in, 120–21, 122, 126
Foti, Salvo, 185
France, 41, 183–4
Franchetti, Andrea, 185, 186–7
Futurist movement, 112, 113

Galen, 175
Galt, John, 20
Garibaldi, Giuseppe, 160, 162
Gemmellaro, Giuseppe, 25
Gemmellaro, Mario, 44
geology of Etna: Calderara Sottana, 187–8; the Chiancone, 39; debate about history of the Earth, 39–40, 41–2; Deep Time, 29, 42, 75; Etna's origins, 15–16, 29–30, 35–9, 41–2, 154, 187–8, 199; explanations of early scientists, 33–4, 39; lateral/flank craters, 10, 42, 46, 48–9, 67; magma chamber, 49; Piano del Lago, 48, 50; tectonic plates, 35–6; University of Catania's geological museum, 32–3; Valle del Bove, 13, 39, 50, 61–2, 63–4, 198, 199 *see also* caves, lava; summit craters
George V, King, 164
Giarre, 17, 27, 39, 113
Giovanna d'Angiò, Queen of Naples, 118
Gloeden, Wilhelm Von, 112
Goethe, Johann Wolfgang, 162
Grand Tour, 3, 30, 40
granita, 102–3, 104, 105, 109, 110, 113–14; at Bar Musumeci (Randazzo), 23; recipe for/making of, 114–15
Grasso, Guglielmo, 147, 148, 149–51
Grazia, Marco De, 185, 186, 187–9
Greece, ancient, 11, 24, 29, 30–34, 103, 127, 152, 179
Guide Vulcanologiche Etna Nord, 45, 198, 199, 200

Hamilton, William, 41
Hesiod, 31
history of Sicily/Etna: Arabic settlers, 103–4, 114, 139–40, 141, 150, 170–71, 174, 175; Carthaginian march on Catania (396 BC), 28–9, 41; eruption as political metaphor, 41; *Fatti di Bronte*, 161–2; feudal system, 18, 155–66; Garibaldi's campaign (1860), 160–62; Grand Tour, 3, 30, 40;

Index

Greek arrival, 30, 127, 152, 179; impact of Unification, 5, 17–18, 160–62; nineteenth century, 6, 155–7, 159–63; Norman invasion, 104, 170; Phoenicians, 23–4, 103; revolutions, 159–60; Second World War, 7, 148, 165, 184; Spanish rule, 53, 55, 57
Homer, *Odyssey*, 31–2, 33
horses, 6, 83, 84, 150, 163
Houël, Jean-Pierre, 70–71, 105, 111, 119
Hutton, James, 42

Ibn-al-Awam, 170
ice cream, 104, 105, 109, 110, 114, 167
International Cooperation for Animal Research Using Space (ICARUS), 72–4
Irvine, William, 110, 111
Islamic Caliphate, 103–4, 114, 139–40, 170–71

labour/workforce, 2, 5–6, 22; in basalt industry, 98–101; *braccianti*, 18, 59, 158, 161; building Circumetnea, 18–19; *contadini*, 18, 59, 156, 157–8, 159, 160–62, 163–4, 165, 166, 180, 181; pistachio industry, 173–6; snow trade, 104–5, 106, 107–8, 111–12; sulphur mines, 18; timber trade, 120–22; vineyards, 190–91
Lachea, Isola, 34
language, 123; Arabic, 4, 11; gendered names for Etna, 4–5; dialect, 4, 129, 190
Latini, Antonio, 109–10
lava: *'a'ā* flows, 47; basalt formed from, 93, 96, 97–8; breaking down of, 152–5; buildings/settlements engulfed by, 10, 13, 52, 53–7, 58–9, 61–2, 63, 113, 180, 184; Chiancone, 39; and Christian rituals, 64–5, 79, 81, 196–7; at coast, 28–30, 31, 33, 34–40, 41–2; *dagale*, 61, 130; detritus in towns/villages, 7, 13–15, 52; diverting the course of flow, 52, 55–6, 60, 62, 63–4; Faraglioni, 29–30, 31, 33, 34–5, 36–8; filming of 1928 eruption, 59; flows in forests, 116–17, 153–4; lava tubes, 62–4, 199; landscape above Milo, 10, 11–13, 16, 198–200; landscape at Ragabo, 10–11; landscape at summit, 38–9, 40, 42, 46–51, 195–6, 200; lapilli, 7, 13–15, 48, 53, 54, 153; lava tubes, 62, 63, 64, 199; magma becomes, 35–6, 57; as metaphor for political ferment, 41; milkvetch growing on, 12–13, 152–3, 199–200; in old riverbeds, 58; *pahoehoe*, 50–51; *pietra cannone*, 116–17; and *Pistacchio Verde di Bronte*, 22, 24, 167–8, 169, 171–6, 178; plant species growing on, 152–3; Platania's painting 1675, 55, 56; 'tephra', 47–8; and the terebinth, 170, 172–3; in Val Calanna, 60–61, 62–3; and Valle del Bove, 13, 39, 50, 61–2, 63–4, 198, 199; and Valle del Leone, 198; and vineyards, 24–5, 185–6, 187–8, 192, 193–4; walking on, 10–11, 12–13, 49, 50, 199–200; on west flank, 22, 157 *see also* magma
Lawrence, D. H., 91, 165
Lentini, 31, 131
Leotta, Giuseppe (Don Puddu), 111–13, 120
Leotta, Salvatore, 112–13
Levi, Carlo, 125, 155, 158, 166
lichens, 152–3, 154

213

Index

Linguaglossa, 25–6, 45, 120, 122–3
Lizzio, Alfio, 137–8, 139
Lizzio, Salvo and Raimondo, 95–101
Lo Faro, Lavinia, 120–21, 122, 126

Macleod, Fiona, 165
Madonie Mountains, 104
Mafia, 97
magma, 1, 35–6, 46, 57, 69; gases in, 67, 68; silica levels in, 67, 68 *see also* lava
Major Risks Commission, 62
malaria, 157, 158
Maletto, 23
Malta, 182; Knights of, 105; snow/ice exports to, 102, 104, 105
Maniace, Castello, 156, 162–6
maps/cartography, 25, 45
marine life, 37
Marinetti, Filippo Tommaso, 112, 113
marriage customs, 6, 138–9
Marsala, port of, 181
Mascali, 57, 58, 59–60, 180, 181, 184, 191
Max Planck Institute of Animal Behaviour, Germany, 72–4
Mazara del Vallo, 103
Mercatanti, Leonardo, 76–7
Messina, city of, 122, 133
Messina Strait, 1, 2, 10, 26, 69
methane, 70
milkvetch, Sicilian (*Astragulus siculus*), 12–13, 152–3, 199–200
Milo, house in, 7–8, 13, 14–15, 34, 42–3; donkey-milk dairy in, 147; earthquake risk in, 16; eruptions above, 52, 60, 61–5, 197–200; Wilhelm Von Gloeden settles in, 112; 'grumbling' of south-east crater above, 14, 68; ICARUS project in, 73–4; lava landscape above, 10, 11–13, 16, 198–200; mountain climate of, 15, 192–4; roadside shrines, 8–9; shops and bars, 9, 10, 43, 91; soil in, 39, 192–4; stray dogs in, 73–4; vineyards, 9, 11, 192–4

Montale, Eugenio, 'I Limoni', 26
mud volcanos, see *salinelle*
Mussolini, Benito, 19, 58, 60, 148, 172
Musumeci, Giovanna, 114–15
myths and legends, 5, 30–33, 34, 45, 78–9, 200

Naples, 40, 68, 110, 118, 156
Napoleonic Wars, 44, 182
National Institute of Geophysics and Volcanology (INGV), Catania, 4, 66–7, 68–73, 74, 75–6, 196
National Research Council, 62
National Volcanology Group (GNV), 62, 64
natural disasters, 3–4; animals' powers of prediction, 72–4; early-warning systems, 4, 75; earthquakes, 16, 38, 53, 56, 69, 93–4, 95; emergency-management plans, 4; flooding, 157; tsunamis, 39, 94
Naxos, 29, 33
Nebrodi Mountains, 148
Nelson, Horatio, 156, 161, 182
Nelson Hood, Alec (son of Alexander), 163, 164, 165
Nelson Hood, Alec (son of Peter), 166
Nelson Hood, Alexander, 162–3
Nelson Hood, Peter, 165–6
Nicolosi, Marco, 193
Nicolosi, 44, 45, 53, 76, 120
Norman invasion, 104, 170

Omodei, Antonio Filotei degli, 123
Ovid, *Metamorphoses*, 31

Index

paganism, 78–9, 82, 83
pagghiari, 125
palaeontology, 31–3
Palermo, 17–18, 133, 159–60
Palermo, University of, 76
Papero, Alfio, 172, 173–4, 176–7
Papero, Nino, 168–9, 172–3
Pappalardo, Diego, 55–6
Parthenopian Republic, 156
Passopisciaro, 185, 189–92
Patanè, Alfio, 121–2, 126, 131
Paternò, 56, 70–72
Peloritani Mountains, 104
people/inhabitants of Etna: and Christianity, 54–5, 64–5, 77, 78–91, 196–7; Circumetnea's impact, 17, 18–19; financial cost of eruptions, 14; hospitality of, 99–100, 168, 190; impact of volcanic ash/lapilli on houses, 7, 13–15; ingenuity and resilience of, 4, 52 80, 88. 90; lives lost to eruptions, 22, 48, 68, 76; and mass emigration, 5, 184; Mercatanti's research, 76–7; relationship with mountain, 3–5, 76–7, 78–92; risk–reward calculation, 3, 5; rural life as changing, 6; Sicani, 30, 125; victims of 1669 eruption, 54–5, 97
Piano dell'Acqua, 63, 64, 65
Piano Provenzana, 10, 13, 25–6
Pino, Zio, 129–30
Pinzirita sheep, 33, 127–8, 149
pistachios: alternate cropping, 172, 173, 176; traditional uses, 170–71, 175; and Etna's soil, 155, 169, 170, 172; grafting of, 6, 170, 172–3; 'green pruning' of, 176; history of cultivation, 169–71; *lochi*, 169, 172–6; *Pistacchio Verde di Bronte*, 22, 24, 167–8, 169, 171–8; *Pistacia vera* tree, 170; pollination, 173; processing machines, 177–8; *smallatura*, 176–7; *Smeraldi di Sicilia*, 167–9, 171–8
Platania, Giacinto, 55–6
Pliny the Elder, 169–70
Pliny the Younger, 103
Polyphemus, 31–2, 33, 127
Pompeii, 68, 116–17
prickly pears (*fichi d'india*), 20–21
Prima, Alfio Di, 137, 140, 141–3, 147
Prima, Maria Di, 137, 138–9, 140–41, 145
Prima, Marica Di, 137, 140, 142–4, 147
Prima, Michele Di, 137, 138–9, 140–41, 142, 144–5
Prima, Sebastiano Di, 140

Quinziano, 81

Ragabo, bosco di, 10–11, 122–4, 153
Ragusa, 148
railways, 2, 18, 19, 58
Randazzo, 13, 23, 24, 73, 74, 114–15, 187, 189
Recupero, Giuseppe, 41–2
resilience, 4, 52, 80, 88, 90, 118
Rifugio Sapienza, 45, 64
Riposto, 17, 26–7, 39, 181–2, 183, 184
roads/streets, 48, 52, 58, 153, 162, 182, 187; *basalto* paving of, 9, 57, 93, 94, 96; of Bronte, 157–8, 159, 166, 172; of Catania, 55, 56, 81–90, 93, 94, 102; Mareneve road, 8, 10, 13, 129–30; of Mascali, 59–60; 'snow streets', 102
Romantic poets, 40–41
Rome, ancient, 19, 103, 155, 169–70, 179, 191–2
Royal Navy, 182
Royal Society, 53

215

Index

rubbish, 8, 74, fly-tipping 96–7
Ruggero, Gran Conte, 104, 107

Salerno, Giuseppe, 66
salinelle, 70–72
Sant' Alfio, 118
Santa Tecla, 41
Saponaria sicula, 153
Saro Ruspa, 63–4
Scappi, Bartolomeo, 171
Scuderi, Salvatore, *Trattato dei Boschi dell'Etna* (1828), 124
Second World War, 148, 165, 184
Seneca, 103, 109
Sestini, Domenico, 180
Sharp, William, 165
shepherds: cheese making by, 6, 9, 127, 128–9, 131–6; grazing in forest areas, 116, 125, 126, 130; high-altitude pastures, 125, 126, 129, 130, 131; modern, 130–33; move to beekeeping, 141; nomadic, 127–9; straddling old and new traditions, 129–30; winters on the Catania plain, 140–41
sherbets, iced, 103–4
Sicani, 30, 125
Sicily: ancient aristocracy, 18; distinctive culture, 2; emigration from, 5, 184; fossilized bones in, 31–2; invention of granita, 114; Ionian coastline, 17, 28–30, 31, 34–5, 36–40, 41–2, 196; nineteenth-century history, 6, 155–7, 159–63; political/economic impact of Unification, 5, 17–18, 160–62; proposals for bridge to, 2; rebuilding after 1693 earthquake, 93, 94–5; as Spanish possession, 53, 55, 57
Simeto river, 155, 157
Simonides, 103
Siracusa, 111
skiing, 10, 25–6, 61–2
Smyth, William H., 183
snow, and trade, 102–3, 104–15; and banqueting in great houses, 109–10; decline and end of, 113; discovery of artificial freezing, 108–9; Don Puddu's business in Fornazzo, 111–13, 120; exports to Malta, 102, 104, 105; history of, 103–5; medicinal uses of, 111; *neviere*, 105, 106, 107–8, 112, 125; precarious nature of, 106–7, 111; shops on Via Neve in Catania, 110–11; stores built into city walls, 108; use of mule trains, 107–8, 111–12; workforce in, 104–5, 106, 107–8, 111–12
soapwort (*Saponaria sicula*), 153
soil, volcanic, 3, 20, 21, 39, 42, 116; breaking down of lava, 152–5; as diverse in *Coltivata*, 154; nutrients/minerals in, 8, 25, 153, 154–5, 176, 181, 188, 192; and pistachios, 155, 169, 170, 172; strawberries grown in, 23, 28; and water supply, 8, 153–4; and winemaking, 155, 179, 180–81, 182, 185–6, 187–8, 192, 193–4
Stefani, Bartolomeo, 171, 172
Strabo, 179
Stromboli, 66
sugar, 114, 117, 139–40
sulphur mines, 18
summit craters, 3, 10, 46, 49; Bocca Nuova, 46, 195–6; north-east crater, 46, 48, 57–8; old central crater, 40, 46; south-east crater, 10, 14, 28, 44, 46–8, 49, 52, 60, 61–2, 65, 68, 197–200; Voragine, 46

Index

Taormina, 9–10, 17, 91, 112, 114; La Falconara in, 164, 165
Tenuta delle Terre Nere wine estate, 185, 187–9, 194
timber trade, 6, 116, 119, 124, 126, 131, 184; ancient rights of *contadini*, 160; Don Puddu's business in, 111; eco-museum in Fornazzo, 120–21, 122, 126; use of oxen, 122; workforce, 120–22
Tocqueville de, Alexis, 180–81
Torrisi, Ketty, 147, 148–50
Trecastagni, 120
trees: ancient specimens on Etna, 117–20; aspens, 61; beech, 124, 125, 160; birch, 124–5, 153, 198–9; Castagno dei Cento Cavalli, 118–20; Etna broom (*Genista aetnensis*), 153; European register of Monumental Trees, 118; false pepper trees (*Schincus molle*), 182; holm oaks, 117–18; Ilice di Carrinu, 117–18; lemon, 26; lime, 10; and mycorrhizal fungi, 153–4; near Etna's summit, 116; oak, 42, 117–18, 160; *pietra cannone*, 116–17; pine, 10–11, 116, 122–4, 153; *Pistacia vera* tree, 170; *Pistacia terebinthus*, 170, 172–3; sweet chestnut, 45, 61, 118–22, 126, 130, 141, 145, 160, 184;
Trewhella, Robert, 18
Trifoglietto volcano, 38, 199

Unification of Italy, 5, 17–18, 160–62

Vaccarini, Giovanni Battista, 94
Verga, Giovanni, 'Libertà', 161
Vesuvius, 40, 41, 66, 67–8; AD 79 eruption, 68, 116–17
Viagrande, 183–4

Virgil, the *Aeneid*, 30–31
Vitellius, Lucius, 169–70
Vittorini, Elio, *La città del mondo*, 133
Vittorio Emanuele lll, King, 58
volcanic ash, 13, 14–15, 47–8, 54, 93, 116–17, 195–6
'Volcano Buster' Operation, 63
volcanology, 39, 41, 44, 45; 1669 eruption, 20, 28, 29, 52, 53–7, 58, 76, 93; 1843 eruption, 22; 1928 eruption, 52, 57–8, 59, 76, 113, 180; 1950 eruption, 11–12; 1971 eruption, 74–5; 1991 eruption, 52, 60, 61–5, 76; 396 BC eruption, 28–9; animals' powers of prediction, 72–4; 'effusive' eruptions, 68, 75; eruption alert levels / warnings, 74; eruptions as frequent, 3, 7, 12, 13, 46, 52, 157; eruptions on west flank, 22, 157; explanations of early scientists, 33–4, 39; 'explosive' eruptions, 68, 75; filming of 1928 eruption, 59; flank eruptions, 10, 13, 53, 58; gases monitored, 67, 68, 70, 71–2; GPS monitors, 69; and Hawaiian words, 47, 51; INGV in Catania, 4, 66–7, 68–73, 74, 75–6, 196; monitoring of Etna, 66–7, 68–74, 75–6; National Volcanology Group (GNV), 62, 64; observing of *salinelle*, 70–72; October 2002 eruption, 10, 11; and *pietra cannone*, 117; and the seabed, 28–30, 33–9; system for predicting eruptions, 66, 67, 68–70, 71–6; thermal-imaging cameras, 69 *see also* lava; summit craters

water supply, 8, 60, 71, 153–4
Wikelski, Martin, 72–3, 74

217

winemaking: *alberello* vineyards, 119, 184, 191–2; 'Barolo Boys', 185; Barone di Villagrande winery, 193–4; Carricante grapes, 192–3; collapse of (from 1880), 184; *Contrade dell'Etna* festival, 186–7; decline in nineteenth century, 182–4; Duchy of Bronte fine wines and brandies, 164; emphyteusis, system, 180; Etna DOC wines, 185–6, 187, 191, 192–3; and Etna's soil, 155, 179, 180–81, 182, 185–6, 187–8, 192, 193–4; history of, 179–83; and lava, 24–5, 185–6, 187–8, 192, 193–4; Milo vineyards, 9, 11, 192–4; Nerello Cappuccio grapes, 191; Nerello Mascalese grapes, 188, 191; and nomadic shepherds, 128; *palmenti*, 181; Passopisciaro wine estate, 185; and phylloxera, 157, 183–4, 189; renaissance of on Etna, 24–5, 179, 184–91; Royal Navy wine stocks, 182; shipping of Etna's wines, 181–2; stability of Etna's wines, 181; Tenuta delle Terre Nere estate, 185, 187–9, 194; varied altitude of vineyards, 186, 187–9; *vendemmia*, 189–91; *Vino di Riposto*, 181–5

Zafferana Etnea, 14, 45, 120, 131; and 1991 eruption, 60, 62, 63, 64–5; as *Città del Miele*, 137, 138, 140–45; and donkey-milk dairy, 147